Contract Management
Body *of* Knowledge
(CMBOK)

3RD EDITION

Contract Management Body of Knowledge
Third Edition

©2011 National Contract Management Association
All rights reserved. Published 2011.
Printed in the United States of America.
ISBN-13: 978-0-9700897-4-8

contents

Preface to the Annotated Edition			i
Acknowledgements			ii
Chapter 1	**The Contract Management Framework**		1
	The Contract Management Profession		2
	Purpose of this Guide to the CMBOK		3
	What is a Contract?		3
	What is Contract Management?		4
	About The Contract Management Profession		5
	About NCMA		6
	Professional Certification		8
	The CMBOK Structure		10
Chapter 2	**The CMBOK: An Overview**		13
	Contract Life Cycle		14
	Contract Stakeholders		14
	Organizational Influences		14
	General Business Competencies		15
	General Contracting Competencies		15
Chapter 3	**The CMBOK Knowledge Areas/Outline of Competencies**		17
	1.0	**Pre-Award**	18
	1.1	Laws and Regulations	18
	1.2	Contract Principles	27
	1.3	Standards of Conduct	27
	1.4	Socioeconomic Programs	29
	1.5	Contract Structures	32
	1.6	Contracting Methods	35
	1.7	Contract Financing	37
	1.8	Intellectual Property	38
	2.0	**Acquisition Planning/Strategy**	39
	2.1	Acquisition Planning	39
	2.2	Acquisition Methodology	41
	2.3	Proposal Preparation	47
	2.4	Negotiation	48
	2.5	Source Selection	52
	2.6	Protests	61
	3.0	**Post-Award**	62
	3.1	Contract Administration	62
	3.2	Contract Performance/Quality Assurance	63
	3.3	Subcontract Administration	65
	3.4	Contract Changes and Modifications	65
	3.5	Property Administration	67
	3.6	Transportation	68

contents

	3.7	Disputes	68
	3.8	Organizational Conflict of Interest	70
	3.9	Contract Closeout	71
	3.10	Contract Termination	72
	4.0	**Specialized Knowledge Areas**	72
	4.1	Research and Development	72
	4.2	Architect-Engineer Services and Construction	74
	4.3	Information Technology	76
	4.4	Major Systems	76
	4.5	Service Contracts	77
	4.6	International Contracting	80
	4.7	State and Local Government	81
	4.8	Supply Chain Management	82
	4.9	Performance-Based Acquisition	83
	4.10	Government Property	83
	4.11	Other Specialized Areas	85
	5.0	**Business**	85
	5.1	Management	85
	5.2	Marketing	87
	5.3	Operations Management	87
	5.4	Financial Analysis	87
	5.5	Accounting	87
	5.6	Economics	88
	5.7	Information Science or Information Technology	88
	5.8	Leadership Skills	88
Chapter 4	**The CMBOK Lexicon**		91
Chapter 5	**NCMA Certification Exams**		113
Appendices			117
	UCC		118
	***FAR* Table of Contents**		132
	Task List from 2010 Job Analysis Study for Contract Managers		138
	Knowledge Domains from 2010 Job Analysis Study for Contract Managers		139
Bibliography			143

The National Contract Management Association (NCMA) was formed in 1959 to foster the professional growth and educational advancement of its members. It is a membership-based professional society whose leadership is composed of volunteers. The NCMA office has a full-time staff to support its members' needs. The NCMA Staff Directory provides information about the Office departments responsible for different services. NCMA is located at 21740 Beaumeade Circle, Suite 125; Ashburn, VA 20147. The office is open between the hours of 8:30 a.m. and 5:00 p.m. (EST).

preface

This document supersedes the National Contract Management Association's (NCMA) *Contract Management Body of Knowledge (CMBOK)*, second edition, published in 2004.

The third edition of the *CMBOK* expands, refines, and reorganizes the information presented in previous editions. It provides further definition of the field of contract management, the framework for the body of knowledge, the practice(s) outlined, the definitions (lexicon), and the processes of contract management. The guide provides procedural steps that apply to the contract management process in general, as well as specialized areas and those that are unique to either federal or commercial contracting.

Readers should note that the guide does not purport to define the body of knowledge, but rather to serve as a compendium and guide to the body of knowledge that has been developing and evolving over the past five decades. Furthermore, this body of knowledge is not static. The guide must, necessarily, develop and evolve as the contract management profession matures. It nevertheless constitutes a valuable source for information on the competencies and knowledge areas required for success in the profession.

acknowledgements

Acknowledgements are made to previous authors and contributors of earlier editions of the CMBOK and *Annotated Guide to the CMBOK*. Acknowledgements and thanks go to the oversight group, task force, and independent reviewers for the 2011 edition, including:

Chuck Woodside	Rene Rendon
Craig Bowers	Sherry Carmichael
Ed Rinkavage	Bill Daniel
Janet Best	Cathy Dixon
Bill Kaplan	David Gragan
Karen Clougherty	DuWayne Jones
Karin Walls	Janet Mattson
Marge Rumbaugh	John Godzac
Michael Fischetti	Morgan Ross
Michael Gauthier	Po Collins
Diane Whitmoyer	Robert Cooper
Andrea Melius	Sean Lingo
Erika Chesson	Karen Reuter
John Wilkinson	Crystal Glenn
Neal Couture	Rose Gazarek
Charles Chadwick	

Acknowledgements and thanks also go to those responding to the Job Analysis Study for Contract Managers.

The Contract Management Framework

chapter one

The Contract Management Profession

What constitutes a profession? Although individual responses to this question may differ, the U.S. Department of Labor has held that a profession has at least five distinct characteristics:

- A professional organization,
- A code of ethics,
- A body of knowledge,
- Research activities, and
- A credentialing arm.

The contract management profession has all five of these characteristics:

- A professional organization (the National Contract Management Association [NCMA], with news of the profession being published in *Contract Management* magazine and monthly electronic newsletters);
- A code of ethics for the profession;
- A body of knowledge, which is updated continuously;
- A research publication (*Journal of Contract Management*);
- A research arm (the Contract Management Institute [CMI]); and
- A viable and highly visible credentialing program (Certified Federal Contracts Manager (CFCM), Certified Commercial Contracts Manager (CCCM), and Certified Professional Contracts Manager (CPCM)).

In 1996, Frank Meneely defined the body of knowledge as:

> ...a conceptual framework that is systematized about a central theme and formulated through the process of definition, classification, and analysis with reference to the discovery of general concepts, theories, laws, and/or principles. The [body of knowledge] is the keystone of a profession and provides the baseline for the development of education and training materials and certification requirements for its membership. It encompasses both theory and practice.

Building on Meneely's definition and borrowing from the Project Management Institute's definition of the project management body of knowledge, the CMBOK offers the following encompassing definition:

> The CMBOK is an inclusive term that describes the sum of knowledge for the profession of contract management. The complete body of knowledge concerning contract management resides both with the practitioners and those who, like academicians and governing bodies, apply and advance contract management. This body of knowledge includes both the generally accepted practices (such as business and finance) that are widely applied, as well as state of the art practices (such as e-commerce and catalog aggregation).

The CMBOK has undergone a number of revisions over the past 15 years. In 1996, the CMBOK was revised and reorganized to make it more relevant and useful to the contracting profession. In 2001, the then-existing Contract Management Certification and Accreditation Board (CMCAB) appointed a CMBOK Committee. This committee was charged with investigating and subsequently updating the CMBOK. The original committee was responsible for the publication of the first edition of the *Guide to the CMBOK*. Another committee added commercial content, and ongoing committee activities continually monitor the profession for changes to this primary document.

The second edition of the CMBOK included an updated lexicon of contracting terms for both federal and commercial areas. A series of charts patterned on a work breakdown structure (WBS) helped the reader understand the relationship among the elements of the CMBOK, as well as the similarities and differences among competencies associated with federal and commercial contract management. The dictionary complemented the charts and defined the terms used. The definitions take the guesswork out of discerning the meaning ascribed to each term.

In 2006, an *Annotated Guide to the CMBOK* further refined and reorganized the information presented in previous editions. The basic WBS pattern was retained, and the content was reordered into a series of chapters. Each chapter discussed a grouping of competencies essential for successful practice. The chapters were arranged from the general to the specific, and also attempted to stress the similarities between government and commercial contracting, as well as unique aspects of each.

Given that no body of knowledge is ever static, periodic reviews are necessary. What new areas of knowledge have emerged that must be mastered? What are the tasks that contract professionals perform on a regular basis and in what knowledge areas must they demonstrate competency? This analysis is generally accomplished via a job analysis, which identifies the tasks performed by contract management professionals as well as the knowledge areas required for performance. In 2009, NCMA empanelled a Job Analysis Task Force (JATF). With the assistance of Professional Examination Services (a company providing a full range of assessment and advisory services to organizations across a broad range of professions in support of professional licensure and certification, training, and continuing professional education), the JATF was charged with creating a contemporary description of the work of contracts managers, consisting of the major performance domains of practice, the tasks performed within the domains, knowledge content areas, and the knowledge used in each of these areas. The intent was to support the development of a structured description of contemporary contracts management practice as well as determine any updates needed for NCMA's Certification Program and the body of knowledge.

Professional Examination Services formulated these tasks and domains into a survey sent to a combination of certified and non-certified members. Those surveyed were asked to rate tasks and knowledge areas in terms of both frequency of use and importance to the practice of the profession. The survey results give us a snapshot of the practice of contract management and enable us to identify gaps in the body of knowledge or areas that should be more or less strongly emphasized. The tasks and knowledge domains are provided in the Appendices.

Of the over 300 respondents, 82 percent held an NCMA certification with 48 percent on the buyer side and 49 percent on the seller side. There was a clear distinction between pre- and post-award activities dependent on whether the respondent was on the buyer or seller side. The only knowledge domain where more than 15 percent of respondents spent more than half their time was the *Manage Contract* domain. Similarly, the most frequently used knowledge was in the post-award areas; however, nearly all respondents indicated the need for knowledge in other areas, even if they did not spend their practice time in those areas. Therefore, it can be said that the contracts professional must have a wide knowledge base and some level of familiarity with many subjects, even if his or her current environment does not require him or her to practice in those fields.

Purpose of This Guide to the CMBOK

Contract management is a mature profession, but still growing. The purpose of this guide is to provide a common understanding of the terms used in the profession. As a basic reference, this document is neither comprehensive nor all-inclusive; but rather, it seeks to provide a tutorial of the contract management process in commercial as well as U.S. government contracting.

This document is also used by NCMA as a basic reference about contract management knowledge and practices for its professional development programs, including NCMA's Certification Program.

What is a Contract?

A "contract" is an agreement between two or more parties, especially one that is written and enforceable by law. For a contract to be valid, both parties must indicate that they agree to the terms. This is accomplished when one party submits an offer that the other accepts within a reasonable time or a stipulated period. If the terms of the acceptance vary from those of the offer, that acceptance legally constitutes a counteroffer; the original offering party may then accept it or reject it. At any time before acceptance, the offer may be rescinded on notice unless the offering party is bound by a separate option contract not to withdraw. Only those terms expressed in the contract can be enforced; secret intentions are not recognized. For a contract to be binding, it must not have an immoral or criminal purpose or intent or be contrary to public policy. Since a contract is an agreement, it may be made only by parties with the capacity to reach an understanding.

Most contracts are "bilateral," consisting of reciprocal promises. Under bilateral contracts, each party has made a promise, has an obligation to perform, and has expectations that the other party will perform. An example is a contract where one party promises to provide services and the other party promises to pay an agreed-to amount of money to receive said services.

There are also "unilateral contracts" where only one party has made a promise and is obligated to perform. An example of this may be a contract that promises monetary reward to find a missing pet. No one is obligated by that contract to search for that pet, but if the pet is found, the party who promised the reward is obligated to pay a reward.

An "express contract" is one in which the terms of the contract are stated in words, either written or spoken, and assented to by both parties. An "implied contract," sometimes called "implied in fact," is one in which the terms of the contract are wholly or partly inferred from conduct or surrounding circumstance. "Quasi contracts," sometimes called "implied in law," are obligations imposed by law to prevent the unjust enrichment of one person at another's expense.

A legally binding contract must contain the following elements:

- It must involve two or more parties that have the capacity to contract;
- It must show agreement, including offer, acceptance, and mutual assent;
- It must show something of value changing hands between the parties to a contract, or other inducement that leads a person to make a promise;
- It must be for a legal purpose; and
- It must be in the correct form.

A contract can be partially or totally unenforceable. If a party to the contract does not have the capacity to contract (such as being underage or having a mental infirmity), a contract is unenforceable. An "illegal contract" is a type of unenforceable contract that violates public policy or statutes. A court will not intervene in the case of illegal contracts; however, the court may divide the contract into legal and illegal portions and consider only the illegal portions void. A contract can also be unenforceable in cases of misrepresentation, duress, undue influence, lack of written evidence of the terms of certain business-related contracts, and in some cases mistakes.

A contract is "executed" when all the parties have fully performed their contractual duties.

What is Contract Management?

"Contract management" is the process of managing contracts, deliverables, deadlines, and contract terms and conditions while ensuring customer satisfaction. Public agencies and private companies know that the purchasing process does not end when the contract is awarded.

Effective post-award contract management is essential to the seamless acceptance of supplies and services. Contract management impacts many areas within an organization and can significantly influence its budget, operations, customer service, and public image.

Procurement and contract management are actually mirror images of each other. Both professions describe the broader process of sales or acquisition between two parties. Some objectives of buyers and sellers are distinctly different, while others are surprisingly similar. A mutually beneficial contract can often be challenging to write. Buyers want the lowest price, whereas sellers want to maximize profit. Both, however, should strive to meet the quality, delivery, and performance expectations of each other. Working together, they form a group of professionals under the "procurement" umbrella.

Popular discussion often differentiates between "acquisition" and "procurement," with procurement often characterized as the mechanical or even clerical fulfillment of acquisition goals. Notwithstanding such periodic variations, this document considers "procurement" at the overarching level, encompassing the whole gamut of actions required to achieve programmatic or organizational goals. Procurement consists of evaluating and selecting suppliers based on availability, reliability, and price to obtain the highest quality products at the lowest price. Buyers conduct market research by attending trade shows and conferences and visiting suppliers' plants to examine products and stay abreast of industry trends. They must develop a working technical knowledge of the goods or services they buy. They often forge a strong working relationship with their supplier counterparts—the contract managers—to optimize the outcome for both parties.

The mission of a contract management organization may read as follows:

> …The …contract management organization's mission is to provide vision, leadership, and professional expertise within the total business team necessary to ensure, at the lowest cost consistent with the significance of the issue or matter, that:
>
> 1) …contracts with its customers are negotiated, managed, and communicated in a manner that satisfies customers' needs and requirements;

2) Working with program and business management functions, the [organization] complies with contractual terms and conditions and applicable laws and regulations;

3) Contractual issues and risks are anticipated, avoided, or mitigated (if possible) and appreciated in making business decisions; and

4) Opportunities to advance or protect the [organization]'s legitimate interests are identified and appropriately pursued.

To be fully effective, contract management services are best developed and provided through full integration and active participation in the business team from the first moment of the business process.[1]

About the Contract Management Profession

"Contract management" is a specialized competency within the procurement profession, but it has a very broad perspective in terms of the responsibilities assigned to a contract manager. The job scope ranges from the administrative skills of managing, organizing, and planning to the excitement and challenge of negotiating a major contract. Both procurement and contract management demand competence in such areas as contract law, administration, accounting, psychology, management, and planning.

The Contract Management Institute (CMI) commissioned two studies on the contract management profession in 1999 and 2001. The first study, conducted by PricewaterhouseCoopers, analyzed the implications of current and future business requirements on contract and business management professionals. An important objective of this research was to reach conclusions gleaned from the insights of active and inactive contract management professionals and others, such as educators, consultants, lawyers, and those working in various related disciplines. Some notable findings of the study included the following:

- Essential core activities of contract managers include structuring business arrangements, contract formation, contract execution, pursuit of innovative contracting or business approaches, decision-making, and building strategic relations.

- More than 80 percent of CMI's respondents believed that the contract professional's role was more time-sensitive, involved more responsibility, and was more team-oriented and more strategic. Contract managers have an increasingly important role to play in cross-functional or integrated process teams.

- In the future, business-related performance metrics would be used to assess practitioner effectiveness.

- Almost 93 percent of CMI's respondents agreed or strongly agreed that a specialized undergraduate degree in contracting/purchasing is the most desirable educational background. However, effective written and verbal communication skills are the most important current and future professional requirements. Analysis and negotiation skills were highly prized in the short term, but would be superseded by computer literacy and problem-solving skills. Business judgment is a competency valued highly, regardless of the time period.

- With respect to education and training opportunities, contract and business managers are largely responsible for guiding their own career development.

- The results showed a high correlation between salary levels and education.

The purpose of a second study commissioned by CMI, conducted by Stratecon, was to provide a better understanding of the performance metrics and performance evaluation systems by which organizations measured the performance of contract managers and purchasing professionals, as well as what standards might be appropriate to use in the future. The study showed that the contract management profession was evolving. Seventy-five percent of survey respondents agreed or strongly agreed that the contract management/purchasing function in their organizations was evolving into a strategic function that interacts with most aspects of an organization's business to include such activities as:

- Building strategic relationships internally and externally,

- Conducting strategic planning and sourcing,

- Collaborating on acquisition planning,

- Participating in cross-functional or integrated process teams,

- Pursuing innovative contracting or business approaches, and

- Making important decisions.

The top 10 metrics chosen by the overall population to evaluate the performance of contract management and purchasing professionals were:

1. Responsiveness,
2. Integrity and adherence to ethical standards,
3. Timeliness,
4. Written communication,
5. Verbal communication,
6. Human relations/interpersonal skills,
7. Problem-solving ability,
8. Education,
9. Internal customer service, and
10. Business judgment.

The 10 top metrics recommended for use in the future to evaluate the performance of contract management and purchasing professionals were:

1. Integrity and adherence to ethical standards,
2. Human relations/interpersonal skills,
3. Business judgment,
4. Decision-making,
5. External customer service,
6. Written communication,
7. Negotiation skills,
8. Customer focus,
9. Problem-solving ability, and
10. Responsiveness.

About NCMA

NCMA is devoted to education, training, research, study, and to a certification program that reflects the highest standards of professional achievement. Guided by a code of ethics, the association is committed to develop and provide programs, products, and services that nurture and enhance contract management competencies through leadership and business management partnering.

NCMA's Mission

NCMA's mission is to advance the contract management profession.

NCMA's Vision for the Profession

Contract management will be viewed by all organizations—public and private—as an essential business management function that directly contributes to organizational success. People will recognize contract management as a challenging and rewarding profession, and will prepare for and seek out positions in the profession. Universities will provide undergraduate and graduate degree programs and courses designed to prepare students for entry into or advancement in the contract management profession.

NCMA's Vision for the Organization

NCMA will lead in defining the standards and the body of knowledge for the contract management profession. NCMA will provide tools that enable the entry, development, and advancement of all contract management professionals. NCMA will be a model for not-for-profit individual membership organizations, recognized for innovation, effective and efficient operations, and agile and responsible governance.

NCMA's Value Propositions

NCMA provides the tools, resources, and leadership opportunities to enhance each member of the profession's performance, career, and accomplishments. NCMA provides the structure, name recognition, and products directly and through chapters to contracting professionals worldwide. NCMA provides employers ready access to skilled human capital, learning resources, best practices, standards, and metrics of the profession. NCMA also enables other entities, such as researchers, consultants, trainers, recruiters, advertisers, and universities, to gain broad access to defined segments of our community of practice and our body of knowledge for the purpose of advancing the profession and fulfilling their individual goals.

NCMA's Values

NCMA is committed to:

- Principled professional conduct and achievement, as dictated by our Code of Ethics;
- An open exchange of ideas in a neutral forum;
- A culturally and professionally diverse membership;
- Excellence in everything we do, especially our

service to our members and the contract management community;
- Continuing education, training, and leadership opportunities through a network of local chapters;
- Remaining the preeminent source of professional development for contract professionals;
- Recognizing and rewarding professional excellence and superior individual achievement in support of the contract management profession;
- Demonstrated professional achievement through certification;
- Quality volunteer leadership; and
- Members' highly principled freedom of action and responsibility to the people and organizations they serve.

Thousands of professionals enhance their knowledge and leverage opportunities in purchasing, procurement, project management, and contract management with NCMA. Comprising individual members and professional groups from nonprofit, industry, and government, NCMA provides unique resources for the contracting community.

For more than 50 years, members have taken advantage of NCMA membership benefits to advance their careers. Practical, proven survival techniques and industry news help members stay informed about current contract management events. NCMA continues to provide vital information about the field through the association's prestigious publications, educational materials, and professional resources.

As in the past, over the next several years, previously unimagined technological changes will produce a new realm for virtually instantaneous business transactions. Over the next decade alone, what now seems farfetched in electronic commerce will become commonplace. Even the most vivid imaginations cannot predict what may occur and affect the contract management profession, NCMA, and its membership. To help prepare for the vagaries of an uncertain future, NCMA continues to monitor the contract management profession and reflects the changing character of that profession in its Certification Program. One such change is the increasing tendency of contract professionals to no longer pursue what can be termed as "traditional career paths," where an employee enters a profession out of college and seeks upward mobility through increasingly higher levels within that same functional area. The new predominant career profile is a person enters a job out of college, and then moves laterally, or diagonally, seeking new challenges and opportunities in adjacent fields. This new progression is typified by:

- Increasing geographic and assignment mobility;
- Pursuing career-broadening experiences;
- Pursuing flexible work arrangements to accommodate lifestyle shifts;
- Working for multiple employers over the course of a career;
- Working in multiple professions;
- Entering, departing, and reentering a specific profession;
- Engaging, disengaging, and reengaging with the association serving the profession; and
- Accepting lower compensation and occasional backward or downward movements, seeking lesser responsibilities.

The term for this model has been referred to as "the career web" or "lattice," which is intended to convey the fact that traditional career paths may have been made obsolete (or perhaps just significantly less common). There is indeed a shift being observed across the global workforce, driven by generational expectations, globalism, and technology. Therefore, the challenge for NCMA is to help an individual understand his or her options within the career web, or to move effectively in a horizontal or diagonal manner between adjacent fields.

NCMA also demonstrates its commitment to the profession through the Contract Management Code of Ethics:

Contract Management Code of Ethics

Each member of the contract management profession ("the profession") accepts the obligation to continuously improve one's professional knowledge and job performance in the field of contract management and to abide by the letter and spirit of the ethical standards set forth below.

Each member of NCMA shall:

- Strive to attain the highest professional standard of job performance, to exercise diligence in carrying out one's professional duties, and to serve the profession to the best of one's ability.

- Conduct oneself in such a manner as to bring credit upon the profession, as well as to maintain trust and confidence in the integrity of the contract management process.
- Avoid engagement in any transaction that might conflict or appear to conflict with the proper discharge of one's professional duties by reason of a financial interest, family relationship, or any other circumstances.
- Comply with all laws and regulations that govern the contract management process in the jurisdictions in which one conducts business, including protection of competition-sensitive and proprietary information from inappropriate disclosure.
- Keep informed of developments in the contract management field, utilizing both formal training and ad hoc means, to continuously increase knowledge, skill, and professional competence.
- Share one's knowledge and experience openly to contribute to the development of other professionals, improve performance quality, and enhance public perception of the profession.
- Not knowingly influence others to commit any act that would constitute a violation of this code.

Professional Certification

NCMA's first professional certification designation, the Certified Professional Contracts Manager (CPCM), was established in 1974. NCMA's leadership, understanding that NCMA needed to establish a method of recognizing professional achievement, worked closely with industry and government professionals to develop a comprehensive program. The CPCM represents a hallmark of professional achievement in the field of contract management. The first CPCM exams were held across the country in 1976, with 23 successful candidates receiving the CPCM designation. Based on a set of stringent educational criteria and years of experience and service, some senior professionals were given a one-time opportunity to receive the CPCM designation without sitting for the examination.

The Certified Associate Contracts Manager (CACM) designation was added in 1980 to certify the mastery of the fundamentals of federal government contracting. In 2002, the CACM designation was renamed the Certified Federal Contracts Manager (CFCM) to more accurately describe its content and focus. All those who were awarded the CACM were automatically re-designated as CFCMs. Eventually, the Certified Commercial Contracts Manager (CCCM) designation was developed to certify knowledge of the Uniform Commercial Code (UCC).

Although these designations were originally developed as methods of recognizing professional achievement among peers, all of them have evolved to be much more. Today, NCMA's professional designations and the standards behind them are widely recognized by both government and industry as a consistent measure of the skills and experience needed by successful contract managers. Across the nation, employment requisitions and advertisements are stating, "NCMA designation preferred." Government agencies are recognizing the value of certification when making promotion decisions. NCMA's designations are seen as a standardized hallmark of excellence across the contract management community.

NCMA's Certification Program

At the start of the new millennium, NCMA began to consider revising and revitalizing its certification programs. From 2001 to 2008, the certification program was managed by a Contract Management Certification and Accreditation Board (CMCAB) and the testing program consisted of several modules. Completion of certain modules led to either a CPCM, CFCM, or CCCM.

Today, NCMA has reduced the complexity of its premier certification program while retaining the stature of the credentials. The biggest change is the implementation of having only one exam per certification. The CPCM, CFCM, and CCCM are certifications awarded to candidates who meet rigorous standards, including experience, education, training, and knowledge. They are professional designations of distinction and carry the respect of their peers in the profession. NCMA certifications are competency-based, legally defensible, and are based on psychometrically sound objective examination of knowledge. The NCMA professional certification program is designed to elevate professional standards, enhance individual performance, and distinguish those who demonstrate knowledge essential to the practice of contract management.

Eligibility Requirements

➢ *CPCM*

A candidate must have a degree from a regionally accredited institution at a bachelor's level, five years

Contract Management Body of Knowledge (CMBOK) Outline of Competencies

1.0 Pre-Award
- 1.1 Laws and Regulations
- 1.2 Contract Principles
- 1.3 Standards of Conduct
- 1.4 Socioeconomic Programs
- 1.5 Contract Structures
- 1.6 Contracting Methods
- 1.7 Contract Financing
- 1.8 Intellectual Property

2.0 Acquisition Planning/Strategy
- 2.1 Acquisition Planning
- 2.2 Acquisition Methodology
- 2.3 Proposal Preparation
- 2.4 Negotiation
- 2.5 Source Selection
- 2.6 Protest

3.0 Post-Award
- 3.1 Contract Administration
- 3.2 Contract Performance/Quality Assurance
- 3.3 Subcontract Management
- 3.4 Contract Changes and Modifications
- 3.5 Property Administration
- 3.6 Transportation
- 3.7 Disputes
- 3.8 Organizational Conflict of Interest
- 3.9 Contract Closeout
- 3.10 Contract Termination

4.0 Specialized Knowledge Areas
- 4.1 Research and Development
- 4.2 Architect-Engineer Services and Construction
- 4.3 Information Technology
- 4.4 Major Systems
- 4.5 Service Contracts
- 4.6 International Contracting
- 4.7 State and Local Government
- 4.8 Supply Chain
- 4.9 Performance-Based Acquisition
- 4.10 Government Property
- 4.11 Other Specialized Areas

5.0 Business
- 5.1 Management
- 5.2 Marketing
- 5.3 Operations Management
- 5.4 Finance Analysis
- 5.5 Accounting
- 5.6 Economics
- 5.7 Information Science or Information Technology
- 5.8 Leadership Skills

FIGURE 1. CMBOK WBS Structure

of relevant experience, and 120 hours of continuing professional education. No waivers are given.

> *CFCM*

Eligibility for the CFCM requires a candidate to have a degree from a regionally accredited institution at the bachelor's level, one year of relevant experience, and 80 hours of continuing professional education. Candidates lacking only the experiential and continuing education requirements may apply for the designation and take the examinations. Upon successful completion of the examinations, the candidate will be awarded the designation ONLY when both experiential and continuing education requirements are met.

> *CCCM*

A candidate must have a degree from a regionally accredited institution at the bachelor's level, one year of experience in the contract management field, and 80 hours of continuing professional education. Candidates lacking only the experiential and continuing education requirements may apply for the designation and take the examinations. Upon successful completion of the examinations, the candidate will be awarded the designation ONLY when both experiential and continuing education requirements are met.

The CMBOK Structure

The CMBOK may be formatted in a work breakdown structure (WBS) that includes broad subject headings (e.g., preaward, post-award, etc.) as well as foundational (or core) competencies, subject matter competencies, and job or task level skills. The same structure can apply to both federal and commercial contract management, with particular emphasis depending on one's orientation.

Foundational competencies are those general competencies needed for success regardless of job or role (American Society for Training and Development (ASTD)), while subject matter competency relates to a particular field or subject. Task level competencies are the ability to perform specific tasks related to the work. For example, foundational competencies list broad knowledge areas, which are part of the full CMBOK. These five competency areas are preaward, acquisition planning/strategy, post-award, specialized

FIGURE 2. CMBOK Outline

knowledge areas, and business (see **FIGURE 1** on page 9).

Subject matter competencies are a subset of the foundational competencies and the specific knowledge areas, which are part of the full CMBOK that contract managers need to know to be effective and do their job well. Subject matter competencies include specific knowledge areas such as 3.4 Contract Changes/Modifications, 4.8 Supply Chain, and 5.9 Leadership Skills.

Task level competencies list a subset of the subject matter competencies as well as the specific knowledge areas within the subject matter competencies. Task level competencies include specific subject matter, such as 1.5.2 Cost Reimbursement Contracts, 2.2.3 Statement of Work, and 3.10.1 Termination for Default.

The CMBOK can be illustrated in a traditional WBS format (as seen on page 9) or in a relationship fashion (as seen in **FIGURE 2** on page 10).

The CMBOK: An Overview

chapter two

Contract Life Cycle

Contracts have a defined beginning and end. The contract life cycle defines these parameters. The contract life cycle is broken down into several contract phases. The phases during the total life cycle can generally be categorized as:

- Pre-award (which includes acquisition planning),
- Contract award, and
- Post-award.

There is also consideration of special competencies required based on the requirement, contract type, and processes employed in the contract life cycle.

The pre-award phase actually begins with acquisition planning. Planning is an essential preliminary component to successfully completing virtually any effort. Acquisition planning is a critical first step in the contract life cycle. Competencies such as conducting market research, selecting the proper contract type, and formulating the acquisition strategy are all part of this phase.

Once the planning is completed, the next phase involves all of the work that leads up to an awarded contract. Some acquisitions are very simple, others are exceedingly complex, and the majority fall somewhere in the middle. This phase includes preparing requirements documents, evaluating proposals, conducting negotiations, and completing source selection.

The award phase is a transitional phase that goes from signing a contract to notifying unsuccessful vendors. The elements of the contract award phase include completing contract award, debriefing of unsuccessful offers, and addressing any mistakes in proposals or any protests or litigation.

Once the award phase is completed, the post-award phase begins. This involves all of the contract management functions known as "contract administration." The contract administration functions will vary greatly depending on the complexity of the contract. However, the basic premise remains the same. Is the seller delivering what the contract requires? The post-award phase includes the necessary contract administration activities in order to ensure performance and bring the contract to a successful conclusion. This includes executing contract modifications; addressing any issues arising during contract performance; and, upon completion of performance, invoicing, and payment, closing out the contract.

Contract Stakeholders

A contract is an agreement between two parties. Because of that, there are contract stakeholders on both sides of the agreement (contract). The party with the requirement, usually the initiating party in the contractual process, has several stakeholders who are directly affected by the contracting process.

The stakeholders begin with the organization that has the requirement for which a contract will ultimately be executed. This stakeholder is generally the end user of the item or service provided under the contract. There is also a program office that is responsible for defining the requirement in a manner that can be readily identifiable, clear, and concise enough to allow for consistent understanding for all parties involved in the contracting process. The program office may be part of the end user's organization, but does not have to be. The finance office may be part of the program office and is responsible for identifying the funding to be used to buy the supply or service. Then there is the contracting officer, who is responsible for executing the contract and ensuring and enforcing contract terms and conditions, including performance or delivery.

The second set of stakeholders is part of the organization receiving the contract and tasked with providing the goods and/or services to the requiring organization. These stakeholders include the company or organization receiving the contract, including the group within tasked with providing the goods or services. The organization may not have the internal capability to provide the total requirements of the contract. In this case, some of the effort would be subcontracted and those subcontractors would also become contract stakeholders.

The organization providing the goods or services must have the financial capability to perform contractual requirements before delivering and receiving payment. That source of funding, whether internal or through creditors, is also a stakeholder in the contract process.

Organizational Influences

Organizational influences have a profound effect on the contracting process. These influences can be internal or external to the organization. Senior management in an organization directly influences the initiation of requirements that are ultimately fulfilled through the contracting process. This influence takes place in several ways.

For example, senior management may adjust or change company focus through strategic planning. This change in focus will commonly result in changing business processes and procedures. This results in new requirements for software, hardware, and can even cause a change in the qualifications of people working for the organization. These changing requirements are generally fulfilled or supported through the contracting process.

Evolving technology has an enormous impact on an organization. It affects business processes, which ultimately can affect organizational structure and enhance organizational performance. To take advantage of evolving technology and its benefits, an efficient and effective contracting process must be in place.

Other competitors can drive the need to maintain awareness of industry best practices and, where possible, develop best practices rather than continually implementing those already developed. Again, an efficient and effective contracting process is required to be an industry leader.

General Business Competencies

The duties and responsibilities of a contracting professional extend well beyond the specialized set of knowledge and experience unique to the profession. Current business and government organizational models are rapidly and continuously changing in pursuit of increased efficiency and decreased cost. Given the ongoing environment of rightsizing, outsourcing, lean management, six sigma, continuous process improvement, balanced scorecards, transformation, and reinvention (just to name a few), one could argue that the people who work in this environment also have to change as well.

Contracting professionals, as well as other professionals in business and government, can no longer perform effectively in the isolation of specialized knowledge and experience. Most organizations rely, to greater or lesser degrees, on various forms of matrix-managed functions, project or program teams, permanent or temporary process improvement groups, and similar types of collaborative entities. These structures exist primarily to bring more attention to the idea that each segment of an organization, whether public or private, needs to make a positive contribution to the business of the business or the mission of the agency.

The team approach to the operation of business and government often results in a smaller and necessarily more proficient and agile staff. The knowledge required to be an effective contracting professional extends beyond the complex and dynamic contracting environment. A contracting professional must also (and some would argue first) be a business professional. One must have a clear understanding of the general functions of business and government and how those functions combine with and compliment each other to achieve organizational goals.

General Contracting Competencies

A contract manager's skills are developed through continuing education and practice. A successful contract manager has developed skills in three main areas:

- Technical,
- Conceptual, and
- Human relations.

Technical skills are demonstrated by competently performing the tasks required, such as preparing and issuing solicitations, preparing bids and proposals, preparing or analyzing terms and conditions, or analyzing procurement requirements and supplier capabilities. Training for these skills can be accomplished in degree, certificate, professional continuing education, or specialized programs.

Conceptual skills relate to the manner in which the contract manager visualizes the contract's organization in terms of the agency's or company's goals. These skills involve the ability to see and use the "big picture" for greater organizational and personal success.

Human relations skills focus on the "people" aspect of contract management. Effective performance requires people to cooperate with each other even when the contract manager has little or no organizational control over them. Dealing with government and contractor representatives from a diverse range of disciplines requires strong relational and communication skills. Many contract managers consider competency in human relations to be the most important skill for the future of their jobs and careers.

The full CMBOK includes knowledge of generally accepted practices, which are widely applied to the practice of contract management. It also includes the knowledge of more innovative and advanced practices, which may be used less often. This knowledge is obtained, in part, by asking professionals in the contracting community—both public and private—and practitioners in the field what competencies and knowledge contract professionals need to do their jobs well.

Knowledge is also gained through a critical review of the myriad activities performed by contract managers. The diagram in **FIGURE 3** below depicts the interrelationships and activities performed daily by contract managers in a corporation with notionally more than 300 people. A contract manager's activities include coordination with those personnel who think they need an item or service and continue through the development of a contract, its administration, and its ultimate successful completion and closeout. Along the way, the contract manager interacts with those who need the item or service, those who know and can describe the item or service, those who are the keepers of the finances, and all the people involved, as well as all the people who are in charge of those involved—the contract manager affects a wide circle.

FIGURE 3. Interrelationships of Contract Managers

The CMBOK Knowledge Areas/Outline of Competencies

chapter three

Knowledge and competencies used by contract management professionals may generally be categorized into five overarching areas:

- Pre-award,
- Post-award,
- Business,
- Legal/regulatory/professional, and
- Specialized.

Within each area are subsets addressing nearly every aspect of contacting. In order to cross-walk earlier editions of the "CMBOK Outline of Competencies," WBS elements 1.0 and 2.0 are considered "Pre-Award"; 3.0 is considered "Post-Award"; and 4.0 and 5.0 remain essentially the same. The former 1.1.2, "Laws and Regulations," becomes its own competency as a new 1.1. Therefore, the revised outline is depicted below:

1.0 Pre-Award
1.1 Laws and Regulations
1.2 Contract Principles
1.3 Standards of Conduct
1.4 Socioeconomic Programs
1.5 Contract Structures
1.6 Contracting Methods
1.7 Contract Financing
1.8 Intellectual Property
2.0 Acquisition Planning/Strategy
2.1 Acquisition Planning
2.2 Acquisition Methodology
2.3 Proposal Preparation
2.4 Negotiation
2.5 Source Selection
2.6 Protests
3.0 Post-Award
3.1 Contract Administration
3.2 Contract Performance/Quality Assurance
3.3 Subcontract Administration
3.4 Contract Changes and Modifications
3.5 Property Administration
3.6 Transportation
3.7 Disputes
3.8 Organizational Conflict of Interest
3.9 Contract Closeout
3.10 Contract Termination
4.0 Specialized Knowledge Areas
4.1 Research and Development
4.2 Architect-Engineer Services and Construction
4.3 Information Technology
4.4 Major Systems
4.5 Service Contracts
4.6 International Contracting
4.7 State and Local Governments
4.8 Supply Chain Management
4.9 Performance-Based Acquisition
4.10 Government Property
4.11 Other Specialized Areas
5.0 Business
5.1 Management
5.2 Marketing
5.3 Operations Management
5.4 Financial Analysis
5.5 Accounting
5.6 Economics
5.7 Information Science or Information Technology
5.8 Leadership Skills

1.0 Pre-Award

1.1 Laws and Regulations

At its core, the contracting profession is about the knowledge and application of laws and regulations. Contracts are legal documents of agreement whose terms and conditions are legally binding and enforceable in various courts of law and other administrative bodies. As such, it is important for the contracting professional to have a good working knowledge of the laws, regulations, and other sources of guidance that define, to a large extent, the environment in which the contracting professional operates. These sources of law and guidance include:

- The Uniform Commercial Code (UCC),
- The *Federal Acquisition Regulation* (*FAR*),
- Laws related to international contracting, and
- Case law.

Commercial Contract Law Basics

The states, not the federal government, are the primary source of law on commercial transactions in the United States. This includes state statutory and common (judge-made) law and private law. Private law principally includes the terms of the agreement between the parties who have exchanged promises for consideration. These terms may override rules established by state law. Statutory law may require some contracts to be put in writing and executed using specific procedures.

Agency

The "law of agency" is important in commercial contracting. It recognizes that most corporations operate exclusively through agents. Agency law is concerned with any principal-agent relationship—a relationship in which one person has legal authority to act for another. This relationship can result from explicit appointment where the principal authorizes the agent to represent his or her interests and perform acts that bind the principal, or this relationship can result by implication where it is implied by the conduct of the parties.

An "agent" acts on behalf of another person and is subject to that person's control. The one for whom action is taken is the "principal"; the one who acts on behalf of the principal is the agent.

A "universal agent" provides broad authority for an agent to act on behalf of the principal. A "general agent" is authorized to conduct a limited series of transactions involving a continuity of service and may be empowered to enter into contracts that are binding on the principal. A "special agent's" power and authority is limited to accomplishing a specific and limited assignment and does not have the power or authority to enter into contracts on behalf of the principal.

Authority

In order to bind the principal, the agent must act within the authority granted by the principal. This authority may be one of the following four types:

- Actual authority—An agent's specific authority that the principal intentionally confers on the agent. It confers a power to the agent to affect legal relations of the principals with third persons.

- Express authority—Authority plainly granted, either verbally or in writing, to an agent by a principal. It is direction provided to the agent by the principal to do specific actions.

- Implied authority—Authority given by a principal to an agent that is not actually expressed or otherwise communicated. This allows the agent to perform all the usual and necessary tasks to exercise the agent's expressed authority. The direction to do something is not provided expressly from the principal's words, but implied from what is understood as customary in the industry.

- Apparent authority—The appearance of being a principal's agent with the power to act for the principal. Corporations are liable for an employee's acts and promises to a third party if it appears to the third party that the employee has been granted authority by his or her corporate employer (principal) to do those acts which bind the corporation.

The Uniform Commercial Code (UCC)

The UCC is a comprehensive set of laws governing commercial transactions within the United States. The fundamental intent of the UCC is to provide a framework in which commercial organizations can conduct business across state or other jurisdictional boundaries with reasonable assurance that the same or similar rules apply. This concept of mutual understanding of commercial terms and practices is essential to an organization's ability to contract effectively. It is important to note that the UCC, as a uniform law, must be adopted as law by each state separately. As a result, there are differences in the UCC from state to state.

The UCC was created as the result of a joint effort by the National Conference of Commissioners on Uniform State Laws and the American Law Institute. The National Conference of Commissioners on Uniform State Laws is a non-profit association, founded in 1892. Its membership consists of attorneys from all 50 U.S. states, the District of Columbia, the Commonwealth of Puerto Rico, and the U.S. Virgin Islands. Each jurisdiction determines how appointments are made. The National Conference is the combined membership of the various state commissions of uniform laws. The principle purpose of the National Conference is to study and review state laws to determine which laws should be uniform. The National Conference also drafts and proposes specific statutes when uniformity is advantageous. The American Law Institute was organized and created in 1923. Its elected membership consists of attorneys, judges, and law professors from all areas of the United States, as well as some foreign countries. The Institute was created "to promote the clarification and simplification of the law and its better adaptation to social needs, secure the better administration of justice, and encourage and carry on scholarly and scientific legal work."[2] In addition to its collaboration with the National Conference on the UCC, the Institute also collaborates with the American Bar Association in a national program of continuing legal education.

The UCC has been enacted in 49 of the 50 states; Louisiana being the exception. Louisiana has enacted most of the UCC, but differences in state law resulting from Louisiana civil law and the Napoleonic Code make complete adoption of the UCC difficult. Some states have not adopted all of the UCC's articles or have enacted modified versions of the UCC. Therefore, when the UCC applies to a transaction, the requirements of each state need to be separately considered as applicable.

The UCC consists of nine articles, most with multiple parts:

The Uniform Commerical Code Articles	
Article 1	General Provisions
Article 2	Sales
Article 2A	Leases
Article 3	Negotiable Instruments
Article 4	Bank Deposit
Article 4A	Funds Transfers
Article 5	Letters of Credit
Article 6	Bulk Transfers and Bulk Sales
Article 7	Warehouse Receipts, Bills of Lading, and Other Documents of Title
Article 8	Investment Securities
Article 9	Secured Transactions

The UCC has long been a primary source of agreement and guidance in the commercial contracting community. The UCC, as with any body of law, is undergoing continual review, refinement, and revision in order to keep pace with changes in the business environment and technological advancements. Further, as the government contracting community continues to expand its use of commercial contracting practices, government contracting professionals should expand their knowledge base to include the UCC and its impact on contracting policy, procedures, and commonly accepted practices.

A more detailed table of contents for the UCC is provided in Appendix A.

The underlying purposes of the UCC, as stated in Section 1-102 of the code, are:

- To simplify, clarify, and modernize the law governing commercial transactions;
- To permit the continued expansion of commercial practices through custom, usage, and agreement of the parties; and
- To make uniform the law among the various jurisdictions.

The overriding philosophy of the UCC is to allow people to make the contracts they want, but to fill in any missing provisions where the agreements they make are silent. Current law governing contracts for the sale of any kind of "goods" between two U.S. corporations is Article 2 of the UCC. The UCC applies to goods, but not services. Services contracts can become voluminous because there are no "missing provisions" or "gap filler" provisions as under the UCC to protect buyers and sellers, so buyers and sellers create provisions that are suitable for their own needs. Article 2 is intended to be the sole source of law governing sales, supplemented by state law only if not addressed by a provision within the UCC.[3] Article 2 addresses such issues as contract formation, nonperformance, and performance of contractual obligations, repudiation of contract, contract termination, the remedies for nonperformance, the cure rights of a party who fails to perform, the implicit and explicit warranties, the waiver or disclaimer of such warranties, and risk of loss.

Underlying Concepts in the UCC
In regards to contracts, the UCC has several underlying concepts:

- Merchants are professionals in their field and should be held to higher standards than a casual buyer.
- Every contract imposes an obligation of good faith in its performance or enforcement.
- What is a reasonable time for taking any action depends on the nature, purpose, and circumstances of such action.

Formation of a Sales Contract
Article 2 states that in order to contract for the sale of goods with a price of $5,000 or more to be enforceable it must be in writing sufficient to indicate that a contract for sale has been made between the parties and signed by the party against whom enforcement is sought or by his or her authorized agent or broker. Article 2 contains three requirements of the written contract:

- It must provide evidence there was a contract for the sale of goods,

- It must be signed by the party to be charged, and
- It must specify a quantity.

This implies that the price, time, and place of payment or delivery; the general quality of the goods or any particular warranties may be omitted; and if the above three requirements are included, the contract is enforceable. Thus, contracts can be written on a cocktail napkin for sufficient evidence of a real transaction.

If not in writing, a contract can also be validated if there is "partial performance" as evidenced that goods have been accepted and payment has been made and accepted. This provides evidence that the contract actually exists. The party receiving the contract must give written notice of objection within 10 days after it is received, or the contract could be enforceable.

A signed offer to buy or sell goods remains irrevocable for a reasonable period not to exceed three months or for the period stated in the offer. Acceptance of the offer may be made by any reasonable manner, including either shipment or a prompt promise to ship or the beginning of performance by an offeree.

Often in commercial transactions, the offeree has a standard boilerplate of terms on which the offer is printed. When the offeror accepts the offer, the offeror states additional terms or different terms from those offered. The UCC allows for those additional terms to be construed as proposals for additional terms to the contract. Such terms are incorporated into the contract unless the offer stated that the offer expressly limits the terms of the offer, the acceptance was expressly made conditional on agreement on different terms, the additional terms materially alter the offer, or an objection of the additional terms is sent within a reasonable time. Article § 2–207 states:

> Subject to Section 2-202, if (i) conduct by both parties recognizes the existence of a contract although their records do not otherwise establish a contract, (ii) a contract is formed by an offer and acceptance, or (iii) a contract formed in any manner is confirmed by a record that contains terms additional to or different from those in the contract being confirmed, the terms of the contract are:
> a) Terms that appear in the records of both parties;
> b) Terms, whether in a record or not, to which both parties agree; and
> c) Terms supplied or incorporated under any provision of this act.

In addition to the express terms of the contract, there are other factors that can be relevant when interpretation of the contract is required. These include the following:

- "Course of performance"—refers to any acts in the performance of the contract by either party that are not objected to. These acts can be interpreted as consistent with the express terms.
- "Course of dealing"—a series of previous conduct between the parties to a particular transaction that can be regarded as establishing a common basis of understanding for terminology and conduct.
- "Usage of trade"—practices or methods of dealing that are regularly observed and justify an expectation that they will apply to the transaction in question.

Contract Modification

Under UCC rules, an existing contract can be modified without consideration, but the modification must satisfy the "statute of frauds" provision. A contract can be modified or rescinded only if done in writing on a form provided by the merchant and signed by the other party. Contract modifications must meet the test of good faith and cannot be used to escape performance obligations under the contract. A modification that does not meet the above requirements can be considered a waiver.

Performance

The general obligation of the seller under the contract is to transfer and deliver; the obligation of the buyer is to accept and pay in accordance with the contract. According to the UCC, the contract "imposes an obligation by the seller to use best efforts to supply the goods and by the buyer to use best efforts to promote their sale."

After the seller has manufactured the product, the seller may be unwilling to forward the product to the buyer until payment is received. Likewise, the buyer may be unwilling to pay until the buyer receives and inspects the product. The concept of "tender" entitles the seller, upon shipment, to the acceptance of goods and to payment according to the terms of the contract. It also entitles the buyer, upon payment, receipt of conforming goods. The seller's goods must conform in all respects to the terms of the contract or the buyer may reject the goods and not perform further. This is in addition to other rights the buyer may have. The concept of "tender" allows each party to be confident that the other party will perform so the seller and buyer can ship the product and make payment respectively.

The UCC states that acceptance of goods occurs when the buyer, "after a reasonable opportunity to inspect the goods, signifies to the seller that the goods are conforming or that he will take or retain them in spite of their non-conformity." Acceptance can also occur when the buyer fails to reject them or commits actions that are inconsistent with rejection.

The buyer has the right to reject the goods if they "fail in any respect to conform to the contract." The seller has a right to cure defects if the time for performance has not run out and the seller can cure the defects within that time, or the seller has reason to believe the buyer would accept nonconforming goods (in which case the seller can take a reasonable amount of extra time, beyond the time for original performance, in curing the defects).

In certain situations a buyer may revoke a prior acceptance of nonconforming goods (as long as the buyer notifies the seller of revocation in a reasonable time after the buyer discovered or should have discovered the nonconformity) when the defect has substantially impaired their value. A prior acceptance can be revoked if acceptance was made on the reasonable assumption that the defects would be cured in a reasonable time but haven't been, acceptance was predicated on the seller's assurances of conformity, or the defect was difficult to discover before acceptance. In order for the revocation to be effective, the goods must be in the same condition they were in when they were delivered to the buyer except for changes caused by the defects themselves. A revocation puts the buyer in the same position as if the buyer had rejected the goods initially.

Implied Warranties

Under the UCC, every sale of goods gives rise to certain implied warranties, including "implied warranty of merchantability" and "implied warranty of fitness for a particular purpose":

- "Implied warranty of merchantability"— Warranty a merchant makes which guarantees that goods are reasonably fit for the general purpose for which they are sold.
- "Implied warranty of fitness for a particular purpose"—Warranty for when a seller knows or has reason to know of a particular purpose for which some item is being purchased by the buyer, the seller is guaranteeing that the item is fit for that particular purpose, and if the buyer is relying on the seller's expertise to select suitable goods.

An implied warranty can be expressly disclaimed but has strict requirements in how it is disclaimed. The phrases "as is" or "with all faults" must appear distinctly in the contract in a different kind of print or font that makes it stand out. A disclaimer of the implied warranty of merchantability must use the word "merchantability." Contractual language can also limit the remedies available for breach of an implied warranty—for example, capping recoverable damages or limiting the remedy to a replacement of a defective item.

Repudiation

"Repudiation" is the refusal, especially by public authorities, to acknowledge a contract or debt. In the case of repudiation, a party can wait a commercially reasonable time for the repudiating party to perform or resort to any remedy for breach, even if it has notified the repudiating party that it is waiting for performance and urges it to retract the repudiation.

The repudiating party can retract the repudiation until its next performance is due unless, since the repudiation, the aggrieved party has cancelled or materially changed its position or the aggrieved party has indicated it considers the repudiation final. A retraction must be accompanied by "adequate assurances" within a reasonable time of the retraction.

Adequate assurances may be demanded in writing by any party when it has reasonable grounds for insecurity with respect to the performance of the other party. Until it receives such assurances, it may suspend its own performance. These adequate assurances would need to make a reasonable merchant believe the promised performance will be forthcoming.

When anticipatory repudiation substantially impairs the value of the contract, the innocent party may resort to any remedy, including suing immediately for breach, even if it is still negotiating with the repudiating party for performance or retraction. The innocent party can, if it so chooses, wait for a commercially reasonable time for the repudiating party to perform. Either way, taking some action now or waiting, the innocent party can suspend its own performance.

The Sarbanes-Oxley Act (SOX)

The SOX (*Public Law* 107-204) was signed into law on July 30, 2002. The substance of the law is to create requirements to prevent companies from accounting for profits not realized in an effort to portray value where none exists. The SOX has had a significant impact on the accounting practices of nearly all companies doing business in the United States. Indirectly, the SOX has had a significant impact on contract management functions as well. A sales contract is typically the primary record underlying a revenue transaction. Before SOX, many large companies did not have standard practices for contract creation or management. Under the SOX, firms could no longer carry a *laissez faire* attitude in how they created, recorded, and managed contracts. Since the SOX was passed into law, a mini-industry for creation and implementation of contract management software systems has boomed, and many firms have devoted more attention to the contract management function than ever before in order to ensure SOX compliance.

The SOX has had a disproportionate impact on commercial companies versus those that do business principally with the U.S. federal government. This is because companies who did substantial business with the government were already required to maintain a higher standard of contract management and cost accounting systems in order to comply with the *Federal Acquisition Regulation* and associated laws and regulations.

Additional information about the SOX can be found at **www.soxinstitute.org**.

Government Contract Law Basics

The U.S. federal government contracting process involves all three branches of the U.S. government: legislative, executive, and judicial. Congress, as the legislative branch, enacts laws that impact the contracting process and provide funding. The agencies, as part of the executive branch, draft regulations implementing the laws, solicit offers, and award and administer contracts. The federal courts, representing the judicial branch, interpret legislation and sometimes resolve disputes. These three branches thus work together to preserve the system of checks and balances necessary for the U.S. government to function properly. Each has an integral function to serve in the procurement process.

Some may argue that as the sovereign, the U.S. government receives special consideration in the contracting process. Although certain conflicts exist between the government as lawmaker and the government as contracting party, the laws have been designed to ensure that there is no special treatment conferred to the government. The government must be treated as other contracting parties in order to maintain a fair and equitable business relationship and to protect those with whom the government deals. Nonetheless, as the sovereign, the government can and does specify exactly how it will conduct its business. This includes how it will use contracting to implement social policy, how it will allow a contract to be canceled (e.g., termination process), and how, when, and in which courts it can be sued. All of these are significant differences between government contracts and commercial contracts.

The origin of the government's authority to enter into contract comes from the U.S. Constitution and is subject to various statutes and regulations. Although the Constitution does not specifically refer to government contracts, the government has the implied power to use contracts to fulfill its responsibilities. For example, Article 1 § 8, Clause 18, gives Congress the power to "[m]ake all laws which shall be necessary and proper for carrying into execution the foregoing powers and all other powers vested by this Constitution of the government of the United States, or in any department or officer thereof."

The clause is called the "necessary and proper" clause and provides, by implication, the power for the government to enter into contracts to fulfill its obligations by providing and paying for the common defense and general welfare of the United States. Additionally, Article I § 8, Clause 12, gives Congress the power to "raise and support armies." Congress also has the authority to appropriate funds to federal agencies to fulfill their obligations. Article I § 9 of the Constitution provides: "No money shall be drawn from the Treasury, but in consequence of appropriations made by law...." This section is the basis of Congress's "power of the purse." It means that no debt may be paid out of public funds unless Congress has made an appropriation for that purpose.

Statutes and Regulations
In addition, many statutory provisions implement the Constitution's requirement for congressional appropriations, and also limit a federal agency's powers. For example, the Anti-Deficiency Act states:

> No officer or employee of the United States shall make or authorize expenditure from or create or authorize an obligation under any appropriation or fund in excess of the amount available therein; nor shall any such officer or employee involve the government in any contract or other obligation, for payment of money for any purpose, in advance of appropriations made for such purpose, unless such contract or obligation is authorized by law.[4]

Congress has extremely broad power to pass laws affecting the procurement process. Many of the laws are substantive (i.e., they describe how the process must be conducted). Examples of these laws would include the Armed Services Procurement Act, the Federal Property and Administrative Services Act, the Competition in Contracting Act, and the Streamlining Acquisition Regulations Act. These acts are a primary means by which Congress grants contracting powers to an agency, as well as to place limitations on the way an agency exercises those powers. Congress also places limitations through authorization and appropriation acts.

Other laws Congress passes each year deal principally with fiscal matters. Each "pot of money" from Congress must pass two key gates. The first is an authorization act. This law authorizes the various congressional committees to propose appropriations within a defined ceiling. The second gate is the appropriation act, which makes the specified funds available to the agencies. Both acts must be followed by agencies. If a particular program is authorized but not funded (i.e., no appropriation made), the program cannot survive. Conversely, if funds are appropriated but the program is not authorized, it likewise cannot survive.

There are certain steps that must be made in the budgeting process. The first step requires agencies to compile a budget from their various commands, installations, or field sites. This is presented to the Office of Management and Budget (OMB), which negotiates with the agencies—in concert with the president's desires—to compile a proposed federal budget. This federal budget is sent to Congress, which holds hearings and debates to finally settle on proper "authorized" and "appropriated" budgets for the various agencies. Once the acts become law by the president's signature, this budget is returned to OMB, which then allocates it to the agencies, which then makes allotments and sub-allotments, as appropriate, to their various segments. In recent years, the budget process has not always been smooth. When consensus on budget issues cannot be reached, continued government operations must be funded by a "continuing resolution," based on a proportion of the prior year's authorized and appropriated budget. While this avoids a potential government shutdown, it can have an extremely adverse impact on contracting, both in terms of performance as well as payment restrictions. Both contracting sides must be aware of the impact to contract requirements.

The funds appropriated by Congress are commonly restricted in two principle ways: by intended use and time of availability. The executive branch has limited ability to reprogram funds to alter their intended use, and no authority to obligate funds beyond their period of availability (usually one year), generally referred to as "the color of money." However, obligating funds should not be confused with actually paying those funds to a contractor. An obligation occurs when the funds are specifically designated to a particular contract or grant by the actual "award" of the contract or grant. Congress requires that all obligations be recorded by some clear documentary evidence.[5] Once obligated, however, it may be some time (sometimes years) before the work is completed and the contractor paid with those funds. Thus, expenditure occurs after the obligation.

If contracting officers are not clear whether a particular use of funds is proper, they can seek the guidance of the Government Accountability Office (GAO), a part of the legislative branch that will issue an opinion that is binding, since GAO has the authority to "settle all accounts" of the government.[6]

The Role of the FAR
Regulations, which implement statutes, are detailed procedures for use in awarding government contracts. An example of such a regulation is the *Federal Acquisition Regulation* (*FAR*). The *FAR* is the principal source of contracting guidance within the federal government.[7]

The *FAR* has been in place since April 1, 1984. The *FAR* system was developed in accordance with the Office of Federal Procurement Policy Act of 1974,[3] as amended by *Public Law* 96-83 and Office of Federal Procurement Policy (OFPP) policy letter 85-1, dated August 19, 1985. The *FAR* system consists of the *FAR* and various agency acquisition regulations that supplement the *FAR*. The *FAR* is prepared, issued, and maintained jointly by the secretary of defense and the administrators of the General Services Administration (GSA) and the National Aeronautics and Space Administration (NASA) via two councils, who must agree to all revisions proposed by either council. The *Defense Acquisition Regulations* Council chair is appointed by the secretary of defense. Remaining council membership includes representatives from the military departments, the Defense Logistics Agency, and NASA.

The Civilian Agency Acquisition Council chair is appointed by the administrator of GSA. Remaining council membership includes representatives from the Departments of Agriculture, Commerce, Energy, Health and Human Services, Homeland Security, Interior, Labor, State, Transportation, and Treasury; and from the Environmental Protection Agency, Social Security Administration, Small Business Administration, and the Department of Veterans Affairs.

The *FAR* is printed, published, and distributed by the *FAR* secretariat, which is controlled by GSA.

A more detailed table of contents for the *FAR* is provided in Appendix B.

Although the *FAR* was intended to be the single comprehensive source of procurement regulations, many agencies have extensive *FAR* supplements (e.g., the *Defense FAR Supplement* [*DFARS*]) and sub-supplements (e.g., the *Army FAR Supplement* [*AFARS*]). In addition, there are OMB circulars, OFPP policy letters, agency directives and instructions, and agency handbooks and manuals.

All of the applicable statutes, regulations, and contract law basics must be used together to effectively manage federal government contracts. Relying solely on the *FAR* may not answer every contract manager's questions about contract law. Generally, contract principles come from case law and court decisions, which are summarized in the *Restatement of the Law, Second, Contracts*. The "*Restatement*" is a presentation of contract law by the American Law Institute. It is regarded as an authoritative reference and is relied upon in judicial opinions.

In addition to the *Restatement*, the UCC is the current legal guideline for commercial transactions. The UCC is a law drafted by the National Conference of Commissioners on Uniform State Laws Governing Commercial Transactions, and is applicable in nearly every state. While the *Restatement* and the UCC are not binding on federal government contracting, they provide useful examples to determine the rights and obligations of contracting parties, and serve as a significant source of legal principles applicable to government contracts.

Ratification

"Ratification" is the act of approving an unauthorized commitment by an official who has the authority to do so.[8] "Unauthorized commitment" is a nonbinding agreement made by a government representative who lacks the authority to enter into the agreement on behalf of the government.[9] The government is not bound by unauthorized acts of its agents. The agent's unauthorized action may become binding, however, if the principal chooses to ratify the agent's act. A principal may ratify an unauthorized act of his or her agent only if the principal could have authorized the agent to act when the agent performed the unauthorized act.

Commitments that cannot be ratified may be subject to extraordinary contractual relief as authorized by *Public Law* 85-804; or may be subject to resolution by GAO under its account settlement authority.

Laws Related to International Contracting

When contracting beyond the governmental limits of the United States, whether with foreign governments or foreign corporations, contracting professionals must be careful to ensure a complete understanding of the legal, regulatory, political, and social consequences of their actions. Some of the more significant issues regarding international contracting include the following.

The Foreign Corrupt Practices Act (FCPA)

The FCPA[10] is primarily concerned with the issues of bribery and other corrupt payments, as well as record-keeping and accounting provisions to facilitate the review or audit of international transactions. The FCPA prohibits the payment or promise of payment of money or other items of value to foreign officials to influence or attempt to influence obtaining business, retaining business, or directing business to anyone. The record-keeping and accounting provisions require that reasonable record systems and accounting controls be present to ensure that all transactions and the disposition of assets are reflected. These requirements apply to domestic as well as foreign operations.

Export Regulations

The Bureau of Export Administration (BXA), a federal bureau in the Department of Commerce, is charged with enforcing the *Export Administration Regulation* (*EAR*). The *EAR* governs the export of commercial goods and data, and the BXA controls such exports by issuing general and specific export licenses. Violations of these regulations can result in civil and criminal penalties for the entire organization, and loss of the organization's exporting privileges in the future. It can also result in debarment from government contracting. It is important to be aware of the applicable *EAR* requirements when entering into a contract.

International Traffic in Arms Regulations (ITAR)

The State Department's Office of Defense Trade Controls (DTC) controls all exports of defense articles, related technical data, and services by issuing licenses and approvals. The U.S. Munitions List, located in Part 121 of the *ITAR*, details the items subject to DTC control. The *ITAR* also provides instructions on the procedures and types of licenses required. Violations of the *ITAR* can result in substantial civil fines and willful violations can result in criminal penalties including up to 10 years of imprisonment and fines up to $1 million. U.S. exporters need to be aware of the *ITAR* status before entering into a contract.

Anti-Boycott Regulations

The U.S. Department of Commerce and the U.S. Department of Treasury both enforce regulatory requirements to prevent U.S. companies from entering into foreign transactions that could be construed as supporting a foreign boycott against a country that is friendly to the United States. Violations can result in fines, imprisonment, and loss of their privilege to export.

Foreign Laws and Customs

In addition to ensuring compliance with applicable U.S. laws and regulations, U.S. firms pursuing or contemplating international contracting need to become knowledgeable regarding the myriad foreign laws, regulations, customs, and practices that may impact their ability or desire to conduct business in foreign countries. Particular care is required when dealing with or in foreign countries whose legal, political, business, and social systems are vastly different from our own.

FIGURE 4. Federal Contracting Cycle

FIGURE 5. GAO's "Best Practices" Project Knowledge Points[11]

1.2 Contract Principles

"Contract principles" are the fundamentals of acquisition that all contracting professionals must comprehend. These may be codified as part of a larger contract framework, such as that promulgated by the Leads Corporation some years ago (the "Federal Contracting Cycle"), and a more generic project life cycle. While the Leads Corporation (see **FIGURE 4**, page 26) postulated specific steps in the process, the life cycle depicted in **FIGURE 5** above is similar to the defense acquisition management framework. Other government agencies and government contractors follow similar forms of the contracts/acquisition model.

1.3 Standards of Conduct

There are many federal, state, and local laws, regulations, and ordinances that provide the legal framework that guides or regulates many activities, including the operation of government and business in general, as well as the contracting profession in particular. In addition to the legal framework, there are other procedural or policy documents that exist to formalize basic concepts and guide employers and employees to do their jobs ethically. These documents are commonly referred to as "Standards of Conduct," "Codes of Ethics," "Statements of Professional Responsibility," "Standards of Ethical Conduct," and similar terms. Typical components of ethical systems may include:

- The formalized, written document that presents the standards of conduct or code of ethics.

- An ethics compliance officer or manager to monitor and enforce the written standards. The ethics compliance officer or manager is frequently a senior staff executive with direct access to the senior executive in the organization.

- A formal training program for employees to provide recurring refresher training in ethics issues.

- An internal information system to respond to general questions and provide specific guidance to employees.

- A complaint system to receive, investigate, and respond to actual or perceived issues of non-ethical behavior. Some of these complaint systems also provide, either internally or internally and externally, information regarding the resolution of ethics complaints. They may also include information about specific actions taken with regards to confirmed ethics violations, though the identities of violators are sometimes not revealed for legal reasons.

- A system to address issues related to:
    o Conflict of interest,
    o Behavior toward competitors,
    o Privacy of information,
    o Gift-giving and receiving,

o Making and receiving political contributions,
o Levels of dedication and work effort required,
o Encouraged behavior, and/or
o Discouraged or prohibited behavior.

Though standards of conduct can sometimes be codified as law when issued by a government agency, and can sometimes be issued by corporations as a requirement of the law, they are also sometimes issued as a matter of policy or preference or to promote an organization's values to the general public. Over 90 percent of the Fortune 500 firms, over 50 percent of all other firms, and virtually all government entities have published standards of conduct or ethical codes.

Ethics

Laws, regulations, and policy documents, such as standards of conduct, provide an authoritative, formalized, written set of guidelines that require certain actions, prohibit others, and define broad goals or desired traits for the proper way to conduct business. Ethics provides an environment of structures, people, concepts, and values that enables an organization, and the individuals in it, to operate in a manner that conforms to the basic norms of society and business.

An excellent working definition of *ethics* was provided in the April 2004 edition of *Contract Management* magazine:

> Ethics are standards by which one should act based on values. Values are core beliefs such as duty, honor, and integrity that motivate attitudes and actions. Not all values are ethical principles.... Ethical principles are values that relate to what is right and wrong and thus take precedence over non-ethical values when making ethical decisions.[12]

Although ethical conduct can be viewed as both the means and the end, there is also a practical application and benefit associated with high ethical standards and conduct: ethics is good for business and the government. Business flourishes in an environment of profitability and sustainability. Government functions best in an environment of service to the governed, efficiency, and trust. Ethics is a critical component to both the business and government models.

For example, the Defense Industry Initiative was formed in 1986 as a result of several procurement scandals and is a nonpartisan, non-profit association of responsible U.S. defense companies committed to conducting business affairs at the highest ethical level and in full compliance with the law. Members are the professional ethics officers, CEOs, and senior officials of 85 top defense and security companies serving the U.S. military. Members have also committed to establish written codes of business ethics and to train employees to comply with the codes.[13]

Government and business organizations generally recognize that ethics-related issues can have a positive or negative impact both internally and externally. They also realize that internal and external influences can have positive as well as adverse impacts on the best-planned ethics compliance system. Therefore, organizations that take ethics seriously seek to instill and influence high ethical standards in their own employees and with other firms and organizations with which they do business. Additionally, they seek to make their clients or customers, as well as the general public, aware of the significant role that ethics plays as a means to foster goodwill and a positive image.

The issue of personal ethics, as opposed to the issue of organizational ethics presented above, is naturally more philosophical than fact-based. Though an organization can implement and maintain a very aggressive and far-reaching ethics function or program, the value of such a program can be easily diminished or severely damaged by the action or inaction of individuals throughout the organization. Personal ethics—i.e., knowing the "right" thing to do, and doing it—is therefore a significant issue. Personal ethics is of particular significance in the contracting profession due to the fiduciary nature of the contracting function, the requirement to build good working relationships both internally and externally, and the effect that contracting can have on an organization's "bottom line" and/or public image.

Contracting professionals are people first, professionals second. One's sense of personal ethics is in no small part defined by one's life experiences. Though not bound exclusively to one's past, what has occurred before often influences what may occur in the future. It is important that, as individuals, we clearly understand the ethical challenges that our profession sometimes presents to us and that we clearly understand corporate or agency requirements or policy related to such challenges. We must then bring our life experiences, as well as societal norms, into the equation to determine if a particular course of action is right or wrong. In some cases, these decisions are so simple that they are made automatically. In other cases, they can be the source of great anxiety and turmoil. Regardless, true professionalism requires that we continuously verify the "true north" of our "ethical compass" and that all our words and deeds proceed along that "right," ethical direction. NCMA members are obligated to adhere to the "Contract Management Code of Ethics." For more information, please refer to John W. Polk's article, "Turning Square Corners," from the January 2008 issue of *Contract Management*.[14]

1.4 Socioeconomic Programs

Socioeconomic programs are designed to benefit particular groups. They represent a multitude of program interests and objectives unrelated to procurement objectives. Some examples of these are preferences for small businesses and for American products, required sources for specific items, and minimum labor pay levels mandated for contractors.

Small Business Programs

It is the policy of the U.S. federal government, as stated in FAR Part 19, to provide the maximum possible acquisition opportunities to small business, veteran-owned small business, service-disabled veteran–owned small business, historically underutilized business zone (HUBZone) small business, small disadvantaged business, and women-owned small business concerns. These businesses must also have the maximum practicable opportunity to participate as subcontractors in the contracts awarded by any executive agency, consistent with efficient contract performance. The Small Business Administration (SBA) counsels and assists small business concerns and assists government contracting personnel to ensure that a fair proportion of contracts for goods and services are placed with small business.

Government contracting professionals are responsible for effectively implementing the small business programs, including achieving program goals. Government contracting offices are required to establish an Office of Small and Disadvantaged Business Utilization.

Small Business Policies

Small businesses must have an equal opportunity to compete for all contracts that they can perform to the extent that is consistent with the government's interest. Federal government contracting officers shall, when appropriate:

- Divide proposed acquisitions, except construction, into reasonable small lots to permit offers on less than the total requirement;

- Plan acquisitions so that more than one small business may do the work, if the work exceeds the amount for which a surety may be guaranteed by SBA against loss;

- Ensure that delivery schedules are established on a realistic basis that will encourage small business participation; and

- Encourage prime contractors to subcontract with small businesses.[15]

Contracting professionals should make every reasonable effort to find additional small business concerns, unless existing lists are excessively long.

Small Business Set-Asides

A small business set-aside reserves an acquisition exclusively for small businesses. A small business set-aside may be open to all small businesses. A small business set-aside may relate to a single acquisition or a class of acquisitions and may be total or partial. For federal government contracts, all acquisitions within a certain dollar range are automatically set-aside for small business. Small business set-asides may be withdrawn by the contracting officer if award would be detrimental to the public interest (e.g., paying more than a fair market price).

Types of Small Businesses

Small Business
A "small business" is a concern, including its affiliates, that is independently owned and operated, not dominant in the field of operation in which it is bidding on government contracts, and qualified as a small business under the criteria and size standards contained in Title 13, Part 121 of the Code of Federal Regulations (CFR).

Small Business 8(a)
An "8(a) small business" is a small business operating in conjunction with SBA's Business Development Program, authorized by Section 8(a) of the Small Business Act.[16] Fundamentally, SBA acts as a prime contractor for other government agencies and issues subcontracts to 8(a) firms.

SBA sometimes delegates contract execution authority to the requiring agency. 8(a) contracts may be awarded competitively or noncompetitively.

Veteran-Owned Small Business

A small business qualifies as a "veteran-owned small business" if not less than 51 percent of the business is owned by one or more veterans or, in the case of publicly owned businesses, not less than 51 percent of the stock is owned by one or more veterans. In addition, the management and daily business operations of the concern must be controlled by one or more veterans.

Service-Disabled Veteran–Owned Small Business

A "service-disabled veteran–owned small business" is a veteran-owned small business in which the 51 percent veteran stipulation refers to veterans with a disability that is service-connected.

Small Disadvantaged Business

A "small disadvantaged business" is a small business that has received certification as a small disadvantaged business consistent with 13 CFR Part 124.

HUBZone Small Business

A "HUBZone" is a small business that operates in a historically underutilized business zone that is in an area located within one or more qualified census tracts, qualified non-metropolitan counties, or lands within the external boundaries of an Indian reservation. The business must also appear on the "List of Qualified HUBZone Small Business Concerns" maintained by SBA.

Women-Owned Small Business

A "women-owned small business" is a small business that is at least 51 percent owned by one or more women; or in the case of a publicly owned business, at least 51 percent of the stock of which is owned by one or more women. In addition, the management and daily business operations of the concern must be controlled by one or more women.

Other Socioeconomic Programs

Federal contracting professionals need to be aware of and comply with federal laws and policies that have some form of socioeconomic implication. Commercial contracting professionals whose organizations perform under federal contracts are also often bound by these laws and policies, which are normally included as terms and conditions in government contracts. Some of the significant socioeconomic programs include the following.

Indian Incentive Program

Government policy states that Indian organizations and Indian-owned economic enterprises, including Alaskan Natives, shall have the maximum practicable opportunity to participate in performing contracts awarded by federal agencies. The policy also provides for incentive payments to Indian-owned economic enterprises that perform as subcontractors.

Disaster or Emergency Assistance Activities

When contracting for disaster or emergency assistance services following a major disaster or emergency, the government provides a preference to organizations, firms, or individuals residing or doing business in the area affected by the disaster or emergency. Such services can include debris clearance, distribution of supplies, or reconstruction.

Historically Black Colleges and Universities and Minority Institutions

The government promotes the participation of historically black colleges and universities and minority institutions in federal procurement, in compliance with Executive Order 12928, particularly for the types of services normally acquired from higher educational institutions.

Diversity

There are also programs designed to encourage a diverse workforce or education and training group, such as programs that prohibit employment or workplace discrimination based on race, color, religion, sex, national origin, age, or disability.

Application of Labor Laws to Federal Government Acquisitions

Labor laws are frequently a matter of concern for contracting professionals, particularly as they relate to service contracts. As a matter of policy, the government seeks to maintain sound relations with both industry and labor and usually remains impartial concerning disputes between labor and contractor management. Some of the significant issues and policies related to the application of labor laws include:

- Restrictions on the use of convict labor;
- The requirement to pay at least the prevailing wage rate for construction contracts subject to the Davis-Bacon Act;

- The Anti-Kickback provisions of the Copeland Act, which make it illegal to require, induce, intimidate, or otherwise force employees on construction contracts to give up any part of their compensation;
- The requirement to pay overtime for work in excess of 40 hours per week as governed by the Contract Work Hours and Safety Standards Act;
- The provisions of the Walsh-Healy Public Contracts Act, which require various stipulations regarding minimum wages, maximum hours, child labor, convict labor, and safe and sanitary working conditions for certain types of supply contracts;
- The provisions of the Service Contract Act of 1965 regarding minimum wages and fringe benefits, safe and sanitary working conditions, and notification to employees of the minimum allowable compensation for contracts covered by the act; and
- Various laws, Executive Orders, and policies that deal with equal employment opportunity, age discrimination, veteran's preference, providing employment opportunities for the disabled, and other related matters.[17]

Workplace and Environmental Considerations

The government implements various workplace and environmental policies through the acquisition process. Additional information is found in FAR Part 23, but includes the following.

Drug-Free Workplace
Contractors are sometimes required to agree to take specified steps—including establishing an ongoing drug awareness program—providing published statements to its employees prohibiting the manufacture, distribution, dispensing, possession, or use of controlled substances, as well as taking appropriate action against employees who violate the policies.

Energy Conservation
Some contracts contain clauses that help implement government policies to acquire goods and services that promote energy and water efficiency, advance the use of renewable energy products, and help foster markets for emerging technology.

Hazardous Materials
Sometimes contractors are required to provide information to the government regarding hazardous materials that may be introduced into the workplace as a result of performance on a government contract.

Recovered Materials
The government seeks to acquire products that meet performance requirements and are composed of the highest percentage of recovered materials practicable.

Ozone-Depleting Substances
Government policy strives to minimize the procurement of materials and substances that contribute to the depletion of stratospheric ozone, and gives preference to the procurement of alternative products that reduce overall risks to human health and the environment.

Privacy and Freedom of Information

The Privacy Act of 1974[18] and the Freedom of Information Act[19] have implications that sometimes affect government contracts. When a contract requires a contractor to design, develop, or operate a system of records on individuals, the contracting agency is required to apply the requirements of the Privacy Act to the contractor and its employees. The Freedom of Information Act generally provides that information contained in government records be made available to the public. There are some exceptions to the general rule that apply to acquisitions. For example, proposals submitted in response to a competitive solicitation may not be released under the Freedom of Information Act. Also, there are exceptions that relate to classified information, trade secrets, confidential commercial or financial information, and other matters.[20]

Contract Types
- Fixed Price
  - Firm-fixed-price
  - Firm-fixed-price, level of effort
  - Fixed price w/ economic price adjustment
  - Fixed-price redetermination (prospective)
  - Fixed-price redetermination (retroactive)
- Cost Reimbursement
  - Cost contract
  - Cost sharing
  - Cost plus fixed fee
- Time and Materials
  - Time and Materials
  - Labor Hour

FIGURE 6. Contract Types

1.5 Contract Structures

"Contract structure" refers to specific pricing arrangements or contract types used to complete the contract. They are specific business arrangements that govern the buyer-seller relationship. Also, they are types of promises or sets of promises that courts will enforce. They may also be referred to as contract "types." Variations of these contract types may be used by both government and commercial entities.

There are two primary "families" of contracts: fixed-price and cost-reimbursable. Fundamentally, the two families of contracts are based on risk to both the buyer and seller. The more risk the seller has, such as untried technology, vague specifications, etc., the less likely the seller will be to accept a fixed-price contract. Conversely, the more specific the requirement, the less likely the buyer will be to accept a cost-reimbursement contract type.

FIGURE 7 below illustrates the risk relationship of the various contract types for both government and industry. It is interesting to note that the contract type with the most risk for one party is the contract type that has the least risk for the other party.

Contract Types Ranked by Highest Government Risk (from highest to lowest):
- Time and Materials
- CPFF
- CPAF
- CPIF
- Cost and cost sharing
- FPIF
- FFP w/EPA
- FFP

Contract Types Ranked by Highest Contractor Risk (from highest to lowest):
- FFP
- FFP w/EPA
- FPIF
- Cost and cost sharing
- CPIF
- CPAF
- CPFF
- Time and Materials

FIGURE 7.

Fixed-Price Contracts

"Fixed-price" refers to a type or group of contracts that require a firm pricing arrangement established by the parties at contract award. Fixed-price contracts typically include:

- Firm-fixed-price;
- Firm-fixed-price, level of effort;
- Fixed-price with economic price adjustment; and
- Fixed-price redetermination.

Firm-Fixed-Price
As the name implies, firm-fixed-price contracts require a price that is not subject to any adjustment based on the contractor's actual cost to perform the contract. This contract type places the maximum performance risk on the contractor as well as full responsibility for all costs and the resulting profit or loss. It provides strong incentives for the contractor to control costs and perform effectively and imposes a minimum administrative burden on the contracting parties. The level of risk assumed by the contractor is often reflected in the contract price.[21]

Firm-Fixed-Price, Level of Effort
This type of contract requires the contractor to provide a specified level of effort, over a stated period of time, on work that can be stated only in general terms. In return for the specified level of effort, the contractor is paid a fixed dollar amount.[22]

Fixed-Price with Economic Price Adjustment
Fixed-price with economic price adjustment contracts provide for upward and downward revision of the stated contract price on the occurrence of specified contingencies. There are three general economic price adjustments:

- Adjustments based on established prices—The price adjustments are based on increases or decreases from an agreed-upon level in published or otherwise established prices of specific items or contract end items.

- Adjustments based on actual costs of labor or material—The price adjustments are based on increases or decreases in specified costs of labor or material that the contractor actually experiences during contract performance.

- Adjustments based on cost indexes of labor or material—The price adjustments are based on increases or decreases in labor or material cost standards or indexes that are specifically identified in the contract.[23]

Fixed-Price Redetermination (Prospective)
These types of fixed-price contracts combine a firm-fixed-price for an initial period of deliveries or performance and a prospective redetermination (at

a stated time or times during performance) of the price for subsequent periods of performance.[24]

Fixed-Price Redetermination (Retroactive)
These types of fixed-price contracts combine a fixed ceiling price and a retroactive price redetermination after completion of the contract. The redetermined price cannot exceed the original ceiling price.[25]

Cost-Reimbursement Contracts

Cost-reimbursement contracts require paying allowable, allocable, and reasonable costs incurred in the performance of a contract to the extent that such costs are prescribed or permitted by the contract. These contracts establish an estimate of total cost to obligate funds and establish a ceiling that the contractor may not exceed (except at its own risk) without the contracting officer's approval. Cost-reimbursement contracts typically include:

- Cost contracts,
- Cost-sharing, and
- Cost-plus-fixed-fee.[26]

Cost Contract
A cost contract is the least complicated type of cost reimbursement contract. It reimburses appropriate costs without profit or fees.[27]

Cost-Sharing Contract
A cost-sharing contract provides for the partial reimbursement of the contractor's allowable costs with no allowances for profit or fees. Both the buyer and the seller share the costs. Cost-sharing contracts are used when both the buyer and the seller will derive some benefit from the contracted effort, and that benefit is sufficient enough that both parties are willing to share the costs and the benefits.[28]

Cost-Plus-Fixed-Fee Contract
A cost-plus-fixed-fee contract requires reimbursing appropriate costs associated with contract performance and paying a fixed fee that is negotiated. The fixed fee does not vary with actual cost, but may be adjusted as a result of changes made in the work to be performed under the contract.[29]

Time-and-Materials Contracts

Time-and-materials contracts are a means of acquiring goods or services based on direct labor hours and the cost of materials required for contract performance. The labor hour rates are negotiated between the parties for each type or category of labor required. Each fixed hourly labor rate is a composite rate that includes wages, overhead, general and administrative expense, and profit. A time-and-materials contract may be used when it is not feasible to accurately estimate the extent or duration of the work or to anticipate costs with any reasonable degree of confidence. Time-and-materials contracts that do not require the contractor to provide materials are also referred to as "labor hour contracts."[30]

Contract Incentives

Contracts containing various forms of incentives may be appropriate when there is a desire or need to provide additional motivation to a contractor/seller to attain specific acquisition objectives that would be unlikely without the incentives. Such objectives might be improved delivery, improved technical performance, improved cost management, or some other significant parameter.[31]

Incentives generally fall into the following four categories.

Cost Incentives
Cost incentives normally take the form of a profit or fee adjustment based on a formula. Cost incentives are intended to motivate the seller to effectively manage costs. Generally, cost incentives must be required before including other types of incentives in a contract.

Performance or Quality Incentives
Performance or quality incentives may be appropriate when the contractor can attain a level of performance or quality over the requirement and provides a desirable enhanced benefit to the buyer. These incentives should be designed to relate profit or fee to results achieved by the seller compared to specified targets.

Delivery Incentives
Delivery incentives are included when receiving the goods or services faster is important to the buyer. The value of the incentive, however, should not exceed the benefit received for the faster delivery.

Multiple Incentives
Include multiple incentives when there is sufficient justification to motivate the seller to strive for outstanding results in multiple areas simultaneously.

Multiple incentives sometimes require the seller to make trade-off decisions among the incentives to achieve the maximum beneficial result. The buyer should be aware of the potential problems inherent in providing multiple incentives and closely monitor these situations to ensure that the primary goals of the acquisition are not compromised.

Contract Incentives (cont.)

Contract incentives can be used in both fixed-price and cost-reimbursement contracts to create the following types of contracts.

Fixed-Price Incentive Contract
A fixed-price incentive contract requires an initial fixed price, and also permits adjusting profit and establishing the final contract price using a formula that compares the relationship of total final negotiated cost to total target cost. The final price is subject to a price ceiling, which is negotiated at the outset. There are two basic forms of fixed-price incentive contracts:

- Fixed-price incentive (firm target)—A fixed-price incentive (firm target) contract specifies a target cost, a target profit, a price ceiling, and a profit adjustment formula.

- Fixed-price incentive (successive targets)—A fixed-price incentive (successive targets) contract requires an initial target cost, an initial target profit, and an initial profit adjustment formula. The targets and the formula are used to establish the firm target profit, including a ceiling and floor for the firm target profit, the production point at which the firm target cost and firm target profit will be renegotiated, and a ceiling price that is the maximum that may be paid to the seller.[32]

Fixed-Price Award Fee Contract
A fixed-price award fee contract is sometimes used when it is difficult to include other incentives because seller performance cannot be measured objectively. A fixed-price award fee contract establishes a fixed price and includes profit (or base fee) paid for satisfactory contract performance. It also establishes an award fee that can be earned by the seller in addition to the fixed price based on the results of periodic evaluations of the seller's performance against an award fee plan.[33]

Cost Plus Incentive Fee Contract
A cost plus incentive fee contract is a cost-reimbursement contract that also provides for an initially negotiated fee, which can be adjusted later by using a formula based on the relationship of total allowable costs to target costs.[34]

Cost Plus Award Fee Contract
A cost plus award fee contract is a cost-reimbursement contract that also provides for an award fee pool that the contractor may earn in whole or in part during performance, based on the results of periodic evaluations of the contractor's performance against an award fee plan.[35]

Other Types of Contracts, Agreements, and Arrangements

In addition to the contract types and incentive options indicated above, there are a number of other contracts, agreements, and arrangements commonly used by contract professionals, including the following.

Basic Agreements
A "basic agreement" is a written instrument of understanding, negotiated between a buyer and a seller, that contains terms and conditions that will apply to future contracts between the parties during the term of the agreement. A basic agreement contemplates separate future contracts that will incorporate, by reference or attachment, the appropriate terms and conditions negotiated in the basic agreement. A basic agreement itself is not a contract.[36]

Basic Ordering Agreement
A "basic ordering agreement" is similar to a basic agreement, but may also include terms and conditions intended to describe the types of goods and services that may be ordered in the future, to define pricing methods that will apply, or to define ordering or delivery procedures. A basic ordering agreement itself is not a contract.[37]

Letter Contract
A "letter contract" is normally a brief, written, preliminary contractual instrument that authorizes a contractor to begin performance immediately. Letter contracts are used to initiate performance when performance is required, but there is insufficient time to negotiate a more formal, complete contract.[38]

Indefinite Delivery/Indefinite Quantity Contracts
Indefinite delivery/indefinite quantity (IDIQ) contracts provide for the purchase of an indefinite quantity of goods or services for a fixed period of time. The indefinite quantity provisions sometimes include a

guaranteed minimum quantity and normally include a maximum quantity. Deliveries or performance is scheduled by placing orders with the contractor. Examples of variations of IDIQ contracts include:

- Delivery order contracts—IDIQ contracts generally used to purchase goods;
- Task order contracts—IDIQ contracts generally used to purchase services;
- Definite quantity contracts—IDIQ contracts generally used to purchase a definite quantity of goods or services, with an indefinite schedule for deliveries or performance; and
- Requirements contracts—IDIQ contracts that are generally used to purchase all required quantities of specified goods or services needed by a buying organization for a specified period of time.[39]

Delivery or performance is accomplished by placing orders with the contractor.

In addition, governmentwide acquisition contracts (GWACs) and multi-agency contracts (MACs) are federal contracts for goods or services issued by one federal contracting entity, but available for use by many or all federal contracting entities.[40]

1.6 Contracting Methods

"Contracting methods" and "contracting methodology" are terms that refer to the processes employed and the means used to solicit, request, or invite offers that will normally result in issuing a contract.

Sealed Bidding

"Sealed bidding" is an acquisition method in which the government issues an invitation for bid (IFB). The IFB is publicized by distributing it to prospective bidders, posting it in public places, and posting it on the FedBizOpps website. Sufficient time must be allowed between the time the IFB is publicized and bids are opened publicly to enable prospective bidders to prepare and submit bids.

An IFB should describe the government's requirements clearly, accurately, and completely. Unnecessarily restrictive specifications or requirements that might unduly limit the number of bidders are prohibited. The invitation includes all documents (whether attached or incorporated by reference) furnished to prospective bidders for bidding purposes. Agencies must use a fixed-price contract for sealed bidding.[41]

Two-Step Sealed Bidding

"Two-step sealed bidding" combines two competitive methods and is sometimes used to obtain the benefits of sealed bidding when adequate specifications, requirements, or descriptions are not available. The first step consists of the solicitation for submitting technical proposals, which are evaluated on technical merits only. The second step involves submitting sealed price bids only by those bidders who submitted acceptable technical proposals in the first step.[42] The solicitation tool normally used for two-step sealed bidding is the request for technical proposal (RFTP). RFTPs are used to pre-qualify bidders relative to their technical capacity to perform.

Negotiation

"Negotiation" is a method of contracting that can be used to solicit proposals either competitively or noncompetitively, and usually includes discussions. Negotiation is a flexible process that includes the receipt of proposals from offerors, permits bargaining, and often affords offerors an opportunity to revise their offers before final evaluation and award of a contract. A contract issued by any method other than sealed bidding is normally considered to be a negotiated contract. The solicitation tool normally used for negotiation is the request for proposal (RFP). The RTFP can also be used in negotiation when the intent is to conduct a two-step negotiation in a manner similar to the intent of two-step sealed bidding.

Simplified Acquisition

"Simplified acquisition" is a less rigorous method for entering into relatively low dollar threshold contracts. Simplified acquisition usually occurs without the elaborate and formal solicitation techniques required by sealed bidding and negotiation. Very small purchases must be made using simplified acquisition tools such as charge cards.

Federal Supply Schedules (FSS)

The FSS is a program directed and managed by the General Services Administration (GSA). The FSS program provides federal agencies, as well as some state and local governmental agencies, with a streamlined process for obtaining commonly used commercial goods and services.

Fundamentally, the supply schedules are a series of pre-negotiated, awarded contracts that can be used by authorized sources to issue orders for required goods or services.

Electronic Commerce

"Electronic commerce" refers to a group of automated processes that can be used to accomplish business transactions. Electronic commerce includes such processes as e-mail or messaging, Internet technology, electronic bulletin boards, electronic funds transfer, electronic data interchange, and similar tools. In the federal sector, the contracting officer must make available through the GPE (Government Portal Entry, commonly FedBizOpps) solicitations synopsized through the GPE, including specifications and other pertinent information determined necessary by the contracting officer. Transmissions to the GPE must be in accordance with the interface description available through the Internet at **www.fbo.gov**.

Modular Contracting

"Modular contracting" refers to the use of at least one, but usually more than one, contract to acquire major information technology (IT) systems in successive, interoperable increments. The intent of modular contracting is to divide the acquisition of complex, major IT systems into a series of smaller, related contracts that are easier to issue and manage than a single, all-inclusive contract would be.

Auctions

"Auctions" are sales transactions in which goods or services are offered and sold to the highest bidder. "Reverse auctions" are purchase transactions in which goods or services are purchased from the lowest bidder.

Request for Quotation

The "request for quotation" (RFQ) is a solicitation document used in negotiated procurements to request information and quotes. The RFQ differs from the RFP in that an RFQ is fundamentally a request for information. Quotations received in response to an RFQ are not offers.[43] The resulting purchase order is either an offer or a counter offer.[44]

Request for Information

A "request for information" (RFI) is a tool sometimes used as a part of market research to gather information from vendors in the marketplace. RFIs are sometimes issued to determine the availability of products and services, and to gather market information on capabilities to perform when less intrusive forms of market research do not produce the desired results.

Unsolicited Proposal

An "unsolicited proposal" is a proposal from a prospective contractor to provide goods or services without a prior formal or informal solicitation from a contracting office.

Point of Sale Transactions

A "point of sale transaction" is a business transaction in which the entire business arrangement between the parties is executed in a single event.

Master Agreements

A "master agreement" is a business arrangement in which the parties determine the underlying commercial parameters governing the relationship, such as terms and conditions, but defer negotiation of specific elements of the contract—such as price or delivery requirements—to a later date based on the occurrence of specific events or transactions.

Sales Contracts

A "sales contract" is a business arrangement in which all elements of the transaction are determined and defined between the parties at the time of contract formation, including mutual assent, exchange of consideration, capacity to contract, and legal purpose.

Framework Pricing Arrangements

A "framework pricing arrangement" is a contract that is definitive in all respects except pricing. The agreement or contract specifies a predetermined index, formula, algorithm, or method (the framework) for the calculation of price at the point of sale.

Performance-Based Contracts

A "performance-based contract" is a contract that is structured around the purpose of the work to be performed, or the goal to be achieved, as opposed to either the manner in which the work is to be performed or a broad, imprecise statement of work. The requirements for performance-based contracts should be clear, complete, and objective, with measurable outcomes.

Single-Source Negotiation

"Single-source negotiation," also known as "sole-source negotiation," refers to contracting with a single provider in lieu of competitive contracting. Single/sole-source negotiation usually occurs because the provider is the only source of the product or service required (or the business relationship with the provider is of strategic importance to the buying organization) and is normally based on a long-term relationship built on mutual trust.

Gap Fillers

"Gap fillers" are other sources of pertinent information that may be used to "fill a gap" when a contract fails to adequately address an issue of concern. The Uniform Commercial Code (UCC) is frequently used as a gap filler, as are memoranda of understanding, letter contracts, and other agreements (when appropriate).

Prequalification

"Prequalification" refers to a buyer's announcement of interest, including criteria for selecting proposals and selecting offerors capable of meeting the requirements.

Broad Agency Announcements

A "broad agency announcement" is a general announcement of an agency's research interests, including criteria for selecting proposals and soliciting the participation of all offerors capable of satisfying the agency's needs.[45]

1.7 Contract Financing

"Contract financing" is the means of obtaining the funds necessary for performing the contract, including payment methods, loan guarantees, advanced payments, progress payments, and contract funding. Contract financing issues are important in both the commercial and government contracting environments.

Commercial Contract Financing

Financing in commercial contracting may include obtaining loans and lines of credit from financial institutions, obtaining advance funding of accounts receivable or funding of purchase orders from private firms, or obtaining funds from venture capitalists. It may also include negotiating favorable payment clauses, such as a sizable down payment or milestone payments as the work progresses.

Commercial contract financing could also include such methods as:

- Commercial advance payments made before performance has begun,
- Commercial interim payments made after some work has been done, and
- Delivery payments made after receiving and accepting a portion of the total work to be performed.

Government Contract Financing

In some cases, successfully completing a government contract may require the government's assistance with some form of contract financing. For example, contract financing might be appropriate in a multimillion-dollar contract for goods that requires the contractor to make substantial initial investments in labor, materials, and production costs. In cases where the government determines that some type of contract financing is appropriate, it usually takes one of two forms, private or government.

According to FAR Part 32, when a contractor requests financing, the government contracting officer is to consider the following order of preference for methods of contract financing:

1. Private financing,
2. Customary contract financing other than loan guarantees,
3. Loan guarantees,
4. Unusual contract financing, and
5. Advance payments.[46]

Private financing without government guarantee includes loans from financial institutions, sale of bonds or stocks, and loans from family members or other private sources. However, the contractor should not be required to obtain private financing at unreasonable terms or from other agencies. In addition, under assignment of claims provisions, a financing institution can receive payments directly from the government in consideration for making a private loan to a contractor.

Progress payments based on incurred costs at customary progress payment rates can be made on the basis of costs incurred by the contractor as work progresses under a fixed-price contract.[47]

If a contractor applies for a conventional loan to finance a government contract, the private financial institution involved may submit an application for a loan guarantee to the Federal Reserve Bank in its district. The Federal Reserve Bank acts as a fiscal agent and transmits the application to the guaranteeing agency. The president has designated seven agencies as guaranteeing agencies:

- Department of Defense,
- Department of Energy,
- Department of Commerce,
- Department of the Interior,
- Department of Agriculture,
- General Services Administration, and
- The National Aeronautics and Space Administration.

The guaranteeing agency makes a determination of eligibility in accordance with the applicable *FAR* provisions. If the loan guarantee is approved, the private financial institution makes the loan and collects interest from the contractor, the guaranteeing agency guarantees the loan, and the Federal Reserve Bank acts as the "intermediary," or fiscal agent that processes the paperwork between the private financial institution and the contractor.[48]

FAR Subpart 32 provides guidance for customary progress payments, i.e., liquidation rates. Any progress payments that do not comply with this guidance for "customary" progress payments are considered "unusual." As such, unusual progress payments require advance agency approval. "Advance payments" are advances of money by the government to a contractor. They are not measured by performance; they are made in anticipation of performance. Advance payments are the least preferred method of contract financing and generally should not be authorized if other types of financing are reasonably available to the contractor in adequate amounts. Loans and credit at excessive interest rates or other exorbitant charges, or loans from other government agencies, are not considered reasonably available financing. Contractors may apply for advance payments before or after the award of a contract. If advance payments are approved, a special bank account may be required. Interest is usually charged on the advance payments and any interest earned is refundable to the government.[49]

1.8 Intellectual Property

"Intellectual property" is the kind of property that results from the fruits of mental labor. Intellectual property rights include any or all of the following: patent, trademark, copyright, trade secret, trade name, service mark, and the like. Contracting professionals should be aware of the various forms of intellectual property, the need for intellectual property that may be part of contract requirements, and the limitations on the use of intellectual property imposed by law. Typical examples of intellectual property include the following.

Patent

A "patent" is a government grant of exclusive rights, issued by the U.S. Patent and Trademark Office, to an inventor that prohibits others from making, using, or selling the invention for a specified period of time. The patent holder has legal remedies available to those who infringe on a patent.

Copyright

A "copyright" is the exclusive right to reproduce, translate, publish, use, and dispose of various forms of written or recorded material or data, and to authorize others to do so. Copyright is of particular interest to contacting professionals as it relates to the appropriate purchase and/or use of computer software.

Trademark

"Trademarks" are distinctive marks of authenticity. They can include words, symbols, devices, or designs affixed to or placed on an article or its container to identify an article offered for sale. The term can also include "service marks," which designate particular manners or modes of service delivery protected as intellectual property.

Data

"Data" is recorded information, regardless of form or the media on which it may be recorded. Rights to use technical data developed by a contractor may vary depending on the source of funds used to develop the item, component, process, software, or software documentation.

Data Rights

In any contract that may involve the production of scientific or technical data, the rights to those data must be clearly ascribed. Generally, a "rights in data" clause will protect the government's right to use and distribute—without limitation, free from payment or royalties, and with immunity against lawsuits for copyright infringement or misuse of data—any data produced under a contract funded by the government.[50]

Licensing

The sale of a license permits the use of patents, trademarks, or other technology to another firm. A license covering a patent, technical or proprietary data, technical assistance, know-how, or any combination of these may be granted by a U.S. firm to a foreign firm or government to produce, co-produce, or sell an article or service within a given sales territory. An exclusive license grants this right without competition from any other licensees or from the licensor. For a nonexclusive license, competition may be permitted with other licensees and/or the licensor. Licensing involves the many procedures administrative agencies perform in conjunction with issuing various types of licenses.

Royalties

"Royalties" include costs or fees that may be charged by the owner of various forms of intellectual property to permit others to use the intellectual property for specified purposes.

Trade Secrets

"Trade secrets" refer to information, processes, or procedures used in business that may give the owner some advantage over its competitors in the marketplace.

Shop Rights

"Shop rights" are the right of an employer to use, without payment of royalties, an invention conceived by an employee in the course of employment or through the use of the employer's facilities if the employee was not hired to perform such work.

Nondisclosure Agreement

A "nondisclosure agreement" is a legally binding document setting forth the conditions under which proprietary information is offered, received, used, and protected between two or more parties.

2.0 Acquisition Planning/Strategy

2.1 Acquisition Planning

"Acquisition planning" is the process by which efforts of all personnel responsible for an acquisition are coordinated and integrated through a comprehensive plan for fulfilling the buyer's need in a timely manner at a reasonable cost. It includes developing the overall strategy for management of the acquisition. Acquisition planning includes all the activities and events required for both buyers and sellers to prepare for, negotiate, and form a binding contractual arrangement.[51]

Planning is an essential preliminary component to successfully completing virtually any effort. In the government and business environments, planning is required to apply scarce resources to the goal-directed activity necessary to accomplish the mission or functions of the organization. As it relates to the contracting profession, planning in general and acquisition planning in particular was a function that was often thought to begin at the point where a customer expressed a need for goods or services, or delivered a requirement to the contracting office.

In the past, the contracting function, as well as other administrative, staff, or overhead functions frequently operated adjacent to, but often not directly with each other, or with line components that performed the core functions of the organization. This historical concept of technical specialization has now been challenged by many factors, including technological advancements in communications and information exchange, an aging workforce, competitive pressures on businesses to enhance profitability, political pressures on government to reduce the cost of providing services, and many others. The new reality requires both public- and private-sector organizations to be leaner, more agile, more productive, less expensive, and (as a result) more collaborative.

Much of the literature in the contracting profession has defined and described the need for the contracting professional to expand beyond the historical boundaries of the contracting office and become a business professional or business broker and part of the multidisciplinary management team. Because of this environment, contracting professionals have had to change the way they perform acquisition planning.

Acquisition planning should be viewed as a team effort, requiring the talents and input of many individuals other than the contracting professional,

FIGURE 8. Acquisition Strategy Competencies

including the customer; budget or finance experts; various technical experts (IT, logistics); legal counsel; and other direct or indirect stakeholders. The planning process should begin before the traditional first customer contact and should have an inward as well as outward focus, particularly as it relates to an important acquisition planning tool—market research.

Market Research

In the expanded role of a business professional, the contracting professional should consider a comprehensive concept of market research. Not only should contracting professionals determine the degree to which external sources could meet requirements, they should also look within the organization for information that might be of value in anticipating future requirements. It is within this context that market research can be viewed as having internal and external components.

Internal Market Research

For contracting professionals to be of maximum value to the management team and to the overall organization, they must be knowledgeable in the business of the business or the mission of the government agency. The contracting professional needs to know what products or services are generated by each segment of the organization; how these products or services are generated; who the organization's customers are; what the organization's goals are; and what structures, processes, and procedures are in place to accomplish the goals. Fundamentally, the contracting professional needs to become immersed in the organization's activities and plans to the maximum extent possible. This level of involvement can usually be accomplished by activities such as:

- Reviewing historical information on prior acquisitions for internal customers;

- Attending regular management meetings of all internal customers;

- Receiving detailed briefings on the functions and processes of internal customers;

- Participating in short-term assignments of customer work units;

- Reading pertinent customer-oriented professional publications;

- Serving on cross-functional process improvement teams, or similar ad hoc teams, addressing issues that may have little or nothing to do with contracting; and

- Sharing information on contracting issues and trends with other managers.

The basic goal of internal market research is to learn as much as possible about the organization; how it does business and how it has used goods and services acquired in the past. A secondary goal of internal market research is to develop good working relationships with the customer base.

External Market Research

External market research normally pertains to research activities undertaken once a requirement has been either defined or at least conceptualized. However, generalized external market research undertaken in the absence of a requirement can also be of value to the contracting professional, particularly when one has also engaged in some level of internal market research. Whether it is used in response to a specific need or not, the external market research effort seeks to gain useful information about capabilities and limitations inherent in the commercial marketplace. The basic intent of external market research is to gain knowledge that will be used in determining the best method to obtain required goods and services consistent with pertinent law, regulation, and/or corporate policy. Just as the contracting professional can use internal market research to better understand and anticipate the actual and potential needs of the customer, external market research should be used to better understand the actual and potential capabilities of external sources of supply. Standard external market research techniques include:

- Reviewing historical information on similar prior acquisitions for related market research information;
- Reviewing pertinent professional news, trade, association, or industry publications;
- Contacting knowledgeable third-party sources of unbiased information regarding potential sources;
- Attending trade or professional association shows and exhibits;
- Contacting customers of potential sources for past performance information;
- Reviewing catalogs and other printed or electronic information published by potential sources;
- Contacting potential sources for specific capabilities information or briefings; and
- Joining pertinent professional organizations and attending their meetings.

Though the amount of external market research conducted will vary according to the complexity of the anticipated effort and other issues, the results should be formally documented for current and future use.

2.2 Acquisition Methodology

"Acquisition methodology" refers to the processes employed and the means used to solicit, request, or invite offers that will normally result in issuing a contract. For the buyer, it is the process by which buyers develop a comprehensive plan for fulfilling requirements for products or services in a timely manner at a reasonable price and includes developing an overall strategy for the purchase, which is accomplished through conducting market research, developing a strategy, drafting the solicitation, and selecting a supplier. For the seller, it is the process by which sellers develop and execute a strategy for obtaining the award of a contract, including market strategies, pricing strategies, and responding to the solicitation.

The Acquisition Plan

The acquisition plan should reflect a collaborative effort involving significant stakeholders. The level of detail provided in the acquisition plan will vary depending on the anticipated dollar value, level of complexity, degree of significance, and other appropriate factors. A written plan may not be required for simple, straightforward, low dollar value purchases. In the absence of a written plan, the contracting professional should ensure that there is a common understanding and consensus among the stakeholders regarding the course of action to be taken. When required, written acquisition plans should clearly explain all pertinent issues relating to the acquisition, including:

- *A description of the need to be satisfied*—The description should be concise, yet complete enough to explain what the need is, how it came to be needed at the current time, any pertinent history of related prior acquisitions, and how they were acquired.
- *An explanation of conditions or constraints that relate to the proposed acquisition*—These conditions or constraints might include the need for compatibility with existing or future

equipment or systems; implementation constraints caused by space, personnel, or other limitations; budget constraints, particularly as they relate to lease vs. purchase decisions; and other known constraints that could influence cost, schedule, capability, or performance issues.

- *The established cost targets for the acquisition, with sufficient explanation to support the targets*—This section should include discussions of the following issues, as appropriate: the make-or-buy decision, estimated life cycle costs, design-to-cost, should-cost analysis, and other cost issues determined to be of significance.

- *The required capabilities or performance to be acquired*—This section should address such issues as speed, accuracy, reliability, ease of use, and other pertinent performance characteristics when acquiring goods. When acquiring services, the required performance standards or knowledge requirements that are required to provide the services should be discussed. This section should also explain how the goods or services being acquired relate to and will satisfy the need.

- *Delivery or performance period requirements*—This section should provide the required delivery date(s) or the required period of performance, as well as an explanation for why the dates or periods were selected. If an emergency or urgent condition exists that has influence on the delivery or performance requirements, explain that relationship, as well as the incremental impact that the emergency may have on cost considerations.

- *Trade-offs related to the previously defined plans for cost, technical performance, capability, and schedule requirements*—Explain what trade-off issues are likely to occur, the degree to which a trade-off decision may impact other plan components, and how trade-offs may impact the overall acquisition plan.

- *A discussion of the level of risk associated with the technical, cost, schedule, and other pertinent aspects of the plan*—This discussion should clearly define the anticipated risks; the strategies or actions planned or taken to eliminate, reduce, or mitigate risk to an acceptable level; and the likely consequences that might result from failure to achieve goals.

- *The contracting plan of action*—Taking into consideration all of the pertinent plan components mentioned above, the contracting plan of action should address such issues as:
  o Proposed sources that can provide the required goods or services;
  o The degree to which the acquisition will be subject to competition;
  o The contract type(s) proposed for use;
  o The source selection process, including an explanation of how the evaluation factors relate to the achievement of the goals of the acquisition;
  o How the contract will be administered after issuance;
  o Milestones or target dates for completion; and
  o Any other pertinent issues of concern.[52]

The need for acquisition plans differs in the public and private sectors. In the public sector, such plans are normally required for significant or complex acquisitions. In the private sector, such plans may be created as the result of corporate policy or as a matter of professionalism or convenience. Regardless of whether they are required or desired, acquisition plans provide valuable information regarding the initial intent of a proposed acquisition and a basic roadmap to check progress against during the acquisition cycle.

Requirements

Preparing requirements, also referred to as "solicitation preparation," is arguably the single most important function in the acquisition cycle. Although acquisition planning activities also have a significant impact on the success or failure of the proposed acquisition, requirements preparation usually provides the last major opportunity for the contracting professional to influence the solicitation package before potential suppliers see it. It is therefore important that the contracting professional, in collaboration with the customer and required internal sources of specific expertise, craft a solicitation package that accurately reflects the customer's needs and communicates those needs and other related information clearly and concisely to potential suppliers. The end goal should always be to satisfy the customer's need, at a fair price, with the minimum acceptable level of risk. This is an area in which contract professionals can be of greatest benefit to the customer by sharing their knowledge of the market; working closely with the program office or primary customer and generally crafting a solicitation package that satisfies a majority of needs.

Some acquisitions are very simple, others are exceedingly complex, and the majority usually fall somewhere in between. The format and content of solicitation packages and the resulting contracts are often mandated by law, regulation, or corporate policy, such as the use of the "Uniform Contract Format" for government contracting professionals. Regardless of the complexity, the solicitation package normally provides the information outlined in **FIGURE 9** below.

Requirements Preparation

- Statement of Work
- Contract Type and Method
- Terms and Conditions
- Evaluation Procedures
- Preparing and Submitting Proposals
- Other Considerations

FIGURE 9. Requirements Preparation

Statement of Work

The statement of work (SOW) is likely the single most important document in the solicitation package. The SOW is the document that describes the goods or services required in sufficient detail to provide potential offerors with a complete understanding of the requirement. Generally, there are three basic types of SOWs:

- Design,
- Performance, and
- Functional.

The differences among them relate to the degree to which the requirement is defined and explained; from specific to general. Each type of SOW has its own advantages and disadvantages, and SOWs often reflect elements of all three basic types in order to completely describe the requirement.

Design SOWs
A design SOW is most often used when the buyer requires a specific manufactured good. Design SOWs are extremely detailed, and usually define all required materials, production processes, and specifications such as size, shape, color, tolerances, etc. Design SOWs also frequently provide specific requirements related to quality, inspection, packaging, and related needs. The basic intent of a design SOW is to document the requirement with such specificity so any competent seller can provide the product, and that the end product will be exactly what the buyer required.

The degree of precision inherent in design SOWs also presents challenges for the contracting professional. Design SOWs may restrict the competitive process by imposing too many specifications that result in no-bid decisions from sellers that might otherwise be willing to provide the product. Design SOWs may also result in higher costs, since the seller may have to use materials and processes that are different from those used in the normal course of business. Additionally, the buyer assumes virtually total performance risk when contracting with design SOWs since the seller is performing based on the buyer's design and specification requirements. As a result of these drawbacks, using design SOWs is commonly discouraged whenever a less restrictive type of SOW can be reasonably expected to provide the results required.

Performance SOWs
Performance SOWs are less restrictive than design SOWs. Performance SOWs define requirements in terms that relate to minimum acceptable standards or ranges of acceptable performance. A performance SOW may require a particular approach or a particular type of product, but it leaves most of the "how" decisions to the contractor. Performance SOWs are normally considered to enhance competition because they enable a contractor to use their company's strengths and creativity to satisfy the requirement.

Functional SOWs
The functional SOW is the least restrictive of the three basic SOW types. Functional SOWs describe requirements in terms of the end purpose, expected result, or final objective, rather than in terms of how the work effort is to be performed. Though the functional SOW may include needed quality standards or minimum essential characteristics, it focuses primarily on the "what" aspects of the requirement. Functional SOWs provide the contractor with the maximum degree of flexibility and innovation in determining how best to satisfy the buying organization's needs. It is for this reason that

functional SOWs are the preferred type of SOW in most government and commercial contracting organizations.

Another alternative with some popularity is the "statement of objectives" (SOO). The SOO provides basic, top-level objectives of an acquisition and is provided in the request for proposal in lieu of a government-written SOW. It provides potential offerors the flexibility to develop cost-effective solutions and the opportunity to propose innovative alternatives. The disadvantage to using this approach is that significantly different technical solutions may be proposed, thus requiring additional evaluation time or specialized evaluation personnel.

In practice, SOWs rarely fall neatly into one of the types discussed above. Most SOWs reflect characteristics of at least two, if not all three SOW types in order to adequately describe the requirement.

Statement of Work (cont.)

Regardless of which type or types are used, SOWs normally contain at least some of the following elements.

Objective
An "objective" is a brief statement of the goal to be achieved, the end product desired, or the basic purpose of the requirement.

Scope
The "scope" is a general statement defining the parameters or boundaries of expected actions, required performance, or products required. Scope statements can be viewed as the "fenced in area" in which the contractor performs.

Description of Work Required
The "description" is a sufficiently detailed explanation of what is required. The description often contains an explanation of interfaces that will impact the work effort, a history of how the required effort came to be needed, required place of performance, issues and problems that require resolution, and other pertinent information. To the maximum extent possible, the description should be outcome-focused, providing the contractor as much flexibility as possible for determining how to accomplish the work required to achieve the objective within the defined scope. When necessary, specific performance elements can be prescribed, but they should be kept to a minimum.

Performance Standards and Reporting Requirements
"Performance standards and reporting requirements" are an explanation of how the contractor's work effort will be evaluated in terms of quantity, quality, frequency, or other appropriate measures. The performance standards should define clearly the expected, required, or acceptable level of performance that will be anticipated from the contractor. The standards need to be achievable and measurable. Reporting requirements should explain how often and in what format any required progress or performance reports will be provided. Both performance standards and reporting requirements should be limited to the minimum necessary to achieve effective and efficient contract administration.

Staffing Requirements
If personnel with certain specific qualifications are required to perform the work (e.g., electrical engineer, Certified Public Accountant, etc.), these qualifications should be included. However, in most cases, the contractor should have the option to propose staffing levels and composition to accomplish the required work.

Resources to be Provided
Specify any space, equipment, materials, services, information, or other resources that will be provided to the contractor.

Appropriate Reference Documents
Provide a list of any pertinent reference documents that may have been discussed in the SOW, or that may be required by the contractor to ensure adequate performance or clarify contract requirements.

As previously mentioned, SOWs may be of varying lengths and levels of complexity, depending on the needs of the buying organization. While not all SOWs will necessarily contain all the elements noted above, each SOW should be constructed to provide a complete, clear, and concise description of the requirement. Well-constructed SOWs reduce risk, enhance competition, and help achieve organizational goals.

Contract Type and Method

The solicitation package should also define the contract type and method that the acquisition will use. An explanation of commonly used contract types and methods was presented earlier in 1.5 and 1.6. As they relate to the solicitation package, the contract type and method used should complement the degree of complexity and risk associated with the overall SOW. The use of certain contract types and methods for specific types of acquisitions is sometimes required by law, regulation, or corporate policy. In other cases, the contract type and method used is a discretionary decision made by the contracting professional. Sometimes the contracting professional must blend more than one contract type into a solicitation, such as including both firm-fixed-price and time-and-material line items when appropriate. The choice of contract type and method is frequently a business decision, influenced by a variety of organizational and marketplace dynamics. The contracting professional should strive to ensure that the contract type and method chosen are:

- Consistent with the level of complexity and uncertainty inherent in the SOW;
- Reflect an acceptable level of risk sharing between the buyer and seller;
- Conform to applicable law, regulation, or corporate policy; and
- Help promote the successful accomplishment of the contracting function and the overall goals of the organization.

Terms and Conditions

In addition to the SOW and contract type and method, terms and conditions are another component of the requirements package that helps define the business relationship between the buyer and seller and the rights and obligations of both parties to the contract. The primary function of terms and conditions is to eliminate or reduce the risk of contract ambiguity, which is often the source of disputes and misunderstandings. Most government and commercial contracting organizations include standard terms and conditions related to certain contract types in all solicitations and resulting contracts. In many cases, the selection of clauses that comprise the terms and conditions is an automated function that occurs within the buyer's contract writing software programs. In other cases, terms and conditions can be selected from a "shopping list" provided for the appropriate contract type. In still other cases, specific clauses must be crafted to meet an individual need, usually with the assistance of legal counsel and other professionals. Though frequently referred to as "boilerplate," and though sometimes included in solicitations as little more than an afterthought, terms and conditions are another risk mitigating tool that contracting professionals can use to enhance the likelihood of success. Carefully reviewing the solicitation's terms and conditions can reveal gaps that could cause confusion, unnecessary terms and conditions that could adversely affect price or performance, or terms and conditions that conflict with each other. Terms and conditions should be reviewed to ensure that each one included serves a legitimate purpose, is required or provides a direct benefit to the acquisition in question, promotes an acceptable level of risk sharing between buyer and seller, and does not impose unreasonable burdens on prospective offerors.

Evaluation Procedures

The solicitation package should clearly indicate the general procedures that the buyers will use to evaluate proposals and the decisions that they will make as the basis for an award. The method of acquisition normally determines the basis for the award. Using an invitation for bids requires that the selection be based on price or price-related factors. Using a request for proposal indicates a negotiated procurement where various factors, with potentially different degrees of relative significance, will serve as the basis for award. The evaluation procedures can influence, either positively or negatively, the quality of bids or proposals received from offerors. Buyers must take great care in determining evaluation factors—too few factors may result in receiving inadequate proposals that are impossible to evaluate; too many factors may result in receiving exceedingly complex proposals or none at all.

Though price will always be included as an evaluation factor, other factors—such as cost realism, technical excellence, management capability, past performance, and other relevant factors—can and should be included as appropriate. Each evaluation factor should be independent of the other factors, again to reduce the potential for confusion. It is also important to advise potential offerors of the relative significance of the evaluation factors to each other. Though it is not required nor may it be desirable to provide all the details of the evaluation plan in the solicitation, it is important for potential offerors to understand how proposals will be evaluated, the factors that will make up the evaluation, and the relative importance of each evaluation factor to each other and to the overall acquisition.

Instructions for Preparing and Submitting Proposals

The final piece of the solicitation package is the instructions provided to potential offerors for preparing and submitting proposals. The purpose of the instructions is to help ensure that uniform (or nearly uniform) submissions are received from offerors to permit a fair and unbiased evaluation process. Offerors usually pay close attention to the instructions since failure to comply with them may result in a proposal not being considered. The instructions can be very specific or very general, depending on the needs of the buying organization.

Instructions usually contain:

- Information regarding page format and page number limitations,
- The order of topic presentation,
- Required content to be addressed,
- Whether separate technical and price proposals are required,
- If the award will be made with or without discussions,
- If verbal presentations will be required,
- The number of copies to submit,
- The media proposals that may be submitted on,
- The place to submit proposals to,
- The due date and time, and
- Similar types of information.

The contracting professional has to balance the need for the information required to be provided in the proposal with the costs offerors will incur in proposal preparation. The instructions should be constructed to enable the offerors to submit the best possible proposals while also ensuring that the information received in the proposals will provide the necessary data for a thorough and appropriate evaluation and award decision.

Other Requirements Preparation Considerations

Once the solicitation package has been completed, there are a number of techniques that the buyer can use to validate the solicitation package's completeness and accuracy before it is formally issued. Some of these techniques include an independent technical review, obtaining marketplace comments, and pre-solicitation notices and conferences.

Independent Technical Review
The solicitation package can be reviewed by technical experts, legal counsel, and other resources within the organization to ensure it is complete and accurate. Normally, this independent technical review team is composed of people who had no prior involvement with the solicitation package.

Obtaining Marketplace Comments
A draft of the solicitation package can be issued to potential offerors requesting review and comments or suggestions. This pre-release review sometimes yields useful suggestions for revision that might otherwise have been overlooked. However, the contracting professional needs to be aware of the possibility that potential offerors may use this opportunity for preliminary marketing purposes and may try to influence content changes in the solicitation that enhance their ability to successfully compete for the contract.

Pre-solicitation Notices and Conferences
Pre-solicitation notices and conferences can be used to help identify potential interested sources and can provide a forum to explain technical or complicated aspects of the solicitation. These efforts can sometimes separate the interested potential sources from the merely curious ones.

Publicizing

Issuing solicitation packages and the degree to which competitive proposals are sought often depends on the buying organization. Government contracting professionals are subject to a law- and regulation-based preference for fully competitive procurements. Though there are a number of authorized exceptions permitting less than full and open competition and sole-source acquisition, the general rule in government contracting is to seek the maximum level of meaningful competition whenever possible. Commercial contracting professionals sometimes work in organizations that also have a preference for competitive acquisition. However, other commercial considerations—such as supply chain agreements, approved source lists, and other business decisions—can sometimes have an influence on the degree to which competition is pursued. When competition is a goal, the buying organization normally uses publicizing as a technique to ensure adequate competition.

Publicizing—Government Agencies
Government contracting organizations are normally required to post solicitation packages exceeding

certain dollar thresholds (i.e., the simplified acquisition threshold) for full and open competition on an official Internet website. Though certain limitations can apply to these postings (including small business set-asides, restricting competition to firms that hold General Services Administration Federal Supply Schedule contracts, and other discriminators), the fundamental intent of these postings at a single location is to provide a uniform source of information to the business community in pursuit of a required or desired level of competition.

Solicitation packages that do not exceed certain dollar thresholds are normally competed by selecting an appropriate number of potential offerors and issuing the solicitation to them. Though the number of firms solicited usually varies depending on the dollar value and complexity of the acquisition, the intent is to seek a level of competition that will reasonably result in the receipt of multiple proposals, which will produce a competitive award and will not cause undue administrative burden to the agency.

Some government agencies also advertise open solicitations on their official Internet websites, usually under a title such as "Business Opportunities," "Current Business Opportunities," "Doing Business With…" or a similar title.

Publicizing—Commercial Organizations

Commercial contracting organizations may advertise their requirements in newspapers, trade journals, professional publications, and similar media. They may also provide the solicitation to capable firms in their supply chain, or as the result of other business agreements. Commercial firms may also advertise business opportunities on their official Internet websites, in much the same manner as government agencies sometimes do.

Although the methods for publicizing active solicitation packages may vary, the basic purpose does not. When competition is required or desired, the solicitation should be advertised uniformly to ensure that the target market of potential offerors is aware of the opportunity. Additionally, some other concepts should be used to make the publicity effort more meaningful.

Solicitations should remain open or active for a period of time sufficient to permit potential offerors enough time to carefully and completely review and analyze all aspects of the requirement, make an informed bid/no-bid decision, and prepare and submit their best proposal. Though the contracting professional often faces internal pressures to reduce the acquisition cycle time, the length of time a solicitation remains open can have a direct impact on the number and quality of proposals received and the success or failure of the overall acquisition. Contracting professionals should normally provide a period of time within the solicitation period for potential offerors to submit written questions and/or to attend pre-proposal conferences. These activities are often very valuable in clarifying the buyer's intent, as well as technical or other complex aspects related to the acquisition. These conferences can sometimes include a "walkthrough" when the contract will be performed at the buyer's location, or other pertinent information that could be of value to potential offerors.

The need for changes or amendments to a solicitation may become evident after responding to written questions or after a pre-proposal conference. When appropriate, the solicitation should be modified to reflect the necessary changes and the due date for proposals should be extended to provide offerors the opportunity to respond to the changes.

The degree to which solicitation packages are publicized usually has a direct impact on both the quality and quantity of competitive proposals received. The solicitation phase is often a target when trying to reduce acquisition cycle time, primarily because a reduction in the length of time a solicitation remains open has little or no immediate adverse impact on the buying organization. Contracting professionals need to remain aware, however, that an inadequate solicitation period often affects the overall quality of the acquisition.

2.3 Proposal Preparation

"Proposal preparation" refers to the activities and events required to submit an offer or quotation, usually in response to a customer request. The first step will be a bid or no-bid decision (i.e., the determination made by the seller's management whether or not to submit an offer). If that determination is positive, proposal preparation includes defining the proposal team (including any teaming decisions), writing the proposal, and submitting the proposal. Typically, specific areas to focus on are the SOW, invoicing and payment, and the contract type.

It is always a good idea to start by addressing the evaluation factors and subfactors with the highest priority or weighting, as identified in the solicitation.

Make clear that the company understands the agency's needs and explain how the company will meet the agency's requirements by providing specific details. Illustrations and graphics are effective ways to explain processes, cause and effect relationships, and management structure. A successful proposal not only responds to the requirements set forth in the request for proposal, but convinces the agency that it has done so better than any other proposal. When writing a proposal, the authors need to keep the customer and its requirement in mind at all times. Some agencies recommend that evaluators quickly skim the proposal before doing a detailed evaluation. The company must show the evaluator during this quick read that the proposal is clear, concise, organized, and easy to evaluate. The proposal should not only meet the request for proposal's requirements, but also be:

- Clearly written, or the evaluators will not understand the company's win strategy;
- Well organized, or the evaluators will not know where to find important information;
- Concisely written, so evaluators are not confused by overly complicated language; and
- Supported with credible statements, or the evaluators will not believe the company's solution will work.[53]

2.4 Negotiation

"Negotiation" is a communication process where two parties attempt to reach agreement. Negotiation does not need to be a process where one party wins at the other's expense. It is possible and preferable that both parties finish negotiations feeling that they have "won." Despite the fact that both parties have different interests, they have a common goal: to negotiate a fair and reasonable contract. This discussion of negotiation is distinct from that of formal source selection under 2.5.

Preparation

Preparation is the most important step in the negotiation process. Buyers and sellers have unique advantages going into negotiations. Buyers know how much money is available and the amount and nature of competition. Sellers know the basis for cost estimates and where there is flexibility in their proposals. Nonetheless, both parties must plan for negotiations. Thorough preparations can lead to smooth negotiations, a good contract, fewer changes, and successful performance.

The first step in the preparation process is understanding the acquisition. Both parties must know what the requirement is, why it is needed, and whether it was bought before. Although it is not always possible for every negotiator to do an in-depth analysis of each acquisition, it is important to get to know as much as possible before beginning. Sellers must also understand the acquisition. They should know the purpose of the acquisition, the buyer's objectives, whether the buyer is the end-user (or if not, who is the end-user), and the end-user's needs.

After the buyer receives the seller's proposal, they review and analyze it in response to the requirements stated in the solicitation. The buyer's first source of information is the offeror's proposal. The buyer compares the data in the proposal to previous contracts of a similar nature. The seller uses its previous experience and the assumptions used to price the proposal to prepare for the negotiation.

The buyer looks at the differences between the offer and previous contracts or the buyer's estimate. The buyer then gathers facts, analyzes the facts, establishes negotiation objectives, and plans the negotiation strategy. Gathering and analyzing facts is done throughout the acquisition cycle. It is important for both parties to document those facts for use in negotiation. Discrepancies are resolved by providing documentation to justify a position. Without adequate documentation, it may be difficult to reach a negotiation objective.

The Negotiation Team

Large and/or complex acquisitions usually require different people to participate in the negotiations, with each person contributing a special skill. Selecting team members depends on the nature of the acquisition and the experience that each member brings to the team. Team members on each side may include, but are not limited to:

- The contract professional,
- Financial analyst,
- Cost analyst,
- Legal counsel,
- Design engineer,
- Production specialist,
- Quality control specialist, and
- Note-taker.

The negotiation teams for the buyer and seller designate a lead negotiator for their team, which is most often the contract professional, depending on the organization's customary practice and line of business. In the case of federal contracting, the lead negotiator is always the contracting officer.

The team members usually have worked together on the acquisition since its early stages from solicitation to proposal submission. After proposal submission, they work together again to reach an agreement with the other party. It can be a long process that takes months or more, so it is important to put together a team that works well together. Each member of the team must understand and agree with the group's goal or the team will be ineffective. The group must function as a team, reporting to the lead negotiator. It is ineffective to have individuals who conduct side negotiations to protect their own interests. This will jeopardize the team's goals.

Negotiation Objectives

The situation is different for each negotiation, even if the acquisition is for the same item as previously purchased. The market may be different, the delivery schedule may be different, and the economy may be different. All of these factors influence pricing decisions and negotiation objectives.

Establishing the negotiation objectives entails more than cost analysis and comparison. Most aspects of a solicitation are negotiable, such as the statement of work, contract type, delivery schedule, warranties, payment terms, terms and conditions, and/or reporting requirements. These aspects may be negotiable depending on the circumstances surrounding the acquisition.

Both buyers and sellers need to establish specific and realistic negotiation objectives. An objective of "the best price we can get" is neither specific nor realistic, as there would be no way of knowing if the result was the best price. Establishing negotiation objectives is an ongoing process because the negotiation objectives will change as the situation changes.

Based on the requirement, proposed costs, delivery schedule, and risks involved, buyers and sellers prepare a negotiation objective based on the best information available. Since the circumstances change, the objective needs to be flexible. A way to ensure flexibility is to develop three positions in preparing an objective: the minimum, objective, and maximum. By doing so, a range is established that permits movement one way or another depending on the situation. When the seller's objective overlaps the buyer's objective, both parties are satisfied with the final agreement.

The tables in **FIGURE 10** below demonstrate examples of a negotiation objective for a firm-fixed-price contract and for a cost-plus-fixed-fee contract.

Negotiation Objective for a Fixed-Price Contract			
	Minimum	Objective	Maximum
Unit Price	$	$	$

Negotiation Objective for a Cost-Plus-Fixed-Fee Contract			
Cost Element	Minimum	Objective	Maximum
Direct	$	$	$
Indirect	$	$	$
Total Cost	$	$	$
Profit	$	$	$
Total Cost	$	$	$

FIGURE 10. Requirements Preparation

For the seller, the minimum position in a firm-fixed-price contract is the lowest acceptable price. For a cost reimbursement contract, the seller's minimum position might be the lowest possible cost, plus a reasonable profit, given a perfect situation. In a fixed-price environment, the buyer will ask for the lowest price as a counter-proposal, which may be based on a previous contract. If the contract is cost type, cost overruns are likely if the price agreement is too low. If the resulting contract is fixed price, the seller may earn an unreasonably low profit or even suffer a potential loss. These risks may result in poor quality or nonperformance. For these reasons, a buyer's objective of the lowest price possible is not always a good idea.

The objective is to arrive at a price that both parties agree upon. It is an amount between the minimum and the maximum of both parties' negotiation objectives. If the parties' objectives are far apart, a final agreement may be difficult to achieve.

The seller's maximum position is the initial proposal. The buyer's maximum position is usually the funding limit. In this instance, the buyer has an advantage because it knows the seller's maximum position (the initial proposal) and the buyer's own funding limit, whereas the seller only knows the initial proposal but not the buyer's funding limitations.

The amount for each position must be defensible. The negotiators must know the exact figures, the reasons for arriving at that number, and the means to justify those figures. Each party should document how they reached the amounts because as the facts surrounding the assumptions change, the positions will change.

The degree of competition, if any, also affects the relevance of negotiation objectives. If the acquisition is competitive, then the competitive forces of the marketplace set the price.

Another step in establishing negotiation objectives is to identify important issues to discuss. Each side must organize and gather facts to support the issues it believes are important. Issues might include requirements in the statement of work, terms and conditions, and cost proposal details (in a cost reimbursement contract). Identifying issues is based on experience with the required work and with the buyer or seller.

Upper management usually makes recommendations on positions by reviewing the documentation and justification before negotiations. Management review of the negotiation objectives is a vital step before entering negotiations. For private firms, it gives the negotiator the authority to agree to a certain price. In private firms, the negotiator may have a continuous delegation of authority to negotiate contracts up to a certain dollar level. A negotiator would need further management review and approval to go beyond that prescribed authority. Negotiators consult with management throughout the process in both commercial and federal contracting, especially when unanticipated problems arise.

Government contracting officers have authority to commit the government up to the amount specified in the contracting officer's warrant, if limited by a specified dollar amount. When contracting officers have an unlimited warrant, they are constrained only by available funds, but they still participate in management reviews nonetheless. A negotiator's authority is the first item discussed in the negotiation. Negotiators must know the limits of their authority before entering into negotiations.

Discussing negotiation objectives during the management review also sets the stage for establishing basic strategies. Presenting pre-negotiation objectives and strategies helps the negotiators prepare for the negotiation by explaining the plan to upper management.

Negotiation Guidelines

Although both parties enter negotiations intending to reach agreement, the fact remains that they approach it from different perspectives. Lack of respect seriously reduces the possibility of reaching agreement. Respect for the individual and his or her authority is paramount to effective negotiations. Each side takes on certain risks when entering a contract, and it is important for the opposing side to not only recognize those risks, but to understand them as well. The first step in understanding is listening carefully to the other side's position and trying to understand it. The only way an agreement can be reached is for both parties to be flexible and compromise.

"Caucus" and "concession" are two techniques employed in negotiations. A caucus is used to break away from formal negotiations for the team to consider a point. When a counter-offer is made, negotiators use a caucus to confer with their team to consider all aspects of the counter-offer. A caucus is useful to discuss anything about the ongoing negotiation that you don't want the other team to hear. Negotiators may also caucus when a team member wants to bring to the negotiator's attention an important fact, if a fact needs to be checked with a team member, or if management approval is necessary in order to make a concession or counter-offer. Concessions are also necessary to the negotiation process. Entering into negotiations without an intention to concede any point will not result in a mutual agreement. Sometimes it is necessary to concede an item if your objectives can be met at the same time.

Strategies and Tactics

In addition to these guidelines, negotiators also use certain strategies or techniques to achieve negotiation objectives. The use and effectiveness of any strategy depends on a number of factors, including the nature of the acquisition and each party's long- and short-term objectives. In addition to the long-

and short-term objectives, the parties must evaluate the nature of their relationship. On the one hand, if a long-term, continuing relationship is important, then strategies and tactics used are usually cooperative. On the other hand, if the relationship is only a one-time, short-term relationship, then a more competitive strategy may be effective.

Four basic tactics include:

- The cooperative mode,
- The competitive mode,
- Time restrictions, and
- Deadlock.

Cooperative Mode

The cooperative mode presumes that reasonable people are needed to achieve reasonable outcomes. The planning before the negotiation includes developing justifications and explanations for a party's position. This allows compromise and cooperation during negotiations because it allows the other party to understand and recognize the reasonableness and validity of the positions. Each party recognizes that the other party might have a position that meets the objectives of both parties, resulting in a mutually agreeable result. This tactic requires patience as the mutually agreeable result may not be presented immediately.

Competitive Mode

The competitive mode is used when each party views the other as an adversary and concessions are gained at the expense of the other party. Lack of planning can lead to this approach, such as not having justifiable reasons for a position. The ability to convincingly apply pressure is helpful in this mode. However, one should be careful not to issue threats; the other party may accept the threat rather than concede a point.

Time Restrictions

Time restrictions are usually present at any negotiation—the contract must be awarded so deliveries can be met or before funds expire. Learning to work under this pressure is important because concessions made due to time limits may not meet negotiation objectives. Extreme deadlines make adequate preparation difficult and may lead unprepared negotiators to make decisions based solely on time constraints. Time restrictions can be worked around by negotiating delivery schedule, inspection requirement, compensated overtime, or a letter contract. Time tactics can range from "my flight's scheduled to leave in an hour" to "the funding will not be available unless the contract is awarded today."

Deadlock

Deadlock is the inability to continue negotiations because the parties cannot or will not be flexible in their positions. If the negotiations break down and there is a deadlock, the party with time on its side usually benefits. Patience is also important when a deadlock occurs because new objectives must be established requiring additional management reviews. While objectives are reestablished, both parties should consider how to allow the other party a "face-saving" way to concede—give the other party an opening, allowing a concession. After a deadlock happens, one party usually welcomes the other party back into negotiations. If the buyer has begun negotiating with a second seller, the position of the seller is greatly reduced when they enter back into negotiations. A deadlock can sometimes be resolved by introducing new people into the negotiation process to allow another perspective.

The Negotiation

Negotiators ask questions of the other party to obtain a common understanding and validate facts. The buyer initiates the process of validating assumptions, also known as "fact-finding." Fact-finding can be done through telephone calls, correspondence, and/or meetings. It can take place before the formal negotiation session or at the very beginning of the session, depending on the circumstances. Fact-finding may affect both parties' objectives. If an assumption for a negotiation objective is invalid or even slightly different, the basis for that objective also changes. Thus, conducting effective fact-finding is a vital element of successful negotiations.

The buyer is usually the host in negotiations and is responsible for ensuring that adequate facilities are available to ensure the negotiations run smoothly. The facilities should include a room large enough to comfortably accommodate everyone, a separate caucus room close to the negotiation room for both parties, a nearby private telephone, notepaper and pencils for everyone, and visual aids such as a projector or white board.

Since negotiations should not be interrupted, the host should ensure that the conference room used is available for the entire negotiation session. The host should find out in advance how many people are going to attend and if there are any special audio/visual requirements.

The negotiation conference begins with a formal introduction of everyone present. The buyer's lead negotiator, as the host, begins the introductions. All the team members are introduced by announcing members' names and roles in the negotiation. The lead negotiators for both teams should indicate whether they have the authority to bind their organization. Some negotiators can verbally bind their organization, but do not have the signature authority for the contract, so they must return to the office to get the appropriate signature. In the case of federal contracting, contracting officers may bind the government up to a certain amount stipulated in their warrant.

The host provides an agenda to everyone present. The agenda establishes the major issues of the negotiation, and both sides may have different ideas of what the major issues are. Sometimes both parties arrive at negotiations with established agendas; and in some cases, negotiations begin by establishing the items to be discussed on the agenda.

The basic format of negotiations is question and answer. The buyer might begin by asking the seller to justify a proposed price or term, and the seller responds by describing their justification. Alternatively, the seller may ask the buyer about an item in the statement of work, and the buyer responds by describing how that item fits into the program. Regardless of who is answering, it is vital that each party be allowed to answer completely. Interruptions not only distract the person from answering, but also prevent listeners from obtaining important information.

It is helpful to get the easy agreements first. List all potential issues to be discussed, and cross off the items on which there is no disagreement. This method narrows down the list of items quickly and makes the issues remaining appear manageable. Each agreement should be documented by writing it down on paper or on a white board so that everyone knows that discussion on that item is considered "closed." Reopening a closed item is considered unethical and should not be done unless additional facts come to light in the interim.

Agreement

As multiple concessions bring the parties closer to the negotiation range, final agreement also becomes closer. Convincing the other party of your counter-proposal's reasonableness takes logic and salesmanship. Not only does one have to present the basis for why it is reasonable, but one also has to convince the other party that it is in their best interest to accept it. As an agreement is reached, both parties must document it. The documentation must explain the facts upon which they based the agreement. The purpose of documentation is to establish that both parties accepted the final agreement. A lot of paperwork is accumulated by the end of negotiations and the negotiation documentation summarizes this documentation. It takes the reader through each step from solicitation to proposal to negotiation objectives to concessions to final agreement.

Although the narrative may have different formats or styles, the following list identifies some basic information that documentation should include:

- A description of the supplies or services to be purchased, quantities, and delivery schedule;
- The solicitation/proposal number;
- The parties involved, including complete names, addresses, and phone numbers;
- The acquisition history, including information gathered;
- The negotiation objectives and their justifications; and
- A negotiation summary, including:
  - Concessions made and their impact on negotiation objectives,
  - Major items discussed and the parties' positions and outcomes,
  - Use of and reliance on data (including but not limited to price and cost) submitted, and
  - A signed copy of the agreed-to final position.

Both parties keep this documentation in the contract file to explain the final agreement and why it is reasonable. It will allow other personnel who were not involved in the negotiations to track how the negotiators reached the final agreement.

2.5 Source Selection

Selecting the "winning" proposal is often referred to as the "source selection," although the term is also used to summarize all activities inherent in the evaluation process. It is a more formal process than just conducting a negotiation and may have specific rules associated with it. It involves numerous participants with defined roles and duties. **FIGURE 11** illustrates a typical source selection structure.

FIGURE 11. Typical Source Selection Structure

The process has several steps, not all of which will be pertinent to each source selection. The chart depicted in **FIGURE 12** on page 54 is a depiction of a typical source selection process. Every procurement is unique, so the sequence or number of events may be slightly different.

Source Selection or Proposal Evaluation Plan

The proposal evaluation plan or source selection plan may incorporate the required elements of an acquisition plan, thus satisfying the requirement. A written source selection plan is particularly important for a complex negotiated acquisition that will take a long time to complete. Organizations normally do not require source selection plans for less costly acquisitions; the dollar thresholds vary by organization as well.

Documenting key elements of the source selection is an important part of the planning process. This documentation can be done either in a separate source selection plan, if required by the agency, or as a supplement to the acquisition plan. The source selection plan should discuss the acquisition strategy, including the requirements, expected competition, and the method of procurement.

The source selection plan serves several purposes, including:

- Defining a specific approach for soliciting and evaluating proposals;
- Describing the evaluation factors and subfactors, their relative importance, and the methodology used to evaluate proposals;
- Providing essential guidance to the request for proposal authors;

Suggested topics to be covered in a source selection plan include the following:

- A description of what the agency is buying;
- The acquisition's goals;
- Evaluation procedures, including whether award will be made based on the identified lowest-priced, technically acceptable offer or on a trade-off evaluation; and
- Proposed evaluation factors and subfactors, their relative importance, and associated standards.

The relative importance of the following factors should also be identified, as applicable:

- Price or cost,
- Technical proficiency,
- Management,
- Past performance, and
- The proposed acquisition strategy, including anticipated contract type.[54]

Typical Evaluation Considerations

As the source selection plan is developed, particular attention is given to the evaluation factors. These are the factors by which the proposals will be measured for compliance. The evaluation process should focus on the price, technical capabilities, management capabilities, and past performance requirements as set forth in the solicitation.

Price
Price (or cost) should always be an evaluation factor. In some cases, such as sealed bidding, price is the

FIGURE 12. Typical Source Selection Process

only factor. In negotiated procurements, price is always included, but may be of secondary or even lesser significance compared to other evaluation criteria.

Technical Considerations
Often required as a separate volume of the proposal, technical considerations relate to how well the offeror understands the requirement and how effective their proposed solution is in achieving the objectives of the acquisition.

Management Considerations
How the offeror intends to manage the work required under contract is often an important evaluation factor. When such information is required by the solicitation, appropriate evaluation factors should evaluate the proposed organization structure, management capability, experience and controls, and other pertinent factors.

Past Performance
Relevant information concerning how well an offeror has performed similar work in the past is often used as a significant evaluation factor. Offerors are normally required to submit past performance data that references other contracts they have performed that are similar in nature to the current requirement. When required by the solicitation, the evaluation plan must address how past performance issues will be evaluated, including the effect (usually neutral) of an offeror having little or no pertinent past performance. Evaluation factors for past performance normally require the evaluators or the contracting professional to attempt to verify the accuracy of past performance information submitted by an offeror. This is usually accomplished by contacting the sources provided by the offeror and obtaining answers to an established set of past performance questions. There are also government databases that compile past performance information (e.g., the Federal Awardee Performance and Integrity Information System (FAPIIS), Contractor Performance

Assessment Reporting System (CPARS), and Past Performance Information Retrieval System (PPIRS)).

Relative Significance of Evaluation Factors

The evaluation plan should also address the relative significance of all evaluation factors to be used as a basis for selection, as well as the relative significance of price factors to non-price factors. This factor-ranking process is particularly important in negotiated procurements because the award is often made to some offeror of other than the lowest price. As with all other evaluation factors, the relative significance of the factors should have also been addressed in the solicitation.

Typical Evaluation Techniques

The intent of the evaluation process is to uniformly rate the quality and content of all proposals received against a clear set of pertinent criteria in order to arrive at an award recommendation decision that provides the maximum benefit to the buying organization. Several methods are often used to help ensure that the evaluation process is logical, unbiased, and defendable. These methods include the following.

Evaluate Technical Aspects Separately

The solicitation package may have required the submission of separate technical and price proposals. However, even if separate proposal volumes were not required, the evaluation team should review technical considerations on their own merits. The proposals can be edited before review to eliminate any pricing information. Since there are defined evaluation criteria, and since price is always included as an evaluation factor, it is important not to allow the evaluation of one factor to be influenced by other evaluation factors at this stage.

Compliance Matrix

Organizations frequently use a prepared evaluation checklist or document to promote uniformity in the evaluation process. This checklist should contain a compliance matrix, which usually consists of:

- All evaluation factors and subfactors;
- The rating scale to be applied;
- Weights to be applied to factors, if appropriate; and
- Room for evaluator comments.

The use of such a matrix can ensure that each proposal received a thorough and comprehensive review. Offerors often use a similar compliance matrix when preparing proposals to ensure they have addressed all pertinent requirements.

Independent Evaluation

Each member of the evaluation team should evaluate each proposal independently, without any input from other team members. Each member of the team brings unique experiences, knowledge, insights, perspectives, and expectations to the evaluation process. These personal differences should be viewed as assets that can be used to enhance the evaluation process. Though a consensus will eventually be required, the initial evaluation phase should normally be as uninhibited as possible. This preferred independence can be enhanced even further by removing the names of the offerors from the proposals, if it is possible to do so.

Uniform Rating Scale

As noted above, the evaluation checklist or documentation will usually include the rating scale, which is used to assign value to the factors evaluated in the proposals. Rating scales often take one of several forms, which include the following.

➢ *Numeric Scales*

Using numeric rating scales, evaluators assign a range of points (0–10, 0–25, 0–100, etc.) to each evaluation factor, with the highest possible rating equaling the sum of the maximum points available for each factor. Numeric scales most easily accommodate weighted evaluation factors. For example, if technical approach is twice as important as past performance, 20 total points can be allocated to technical approach and 10 points to past performance. Numeric scales are often preferred by evaluators because they are most easily understood and yield a definitive "answer"—i.e., the score. Many contracting professionals do not favor the numeric scoring method because they understand that the definitive score it provides can often be much more subjective that it appears on its face. In addition, unless specific whole numbers are used on a scale (e.g., 20, 25, etc.), potential gradations (23 vs. 26) can seriously complicate the process.

➢ *Color Scales*

Many contracting professionals, most notably in the Department of Defense, use a color-based scale to evaluate proposals. Color scales are normally constructed with three, four, or five ranges. A three-range scale might consist of "Red" for

"Unsatisfactory," "Yellow" for "Satisfactory," and "Green" for "Excellent." For four- and five-range scales, more colors and related scoring ranges are added. The rationale for assigning a particular color rating is usually provided in the source selection plan and instructions to evaluators.

There are very specific definitions for each color rating. Color scales yield results that are easy to compare, but may be difficult to defend if the comments that support the rating are inadequate. For example, the difference between a green and yellow score is difficult to discern if the evaluators do not have specific and definitive reasons for their score.

> *Adjectival Scales*

Adjectival scales are very similar to color scales, but they use adjectives indicating the value assigned. As with color scales, adjectival scales usually have three, four, or five ranges and descriptions that often include: "Unsatisfactory," "Marginal," "Satisfactory," "Highly Satisfactory," and "Exceptional"; "Good," "Better," and "Exceptional"; etc. The evaluators must provide comments to support the ratings in a manner similar to that when using color scales. Adjectival scales are sometimes thought to produce results that are more consistent and defendable, primarily because they do not rely on visual or numeric devices to describe a score. However, the overall quality of the rating is still dependent on the quality of the evaluators' comments. The table in **FIGURE 13** below is a sample of a typical adjectival evaluation rating system.

Compare Results and Reach Consensus

After each member of the evaluation team has completed their individual ratings, the team should come together and compare results. This process will often reveal significant differences in perceptions among team members concerning the relative quality of the proposals. These differences should be viewed as positive because they should require a spirited and collaborative deliberation process. Evaluation team members should avoid simply averaging individual scores, as this diminishes the benefits gained from the individual review process. Rather, each team member should both share and solicit information regarding how ratings were derived. The resulting consensus should be documented thoroughly, with the strengths and weaknesses of each proposal explained. Sometimes proposals are also ranked in order of preference by the evaluation team. It is also important to thoroughly document problems, issues requiring clarification, and other unresolved matters related to each proposal since these often serve as the basis for negotiations with the offerors.

Proposal evaluation involves assessing the content of a proposal against established evaluation factors and determining whether the offeror will be able to perform the prospective contract successfully.

Adjectival Evaluation Rating System	
Adjective	**Explanation**
Excellent (E)	• Thorough and comprehensive ability to meet the criteria.
	• Exceptional added value that will have a significant favorable effect on the government's ability to accomplish its mission, as reflected by the presence of numerous major strengths and no major weaknesses.
Very Good (VG)	• Thorough and comprehensive ability to meet the criteria.
	• Added value that will have a favorable effect on the government's ability to accomplish its mission, as reflected by the presence of numerous major strengths and no major weaknesses.
Good (G)	• Thorough ability to meet the criteria.
	• Offers some value and will have a favorable effect on the government's ability to accomplish its mission.
Minimally Acceptable (MA)	• Ability to meet all of the minimum requirements set forth in the criteria, but offers no added value.
Unacceptable (U)	• Inability to meet all of the minimum requirements set forth in the criteria.

FIGURE 13. Sample Adjectival Evaluation Rating System

Evaluators identify the relative strengths, deficiencies, significant weaknesses, and risks in each proposal and document their assessments. In so doing, evaluators must assess only what each offeror submits in its proposal.

It is important to note that although the evaluators score the proposals, these scores do not make the source selection decision. Scores must not be used as the primary justification for contract award. Rather, the evaluators' written narratives, which identify the proposal strengths, weaknesses, and risks upon which the scores are based, are the primary justification for contract award.

As evaluators read each proposal, they should note anything that could be a problem. Generally, problems in proposals are categorized as deficiencies, significant weaknesses, or weaknesses. The proposal evaluation process comprises four general steps:

1. Identify and document proposal uncertainties, such as:
- Ambiguous language.
- Sections in which the offeror didn't provide sufficient information to determine whether:
    o The proposal should be in the competitive range; or
    o The offeror should win the contract, if the agency doesn't anticipate conducting discussions.
- The contracting officer may ask an offeror to provide additional information to help the government better understand its proposal. Initial ratings reflect the proposal as submitted, but these ratings may be revised when the offeror responds to the clarification request.
2. Identify and document proposal strengths, weaknesses, risks, and deficiencies. These will be discussed during negotiations/discussions, if applicable.
3. Assign ratings for non-cost evaluation factors (when using the trade-off process). Source selection team members independently evaluate each offeror's past performance and technical/management and cost/price proposals. After the individual evaluations, each team convenes to discuss the evaluator's assessment of the proposal's strengths, weaknesses, risks, and deficiencies relative to the evaluation factor(s) or subfactor(s). Then the panel determines a final consensus rating for each factor and subfactor.

4. Prepare a summary evaluation report. Once evaluators finish assessing each proposal, the evaluation team chairperson prepares a summary report that includes the evaluated price, the final rating for each evaluation factor and subfactor, and a discussion of the strengths, weaknesses, deficiencies, and risks of each proposal.[55]

The evaluation report and associated award recommendation is presented to the source selection official. The source selection decision may be made by the contracting professional or the senior contracting professional in the organization, a senior manager in the customer's organization, or a neutral senior manager that has had no prior involvement in the acquisition process. Regardless of who makes the selection, the source selection decision reflects the independent judgment of the source selection official.

Although the source selection official usually relies on the evaluation team's analysis and recommendations, there is no requirement that they concur with the recommendations. The source selection official must document the reasons for the selection made and explain additional considerations of the source selection process, such as a justification for paying more for higher quality.

If the evaluation team does everything right (e.g., evaluations are consistent with the acquisition plan, the solicitation, and the evaluation plan; and their recommendation is logical, reasonable, and supportable), the selection official will likely concur with their recommendation for award. Once a source is selected, additional actions must take place before actual award. Though some of the following discussion more closely relates to government contracting operations, commercial contracting professionals can also utilize some of the information presented, consistent with their corporate goals, processes, and procedures.

Award

The notification of award to the successful offeror should normally occur immediately after the conclusion of all source selection activities. Though the notification is usually made by issuing the contract, in some cases the award notification is made by separate correspondence or by a telephone call or e-mail, followed by the written contract or official correspondence. In any event, there should be little or no delay in making the award once the source selection process has been completed. In the case

FIGURE 14.

of contracts awarded by the government, congressional notification may be required in advance of notice to the successful offeror.

Preparing the Contract

The contract is prepared to document the terms of the agreement and the expectations of each party. The enforceability of the contract and the nature of the parties' obligations can be greatly affected by the form the contract is written in and the language used to express the agreement. Agreements made during preliminary negotiations may not be evident in the written contract and therefore be unenforceable. The terms and conditions within the contract will dictate its legal effect. Ambiguities in a written contract may cause differences in interpretation of the contract requirements. Internal conflict in the terms and conditions of a contract may lead to disagreement between the parties on which term should prevail. It is important to prepare a contract that accurately and concisely reflects the agreement between the two parties.

The contract is prepared using the appropriate format and terms and conditions for the type of contract being awarded and the type of organization awarding the document. The contract may contain standard contract language that has been formulated for the specific type of purchase or it may be necessary to write new contract language to fit the unique requirements of the contract. A great number of commercial contracts are form contracts. Commercial contracts for products, as a common practice in the everyday transactions under the Uniform Commercial Code, include the quantity of goods to be purchased, the time for performance, terms related to payment, delivery, passage of title, risk of loss terms, interest in goods, warranty, and returns of goods.

In the case of more complex requirements, a contract may include a statement of work, specifications, management plan, quality control plan, list of contract deliverables, licensing agreements, subcontracting plans, program and financial reporting requirements, and so on.

In the case of the federal government, a standard uniform contract format is used for most procurements, excluding basic agreements and construction or architect-engineering contracts. The sections in this format are as follows:

- Section A: Solicitation/Contract Form;
- Section B: Supplies or Services and Prices/Cost Schedule;
- Section C: Statement of Work or Other Description of Item Purchased;
- Section D: Packaging and Marking;
- Section E: Inspection and Acceptance;
- Section F: Deliveries or Performance;
- Section G: Contract Administration Data;
- Section H: Special Contract Requirements;
- Section I: Contract Clauses;
- Section J: List of Attachments;
- Section K: Representations, Certifications, and Other Statements of Offerors (incorporated by reference in a resultant contract);
- Section L: Instructions, Conditions, and Notices to Offerors (self-deleting in a resultant contract); and
- Section M: Evaluation Factors for Award (self-deleting in a resultant contract).

A successful contract reflects the agreed-to business transaction and addresses areas where there may be ambiguities regarding the expected performance of each party. If a contract does not adequately address these areas, the parties may end up in legal proceedings asking for the court's interpretation of the contract's terms. The goal of the contract professional is to prepare a document that minimizes the risk to his or her organization, reflects the agreed-to understanding between the parties, and successfully closes the business deal.

After the contract is signed and performance begins, the parties may realize that their agreement is not as clear as first thought. Thus, contract interpretation becomes necessary. "Contract interpretation" refers to determining the meaning of a contract or a term in the contract based on the original intent of the parties. Contract interpretation may begin by attempting to give all parts of the contract some meaning (as opposed to some sections being rendered meaningless through certain interpretations), and by the assertion of the specific over the general.

Most organizations have an instituted process for review of the contract document or items within by various stakeholders in the process. It is usually the responsibility of the contract professional to coordinate this review and obtain any necessary approvals within the organization before the document is signed. Often in organizations, the level of approval and review necessary is dependent on the dollar value of the contract.

Contract File
It is important that all contracts, regardless of dollar value, be properly documented so a complete record of pre-solicitation activities; the solicitation, evaluation, and award process; and the administration of the contract through closeout is provided. Often, a contract file has a table of contents organized in chronological order; for example, it could have six separate sections for pre-solicitation documents, solicitation documents, evaluation documents, award documents, administration documents, and contract closeout documents. Depending on the size of the contract, a separate contract file can be maintained for modifications or orders.

In addition to the contract document itself, pertinent items often assembled in the file might include such solicitation documentation as:

- Sole-source justification or consultant justifications,
- Purchase requests,
- Initial statement of work,
- Specifications,
- Drawings,
- Independent cost estimate detail,
- Make-buy documentation,
- Request for information,
- Acquisition planning/market survey,
- Evaluation plan,
- Solicitation revisions,
- Miscellaneous correspondence,
- Pre-proposal conference minutes and agenda, and
- Proposals received.

Contract award documentation may include:

- Abstract of purchase;
- Technical evaluation;
- Cost/price analysis report;
- Pre-award audit report;
- Subcontracting plan with approval;
- Pre-negotiation plan;
- Record of negotiations;
- Financial approval;
- Regret letters;
- Legal approval;
- Other supporting documentation (i.e., undefinitized terms or revision documentation), including:
  o Audits,
  o Procurement action summaries,
  o Winning proposals and revisions,
  o Non-winning proposals, and
  o Supplier's correspondence; and
- Contract administration information, such as:
  o Invoice actions,
  o Shipments,
  o Cost forecasting/status reports,
  o General correspondence,

- o Contract closeout documentation, and
- o Fee documentation.

The contract professional should review each proposed contractual document and its supporting file for completeness and accuracy. Each contract file should contain all pertinent information applicable to the proposed action. Each contract file should be in sufficient detail to permit reconstruction of all significant events by any subsequent reviewer without referral to the individual responsible for the contractual action.

Post-Award Conference

A post-award conference, meeting, or some other form of post-award contact between the contracting professional and the contractor is sometimes held, particularly if the contract is complex, represents a significant undertaking, or has a high dollar value. The intent of the post-award conference should be to help promote a good working relationship between the buyer and seller, to ensure that both parties to the contract have a clear and complete understanding of all contract requirements, and to identify and resolve questions, issues, and potential problems that may exist. However, the post-award conference is not intended to be, and should not be used as, a forum to "fix" problems that should more appropriately have been resolved in the pre-award phase. The contracting professional representing the buyer needs to be careful to ensure that the contractor does not use the post-award conference as a means to reopen negotiations. The decision to have a post-award conference, as well as all arrangements and agenda items related to the conference, normally remain under the control of the buyer's contracting professional. Post-award conferences are usually attended by representatives of the buyer's and seller's contracting function, the buyer's customer, and the seller's staff that will be performing the work. In lieu of an actual meeting, the exchange of correspondence or teleconferences is sometimes used to convey post-award communication.

Notification

In addition to the prompt notification of the successful offeror, all unsuccessful offerors should be notified of their status immediately or very soon after award. In some cases, notification is provided to offerors who have been eliminated from competition before the award decision.

Award Practices Unique to Federal Contracting

Pre-Award Notification

When an offeror has been eliminated from competition before an award decision has been made, the contracting officer should promptly notify the offeror in writing of their exclusion and the underlying reason for the decision. Pre-award notifications are normally made when elimination from further competition was made based on the offeror's exclusion from a predetermined competitive range or for other appropriate reasons.[56]

Post-Award Notification

Each unsuccessful offeror usually receives written correspondence from the contracting officer that notifies the offeror of their non-selection and provides additional information concerning:

- The number of offerors solicited, if known;
- The number of proposals received;
- The name and address of the successful offeror;
- A list of items, quantities, and unit prices in the award, or the total dollar value of the award if listing items is not practical; and
- The general reason(s) that the offeror's proposal was not selected for award, unless the price paid provides the obvious reason.

The contracting officer should take care not to reveal proprietary information, trade secrets, detailed financial breakdowns, or any other confidential or sensitive data related to the successful offeror's proposal or related to any other unsuccessful offeror's proposal when providing this notice to unsuccessful offerors. The contracting professional should also be aware that this notice often serves as the prelude to a request for a formal debriefing.[57]

Debriefing

Once notified, an unsuccessful offeror may request a formal debriefing. Normally, such a request should be received by the contracting officer within three days of the initial notification of non-selection or pre-award elimination. The types of information appropriate for sharing depends on whether the debriefing occurs pre-award or post-award.

➢ Pre-Award Debriefing

An unsuccessful offeror may request a debriefing before contract award when the offeror has been notified of its elimination from the competitive range, or has otherwise been eliminated from further competition. The offeror may also elect to defer the debriefing until an award has been made. Under certain circumstances, the contracting officer may deny a request for a pre-award briefing in favor of a post-award debriefing. When conducted, pre-award debriefings are somewhat more restrictive than post-award debriefings. The debriefing may be conducted in person, by written correspondence, or by any other manner deemed appropriate by the contracting professional. Pre-award debriefings usually include information concerning the result of the evaluation of significant elements contained in the offeror's proposal. It usually includes a summary of the reasons that the offeror's proposal was eliminated from the competition. Reasonable responses to pertinent questions are also usually given concerning the degree to which source selection procedures defined in the solicitation were actually followed.

It is important to note that information in the pre-award debriefing is restricted to conversations related only to the offeror's proposal and how it was evaluated.[58]

> *Post-Award Debriefing*

Post-award debriefings are requested by unsuccessful offerors in much the same manner as pre-award debriefings. However, the permissible content of post-award debriefings is somewhat more extensive. The debriefing may be conducted in person, by written correspondence, or by any other manner deemed appropriate by the contracting professional.

Post-award debriefings usually include information concerning the evaluation of significant weaknesses or deficiencies in the offeror's proposal, the price and technical ratings of the successful offeror (as well as that of the unsuccessful offeror), and the overall ranking of all offerors if a ranking process was used. The debriefing also usually includes a summary of the rationale used to select the successful offeror and reasonable responses to pertinent questions concerning the degree to which source selection procedures defined in the solicitation were actually followed.

It is important to emphasize that the purpose of a debriefing is to provide useful information to an unsuccessful offeror so that it is aware of how it might improve its chances for selection in future acquisitions. Debriefings are not intended to provide an unsuccessful offeror with the opportunity to perform a complete and detailed analysis of the relative strengths and weaknesses of all aspects of its proposal as compared to the successful offeror or to other unsuccessful offerors. The contracting professional should also be aware of the need to protect proprietary information, trade secrets, financial data, and other sensitive information of all offerors in the same manner as done in the notification process.[59]

2.6 Protests

The period immediately following contract award is the timeframe when contracting professionals may suddenly find themselves confronted with unexpected (and unwanted) issues, sometimes generated by both the successful offeror as well as unsuccessful offerors. These issues are usually presented by offerors as either mistakes or protests. Though they can also surface in the pre-award phase, charges of mistakes or protests are usually reserved for the immediate post-award period. This section will not deal with the detailed and rigorous processes and venues used to resolve mistakes and protests; but rather, will briefly discuss some of the more common reasons for mistakes and protests. Contracting professionals should be aware of common types of mistake- and protest-related issues when crafting solicitation packages to hopefully avoid ambiguities and prevent or reduce the frequency of such issues arising in the post-award environment.

If a contractor alleges a mistake, it is incumbent upon the contractor to present clear and convincing evidence to support the allegation that a mistake was made. Depending on the extent and quality of the evidence provided by the contractor, the contracting professional normally resolves the issue in one of the following manners:

- The mistake can be corrected by issuing a contract modification, provided that the modification would be favorable to the buyer and does not materially alter the essential requirements of the contract.

- If the mistake was mutual or if unilateral by the contractor and so apparent that the contracting officer should have realized the likelihood of a mistake, then the contract can be rescinded or re-formed to eliminate the mistake. Re-formed contracts may result in a price increase, but that increase may not exceed the price of the next most acceptable proposal.

- The contract can remain unchanged if the evidence presented by the contractor is insufficient to substantiate the mistake.

Protests are formal challenges to some aspect or aspects of the acquisition process. Like mistakes, protests can be lodged in either the pre-award or post-award phase. Though the specific grounds for a protest can vary widely and will depend on the particular circumstances of an acquisition and the contractor's perceptions, protests generally relate to some of the following issues.

Typical Pre-Award Protest Issues
- *Restrictive requirements*—The protestor may claim that the requirements or specifications are unnecessarily restrictive and thereby prohibit or limit meaningful competition.
- *Inappropriate sole-source requirement*—A protestor may claim that a requirement advertised as a sole-source procurement is not, in fact, a valid use of sole source authority and that the possibility for competition exists.
- *Ambiguous or erroneous evaluation criteria*—A protestor may claim that the criteria to be used to evaluate proposals is flawed, or inaccurate, or ambiguous in some material way so as to negatively impact the protestor's ability to fairly compete.
- *Ambiguous or incomplete requirements*—The protestor may claim that the statement of work is so incomplete or ambiguous so as to preclude a clear understanding of the full nature and scope of the requirement to be performed.
- *Exclusion from the competitive range*—A protestor may claim that their exclusion from the competitive range, when such a range was pre-established, was inappropriate or that the establishment of a competitive range was not revealed or sufficiently clear in the solicitation.

Typical Post-Award Protest Issues
- *Unfair evaluation criteria*—The protestor may assert that one or more of the criteria used to evaluate proposals was unreasonable, unfair, or otherwise inappropriate.
- *Failure to evaluate as advertised*—The protestor may claim that the method used to actually evaluate proposals was significantly different than the evaluation criteria specified in the solicitation.
- *Unreasonable best value analysis*—A protestor may indicate that, in a best value procurement, the cost/technical tradeoff analysis used to justify an award to other than the highest-rated or lowest-price proposal was flawed, inaccurate, or otherwise unreasonable in some material way.
- *Unequal treatment*—A protestor may claim that other offerors received some form of special treatment or that all offerors were not treated equally, thereby adversely impacting the protestor's ability to compete effectively.
- *Failure to conduct meaningful discussions*—A protestor may claim that they were not the recipient of meaningful discussions during pre-award negotiations, which unfairly prevented them from having the opportunity to submit a more competitive, revised proposal.

Regardless of the specific nature of a pre-award or post-award protest, the underlying issue usually relates to some real or perceived flaw, error, or shortcoming in some facet of the pre-award process. A thorough and comprehensive acquisition-planning effort and the logical implementation of the acquisition plan in the solicitation phase can result in a better procurement and fewer post-award issues to resolve. Once a protest is received, the contracting professional should take all reasonable and appropriate steps necessary to resolve the issue at the lowest possible level.

3.0 Post Award

The acquisition strategy, pre-award, and award competencies discussed in previous sections are arguably the most intense aspects of contract management. In many organizations, the bulk of the professional contracting resources are devoted to "getting the contract issued," or "winning the award." However, once a contract has been awarded, there are many significant and important activities required that often determine how successful the contractual relationship will be. Post-award competencies are equally as critical to successful performance. See **FIGURE 15** on page 63.

3.1 Contract Administration

Once contract award is complete, and unsuccessful offerors didn't file a protest, the tasks associated with ensuring appropriate contract performance begin. These tasks are usually referred to using the generic term "contract administration." The range and extent of contract administration activities required will vary greatly, depending primarily on the complexity, dollar value, and organizational significance of the contract. It is also important to note that effective contract administration is a shared responsibility of both the buyer and seller. The contract specifies the duties, obligations, and benefits that both parties are

FIGURE 15. Post-Award Competencies

responsible for and entitled to. The contract administration function provides the oversight required to ensure that contractual promises are kept. Contract administration can be straightforward, particularly when the contracting parties are individuals or small organizations. The complexities often associated with effective contract administration tend to be more prevalent and important as the size and complexity of the buyer's and seller's organizations increase. Contracting professionals in large, complex organizations frequently find themselves simultaneously responsible for administration activities on multiple contracts, and usually require some technical assistance and ongoing input from their internal customers, internal professional resources, management, and other stakeholders. The increasing level of complexity and the dependence on resources external to the contracting function frequently present significant contract challenges for the contracting professionals for both the buyer and seller.

3.2 Contract Performance/Quality Assurance

Effective Communication

An essential element of successful contract administration is establishing and maintaining effective communications. Maintaining a productive, two-way professional dialogue between buyer and seller during the period of contract performance is perhaps the most difficult, but potentially the most beneficial, aspect of contract administration. All too often, other business priorities and demands seem to force the contracting professional to relegate many administration activities to the "back burner." When this occurs, it is usually the customers in both the buyer's and seller's organizations who "pick up the slack" and run with the contract. Since these individuals often have little or no contracting experience, the results of inadequate oversight can be problematic.

Post-Award Kick-Off Meeting

A post-award meeting can help mitigate the potential for issues and problems during contract performance. In addition to the benefits of conducting a post-award conference, a more comprehensive post-award, pre-performance meeting can set the foundation for good communication between the buyer and seller. When conducted, this meeting should be chaired by contracting professionals from the buyer and seller and include appropriate managers and staff personnel from the buyer's organization (i.e., the customer who will interface with and receive the benefits from the contractor's work) and appropriate managers and staff personnel from the seller's organization (i.e., the contactor's resources that will interface with and perform work for the customer).

A post-award meeting would include a detailed review of the contract, including all work to be performed and related terms and conditions. The intent of this review is to achieve a clear, mutual understanding of what needs to be done and who will do the work. It could include the development of a procedure for continuing written and verbal communications. This procedure should clearly specify, for both the buyer and seller:

- Who is authorized to communicate,
- The subject matter appropriate for communication,
- The subject matter inappropriate for communication,
- The level of negotiation authority of the communicator (if any), and
- The form and format such communication should take.

Since many of the players on both sides will not be contracting professionals, this agreement can be of significant value in reducing or eliminating issues related to constructive changes, apparent authority, etc. At the post-award meeting, there is usually discussion and agreement on progress reporting requirements to include the frequency, format, and content of required reports; procedures for reporting unusual or urgent issues; and similar subjects. There is also discussion and agreement on methods and processes to be used to resolve minor disagreements or questions about contract interpretation, with provisions for escalation when appropriate. The subjects discussed and agreements reached during these meetings should be thoroughly documented, approved by both the buyer and seller, and distributed throughout both organizations.

Periodic Status Review Meetings

Updated information on status, issues, and concerns should be shared between the buyer and seller during periodic face-to-face meetings. The frequency, content, and required attendees for these meetings should be mutually agreed to, and each should have a written agenda. These meetings should augment any written reports required and help serve as a means to continue an open and honest dialogue for issues related to contract performance.

Written Status Reports

When appropriate and useful, the contractor should provide written status reports to keep the buyer's contracting professionals and customers aware of progress and issues. These reports can be narrative, statistical, or a combination of the two, consistent with the need for the information. These types of reporting requirements, as well as the pre-performance meeting and periodic status meetings discussed above, are normally included in the contract language as required deliverables. All reporting requirements should directly relate to some aspect of required performance, create the smallest administrative burden possible, and only be required when the information they contain will actually be used for some legitimate contract management purpose.

Observation

In addition to the information provided by a contractor in various meetings and reports, observation is a tool often used by the buyer's contract professionals and management staff to validate information received from other sources. Indirect observation is usually obtained through the receipt of various types of reports from the contractor, reviews or audits performed by either the buyer's management staff or by internal or external auditors, various forms of pre- and post-production testing and sampling, and a variety of other methods. Indirect observation can provide valuable information regarding issues such as cost, schedule, and quality that might not otherwise be available. If the work effort is primarily physical in nature, indirect observation is often augmented by direct observation. "Direct observation" is the actual physical presence of the contracting professional or other appropriate manager on site to visually check on progress or compare actual work completed to planned work completed.

Documentation

A continuous stream of pertinent documentation should be generated and maintained throughout the life of the contract. The documentation can take many forms: formal correspondence, memoranda for the record, telephone logs, e-mails, personal notes, journal entries, etc. The documentation serves as a written record of all meetings, discussions, issues, problems, solutions, and agreements. The record can be used as a ready reference source to reflect the intent of the parties over time as a means to guide future actions based on agreements reached in the past or as evidence in the event of litigation. Creating such documentation is effective only if the requesting organization actually reads the reports provided. Simply filing reports without reading them is not effective contract administration.

The communications, reporting, and observation aspects of contract administration form the basis for many of the other administration functions to be discussed later in this chapter.

3.3 Subcontract Administration

When the contract includes subcontractors, the buying organization needs to exercise a degree of caution because the buyer has no privity of contract with the seller's subcontractors. The buyer should therefore be careful regarding the communications with subcontractors. The prime contractor should always be the conduit through which information from both the buyer and the subcontractor is relayed to the other party. The buyer should not allow a subcontractor to bring issues or problems with the seller to the buyer for resolution. The buyer should normally not meet with the subcontractor without the seller's representatives present. The buyer should, by word and deed, clearly communicate to the subcontractor that the buyer's contractual relationship with the seller forms the framework for the relationship. The buyer should also be careful not to give the appearance of undercutting the authority of the seller over its subcontractors.

Even though the contractual relationship between the buyer and the seller (i.e., the prime contract) is normally the most important aspect of contract administration, the buying contract professional also needs to pay attention to the relationship between the seller and its subcontractors. In many cases, the ability of a prime contractor to successfully meet contractual obligations is at least partially, and sometimes significantly, dependent upon the ability of subcontractors to meet contractual obligations to the seller. In some cases the subcontractor is simply a supplier of goods or raw materials to the seller for use in production or fabrication. In other cases, the subcontractor may provide specialized services or perform highly technical work for a seller in direct support of the seller's contract with the buyer. Though in both cases the seller's ability to successfully perform is dependent upon the action of its subcontractors, the buyer's contracting professionals should normally be more attuned to and concerned with subcontractor performance when that performance plays a direct and significant role in the overall contract performance.

In some cases, particularly in certain types of government contracting, the buying government organization may require that it consent to subcontracts anticipated by the prime contractor. In other cases, the government may require that the seller's purchasing system be periodically reviewed by government personnel. In both these cases, the primary intent of the oversight is to ensure that government funds provided to the prime are used appropriately.

In other cases, it may be a matter of prudent management, whether in the public or private sector, for a buyer to be cognizant of the relationships between sellers and their subcontractors. When the performance of subcontractors is anticipated to have a significant impact on the ability of the prime contractor to perform, the buying organization may consider including subcontractors in some or all of the communications-related activities mentioned previously, particularly the face-to-face meetings.

Including the subcontractor in meetings can:

- Enhance the level of open communications,
- Provide both the buyer and seller with a more complete understanding of all actions required for performance,
- Alert both the buyer and seller to issues and potential subcontractor problems that may be referred to their level,
- Encourage the seller to maintain an effective relationship with their subcontractors,
- Provide the subcontractor with valuable insight regarding the nature of the relationship between the prime contractor and the buyer, and
- Assist the subcontractor in understanding how its performance affects the seller and the overall achievement of the contractual relationship between the buyer and seller.

3.4 Contract Changes and Modifications

In a perfect world, the buyer and seller negotiate and agree on all aspects of a contractual action, the contract is issued, the contractor performs flawlessly, all required work is completed on or ahead of schedule and at or below expected cost, all goods and services are received, the contractor is paid accurately and promptly, and both sides happily move on to the next matter of business. Though the perfect contract is a goal both buyers and sellers should pursue, the reality is that we live in an imperfect world and contracting parties need to deal with inevitable changes that may occur during the course of the contract. Generally, there are three types of changes:

- Directed changes,
- Constructive changes, and
- Cardinal changes.

Most contracts contain a changes clause that gives the buyer the right to "direct changes" during contract performance. The clause describes what types of changes the buyer can direct, the procedures for ordering the changes, and a provision for "equitable adjustment" to the contract amount or period of performance if there is a resultant change in cost or schedule. A directed change must be within the scope of the original contract.

A "constructive change" is a change resulting from the buyer's actions or directives that impacts the cost or schedule for performance that is construed to have the same effect as a formal change order. A constructive change generally occurs when the buyer implies or expressly orders the seller to perform work that is not in the contract. In government contracting, equitable adjustment is granted for constructive changes only if the change caused injury or liability to the seller.

"Cardinal changes" are changes that are beyond the scope of the contract and materially alter the nature of the contract that the parties entered into. A cardinal change could be considered as breach of contract.

Accordingly, both parties to a contract should adhere to an agreed upon change management process that seeks to fairly and equitably deal with the impacts of change on contracts.

Prompt Notification of Apparent Noncompliance

Both parties should require their respective staffs of the need to promptly report, preferably in writing, any perceived action or lack of action that appears to be in conflict with contractual requirements. Both parties should notify the other promptly, in writing, of the issues and request an explanation. These issues are often a sign that there is a need for a change; and, if left unattended, can cause relatively insignificant issues to become major roadblocks to performance.

Early Identification of Potential Changes

Exchanging pertinent information honestly and openly in meetings, reports, and other communications can often result in identifying issues early that may result in contract changes. Though both parties may be initially reluctant to share potentially "bad" information, or may be tempted to "spin" a positive face onto potentially negative information, the long-term effects of hiding important facts are often more damaging to the contract and the relationship. For the buyer, such data as the potential for funding reductions, project cancellation, downsizing, and related issues should be shared with the seller to the maximum extent permitted by government regulation or corporate policy. For the seller, information related to the loss of key personnel, problems with subcontractors, new contracts that strain available resources, corporate mergers, changes in the economic environment, and other related matters should be shared with the buyer as openly as possible. However, both the buyer and seller should be sensitive to the possibility that such information, once shared, could be used in a manner they had not intended. Trust and honesty are essential elements that will dictate the extent to which important information is shared.

Authorized Individuals

It is critical that both the buyer and seller clearly identify the individuals in their respective organizations who have the requisite authority to make changes. Many times, individuals from both organizations who lack the authority to legally bind their organization contractually will nonetheless make verbal agreements and other arrangements that inappropriately alter the fundamental structure of the contract. If the buyer and seller agree, in advance, to honor only those changes made by authorized personnel, and to promptly notify the other if unauthorized personnel attempt to make changes, many problems can be avoided.

Agreement on Estimating Processes

Buyers and sellers can minimize difficult negotiations about the impact of the change and who will pay for it if they can agree on a process to estimate the financial, quality, schedule, and other potential consequences of a possible change. They can carry this cooperation a step further if the parties agree to perform this analysis jointly rather than separately. The buyer and seller should be more likely to agree with the results of an analysis, even though the results are less than pleasurable, if the results were determined together.

Providing Written Concurrence

Both parties should provide written agreement on the nature, scope, cost, and effect of any change before the change is implemented to prevent the possibility of confusion later regarding the content of the agreement. Changes that are agreed to should be formally issued as contract modifications, with bilateral signatures indicating mutual agreement on the change.

It is imperative that the contract provides an accurate and current written record of the totality of the agreement at any point in time. Both the buyer and seller should maintain current copies of the contract (incorporating all modifications, known as a "conformed" copy) and distribute it internally to appropriate personnel who have a continuing need for access to it. The completeness of distributed copies should be periodically verified. The original signed copy of the contract and all modifications should always be retained by the buyer's contracting professional.

3.5 Property Administration

Generally speaking, most contracts require total performance from the contractor. That is, under the requirements and terms and conditions contained in the contract, the contractor is usually required to provide all the resources required for successful performance. In some cases, however, the buyer can provide various forms of property to a contractor or subcontractor. The fundamental reason for the buyer to provide property to the seller is cost savings. It may be less expensive for a buyer to provide property to a contractor for use during performance than it would be for the contractor to purchase the property, particularly when the property can be reused for future contracts.

The post-award administration of property is a highly specialized aspect of contract administration, normally handled by a trained sub-specialist within the buyer's contracting organization. However, there are some general concepts related to property that are important, including:

- Ownership,
- Accountability,
- Competitive advantage, and
- Property administration.

Ownership

Usually, the buyer retains ownership of and all rights to buyer-provided property. The question of ownership of property acquired by the seller to perform the contract is sometimes more complex, and may be dependent upon the type of contract under which the seller is performing.

Accountability

The buying organization usually retains internal organizational accountability for all property the buyer provides to a seller. But the seller is required to document the property receipt and record relevant facts about the property, such as its condition if overages, shortages, or damages occurred. In addition, the seller should maintain the property in its possession. The contractor's maintenance program shall enable the identification, disclosure, and performance of normal and routine preventative maintenance and repair.[60]

Competitive Advantage

Particularly as it relates to government contracting, the possession of buyer-furnished property can provide an incumbent contractor with a competitive advantage when competing with other sellers for future contracts. Contracting professionals often "level the playing field" in such cases by taking the value of the property into account when evaluating competing offers.

Property Administration

When a buyer furnishes property to a contractor, several property administration issues are normally part of the acquisition. The availability of buyer-furnished property is usually included in the solicitation, and potential offerors are normally provided an opportunity to review and inspect the property to verify its existence and condition.

The buyer is most often responsible for delivering buyer-furnished property to the contractor. The buyer should be careful to ensure that delivery delays do not occur, since that may adversely affect contractor performance.

The contractor is usually required to have a system in place to ensure that all property provided by the buyer is accounted for, maintained as appropriate, and used as specified in the contract. Both the buyer and seller should periodically review or audit these control systems to ensure they are operating properly.

Upon completion or termination of a contract, the contractor is usually held responsible for requesting property disposition instructions from the buyer for disposing of the property as directed.

3.6 Transportation

When contracting for goods, the costs associated with transportation are sometimes little more than a minor afterthought for many contracting professionals. However, transportation issues can sometimes represent a significant expense, particularly when the buyer purchases a large quantity of goods or when the goods are extremely heavy, cumbersome, fragile, subject to spoilage, or otherwise difficult to transport. Transportation is another technical sub-specialty and many organizations have experts in their transportation, logistics, or shipping and receiving department whom the contracting professional can consult to help evaluate the cost considerations of various transportation options.

Some of the more common transportation considerations include required receipt dates, mode of transportation, transportation-related services, and responsibility for transportation charges.

Required Receipt Dates

The date and place that the buyer requires the items to be received sometimes determines transportation costs. The contracting professional should be aware of the potential for increased transportation costs that may be a result of a specific receipt date, particularly when the delivery schedule is aggressive or when the delivery schedule is accelerated by modification due to a change in plans or to overcome some issue or problem in production.

Mode of Transportation

The mode of transportation (i.e., rail, motor freight, air, etc.) is sometimes dictated by the nature of the goods being purchased and is always a factor in determining appropriate transportation methods. Consistent with other contract requirements and industry standards, the mode of transportation selected should reflect a thoughtful balance between speed, reliability, need, and cost.

Transportation-Related Services

Additional transportation considerations sometime result from the need for transportation-related services, which may include storing, packing, marking, loading, unloading, etc.

Responsibility for Transportation Charges

Costs associated with the transportation of goods can be the responsibility of either the buyer or the seller. The responsibility is defined by the applicable clause in the contract. If the contract stipulates "free-on-board destination," the seller is responsible for payment of transportation costs associated with delivering the contract. Such costs are normally included in the seller's price. An advantage to the buyer is that the title to the goods does not pass from the seller to the buyer until the goods have been received, thereby insulating the buyer from in-transit loss or damage issues.

If the contract stipulates "free-on-board origin," the buyer is responsible for payment of transportation costs associated with delivering the goods from the seller's facility to the place or places specified by the buyer in the contract. This option may be advantageous to the buyer when the buyer can obtain the transportation at lower costs than the seller could, or when the buyer has its own transportation capability. Title to the goods transfers from the seller to the buyer when the goods leave the seller's facility.

3.7 Disputes

Notwithstanding the advantages that can result from the buyer and seller adopting a collaborative and cooperative approach toward all aspects of contract management, sometimes issues arise in performing contract requirements that are difficult to resolve. As a general rule, contracting professionals should always seek to resolve differences in the least formal and most collaborative manner possible. Though formal legal action is always a possibility, both buyers and sellers should be hesitant to pursue resolution through legal proceedings for many excellent reasons, including time, expense, uncertainty of outcome, and the effect on the business relationship.

Formal legal proceedings often require many months or years to achieve a resolution. Preparing for and participating in legal proceedings can require spending substantial amounts of funds, which can sometimes have a negative impact on other aspects of the organization's business. Few, if any, organizations will pursue legal action if they do not believe they will prevail. In most actions, however, there are winners and losers, and parties to litigation often find themselves the recipient of unpleasant surprises. Since legal proceedings are, by nature, adversarial, they can have a permanently negative effect on the relationship between the litigants. This negative effect can prevent the parties from engaging in mutually beneficial business relationships in the future.

In recent years, both government and commercial contracting organizations have made progress toward pursuing a variety of informal, less formal, and formal dispute resolution methods in lieu of formal legal proceedings, including:

- Informal collaboration,
- Negotiation, and
- Alternative dispute resolution.

Informal Collaboration

When buyers and sellers share information collaboratively, they can avoid issues and potential problems to quickly resolve differences informally.

Negotiation

Negotiation is another method preferred by both buyers and sellers to resolve disputes. Negotiation is often preferred because most parties are familiar with and experienced in the process, and because it is much more efficient and less expensive than other dispute resolution processes. Agreements resulting from negotiations can be easily implemented as contract modifications.

Alternative Dispute Resolution

When the less formal methods of collaboration and negotiation between the parties does not produce a satisfactory result, alternative dispute resolution procedures can often be used to arrive at a mutually agreeable solution. Alternative dispute resolution encompasses practices for managing and quickly resolving disputes at modest cost and with minimal adverse impact on the relationship between the contracting parties.

These processes significantly broaden dispute resolution options beyond litigation or traditional unassisted negotiation. Some alternative dispute resolution procedures, such as binding arbitration and private judging, are similar to expedited litigation in that they involve a third-party decision-maker with authority to impose a resolution if the parties so desire. Other procedures, such as mediation and the mini-trial, are collaborative, with a neutral third party helping a group of individuals or entities with divergent views to reach a goal or complete a task to their mutual satisfaction.

Some examples of alternative dispute resolution techniques include:

- Interest-based negotiation,
- Mediation,
- Mini-trial,
- Nonbinding arbitration, and
- Binding arbitration.

Interest-Based Negotiation

Traditional negotiation involves each side beginning with a proposed solution, followed by a series of counter-proposals, offers and counteroffers, arguments, persuasions, and concessions until an acceptable compromise is reached. "Interest-based negotiation" is a more collaborative process that involves the parties becoming educated about the needs, concerns, and interests of the other, followed by joint problem solving to identify the most acceptable way to meet all or most of the interests of both parties.

Mediation

"Mediation" is a private, informal process in which the parties are assisted by one or more neutral third parties in efforts to achieve settlement. Mediators do not judge or arbitrate; rather, they advise and consult impartially with the parties in an attempt to bring about a mutually agreeable resolution.

Mini-Trial

A "mini-trial" is a structured process where the attorney for each party presents an abbreviated version of that side's case. This information exchange allows each party to hear the strength and weaknesses of the other party's case as well as their own. Following the presentation, the attorneys meet to see if they can negotiate a settlement. A neutral party can oversee the process, if desired, and provide an opinion on what the potential court outcome might be.

Nonbinding Arbitration

"Nonbinding arbitration" involves an evidentiary hearing before a third party, composed of one or more arbitrators, that draws conclusions regarding the issues in dispute. These hearings typically include broad fact-finding activities, which assist in educating the third party about the matters in dispute. Upon completion of presentations by each party, the third party renders its decision. The parties are not bound by the arbitrator's decision, and either or both sides may reject it. The intent of nonbinding arbitration is to predict the likely adjudicated outcome of the case as an aid to settlement.

Binding Arbitration

Parties that submit to "binding arbitration" submit their disputes to a neutral third person or panel for a decision that both parties must accept. Binding arbitration is commonly used in private sector contracting, but is rarely used in government contracting, due to the absolute nature of the binding decision.

Resolution Through Available Legal Means

When the parties cannot resolve or accommodate disagreements about the meaning of terms of an agreement, a court may be required to decide what the contract requires. Both commercial and government contracting allows resolution utilizing available legal means.

Government contracting allows the filing of claims and appeal to the boards and courts when less formal methods do not produce satisfactory results. A contractor may submit a claim with the government contracting officer who issued the contract. There are a number of procedural and time-sensitive requirements imposed on both the contractor and the government contracting officer when a claim is submitted. The government contracting officer is required to formally accept or reject the claim, in writing, within a specified period of time. When a government contracting officer denies a claim, the contractor may appeal that decision to the appropriate agency Board of Contract Appeals or to the U.S. Court of Federal Claims.

Depending on the type of agreement and facts of the case, there are a variety of remedies available to a party who prevails in a lawsuit for breach of contract. These include "money damages" and "equitable remedies."

Money Damages

Money damages include compensatory damages for the purpose of putting the non-breaching party in the position it would have been in if the contract had not been breached. "Consequential damages" are those damages not directly associated with the seller's breach, but traceable to it nonetheless because the seller had reason to know of the buyer's general or particular needs at the time of contracting. Consequential damages also include injury to person or property proximately resulting from any breach of warranty. "Incidental damages" include damages resulting from the seller's breach; for example, expenses reasonably incurred in inspection; receipt; transportation, care, and custody of goods rightfully rejected; any commercially reasonable charges; expenses or commissions in connection with effecting cover; and any other reasonable expense incident to the delay or other breach. In the case of fraud or malice, punitive damages may be awarded to the non-breaching party to punish the party that breached, which is meant to discourage the offending party from committing the same offense again. "Liquidated damages" are those money damages the parties agreed to in their contract should breach of contract occur.

Equitable Remedies

Equitable remedies include an order of specific performance, restitution, and rescission. In the case of goods or real property, an order of specific performance can require the breaching party to perform in accordance with the contract. Restitution, as an equitable remedy, seeks to restore the non-breaching party to the position it was in before the formation of the contract. Rescission, as an equitable remedy, allows the cancellation of the contract, usually when mutually agreed to between the parties. In some cases, the contract or statutes allow unilateral rescission for a specified period of time, such as in the case of mortgages and real estate purchases.

In the case of commercial contracts, questions involving the legality or interpretation of a contract are generally governed by the law of the state where the contract was made. Questions related to contract performance are generally governed by the law of the state where such performance occurs.

Regardless of whether the contracting professional is operating in the government or commercial arena, the prompt and efficient resolution of all disputes, at the lowest organizational level possible, should always be the goal.

3.8 Organizational Conflict of Interest

Given the number of mergers, acquisitions, and consolidations that have taken place in recent years, contractors face being told they are ineligible to compete for a contract because they—or their predecessors—have an unfair competitive advantage over other firms. Buyers should identify and evaluate potential organizational conflicts of interest as early in the acquisition process as possible and to avoid, neutralize, or mitigate potential significant conflicts of interest before contract award.

It is essential that a potential organizational conflict of interest be identified during the initial phase of an acquisition process so steps can be taken to avoid, mitigate, or neutralize the organizational conflict of interest. Early identification of a potential organizational conflict of interest will reduce the possibility of delays and disruptions during the acquisition process.

Most organizational conflict of interest mitigation plans tend to be made up of similar elements, as discussed below.

Disclosure of Relevant Information

Several agencies are requiring offerors to disclose all information relative to an organizational conflict of interest determination. This requirement tends to dictate that companies have systems in place to be able to screen not only new work against contracts already in place containing organizational conflict of interest provisions, but also new solicitations with organizational conflict of interest provisions that might conflict with future plans of other parts of the business.

Firewalls

The written agreement between the conflicted entities usually relies on a combination of procedures and physical security to establish organizational "firewalls" to avoid potential, real, or perceived organizational conflicts of interest from affecting the business activities of either party.

Confidentiality Agreements

Employees are required to execute special confidentiality agreements with penalties for noncompliance ranging from disciplinary action up to termination. Confidentiality agreements require the employee to notify a high-ranking corporate official should any person not working on the contract attempt to solicit information or influence the work being performed under the contract.

Separation of Personnel

Eliminating communication between personnel from the conflicted entity and the organization can effectively eliminate the potential for bias.

Divestiture of a Company

A new company can be created with a completely separate board of directors.

Removal of Conflict

Often, staff members have been supporting a particular program or agency for most of their careers, and their particular expertise and knowledge would have dire consequences for the program should their efforts be interrupted. In these cases, the affected individual(s) can be hired by another, non-conflicted entity to perform the same work. However, the buyer must be careful to keep the employees "whole" (from a salary and benefits perspective).

Work-Switch

Depending on who has the conflict, work can be switched between the prime and the subcontractor.[61]

3.9 Contract Closeout

Contracting activities are responsible for initiating each contract closeout. This administrative process should begin as soon as possible after the contract is physically completed, which means that the seller has delivered the required supplies and the buyer has inspected and accepted them—or the seller has performed and the buyer has accepted all services required by the contract—and the base period and any option periods exercised have expired.

"Contract closeout" consists of completing a number of procedural and administrative tasks to change the status of a contract from "active" to "complete." These required tasks normally include:

- Verifying that all required goods or services have been received and accepted;
- Verifying that all contractor invoices have been received and paid;
- Returning or disposing any buyer-furnished property;
- Closing subcontracts by the seller;
- Agreeing that no claims, issues, or unresolved matters exist;
- Signing a formal notice of contract completion; and
- De-obligating excess funds remaining on the contract (federal contracting) by the buyer.

Upon completion of all required closeout actions, completed contract files should be retained for the appropriate period of time required by law, regulation, or corporate policy.

3.10 Contract Termination

In some cases, it becomes necessary to end performance on a contract before the contractual period of performance ends. This premature ending of a contract is referred to as a "termination," and usually takes one of the following forms.

Termination for Default

"Termination for default," also referred to as "termination for cause," is normally a right of law as well as a right vested as the result of including appropriate terms and conditions in the contract. Termination for default can result from one party's failure to perform one or more actions required by the contract. Typical reasons to terminate for default include the following:

- *Failure to perform*—The seller's failure to provide the goods or services contracted for is a valid reason to terminate for default.

- *Failure to adhere to schedule*—If a seller fails to completely perform during the specified period of performance, that failure may be justification for a termination for default. The buyer should exercise good business judgment in this situation to determine if the failure is significant enough to justify the termination.

- *Failure to comply with other terms and conditions*—The seller's failure to comply with other significant terms and conditions contained in the contract can justify termination for default. This is another area in which the buyer should exercise sound business judgment and good faith in determining if the seller's failures are damaging enough to warrant termination.

- *Repudiation*—A contract may be terminated for default if either the buyer or seller clearly indicates to the other party, by word or deed, that it cannot or will not perform.

Termination for Convenience

In government contracting, the government buyer always has the unilateral right to terminate a contract for the convenience of the government when the contract no longer serves the best interests of the government. Terminations for convenience often result from a change in government priorities, program termination or downsizing, or other significant events that were not anticipated at the time of contract formation. When the government pursues a termination for convenience, a termination settlement is negotiated with the seller.

Termination by Mutual Consent

Commonly used in the commercial contracting environment, "termination by mutual consent" is a bilateral agreement indicating that the parties no longer wish to be bound by the contract and terminates both parties respective rights and obligations. Termination by mutual consent clauses are sometimes included in the initial contract, though they can also be negotiated and executed during the period of performance.

No-Cost Cancellation

A no-cost cancellation is a type of quasi-termination that usually occurs shortly after contract execution, often because the seller realizes that it will be unable to perform. If both parties agree, no debts or obligations are due, and if the buyer can obtain performance from other sources, a no-cost cancellation can be a quick and efficient way to sever a contractual relationship.

4.0 Specialized Knowledge Areas

Certain types of contracting actions require highly specialized experience and knowledge to perform effectively. This section presents a brief overview of various contracting specialty areas. Some of the areas relate exclusively to government contracting, others relate exclusively to commercial contracting, and some have a degree of application to both the government and commercial sectors.

4.1 Research and Development

When a buyer procures research and development services, it is generally difficult to define the requirement other than to describe the problem the buyer wants to solve. This is a different situation and deviates from the general guideline used when contracting for other types of products or services that prefers more precise statements of work. The contract professional cannot clearly define the requirement, define specific acceptance criteria, or negotiate a low price based on the market. Research and development contracting necessitates a different philosophy than is necessary for other types of procurement. There are differences between commercial research and development and government research and development. Each is discussed below.

Commercial Research and Development

In the commercial world, the phrase "research and development" has a special commercial significance apart from its conventional meaning of research and technological development. In the context of commerce, research and development normally refers to future-oriented, longer-term activities in science and technology. Profits are not realized until after a successful discovery, development, and application of a new technology, which only occurs after diligent and systematic research.

During a company's lengthy product development phase, it takes large amounts of capital to fund research and development activities. Most companies prefer to perform research and development internally so they own the resultant technology. To share the burden, a company may purchase a non-controlling equity stake in another company as part of a strategic alliance with the other company to conduct research and develop products jointly. Alternatively, they may choose to use public funds for research in their areas of interest and provide research and development services to the government.

If a corporation contracts for research and development services from another corporation, the most important issues become acceptable clauses in the areas of intellectual data, data rights, ownership of inventions, license-to-use, and patents. These clauses are also important when a commercial company enters a contract to provide these services to the government. The vast majority of research and development contracts are between commercial firms contracting with the federal, state, or local governments.

Government Research and Development

When used by the government, the primary purpose of research and development contracts and programs is to advance scientific and technical knowledge and apply that knowledge to achieve organizational and national goals. Unlike most other types of contracts, research and development contracts are intended to achieve objectives for which the work or methods cannot be precisely defined in advance. It is also frequently difficult to estimate the effort required for various research and development technical approaches, particularly when some of the approaches may offer little or no early indications or assurances that they will be successful. Due to this level of uncertainty, contracting professionals should use research and development contracting in a manner that will encourage the best scientific and industrial sources to participate and the contracts should be structured so that they provide an environment in which the work can be pursued with reasonable flexibility and minimum administrative burden.[62]

Publicizing Requirements

As is the case for any competitive requirement, research and development requirements should be publicized as widely as possible. Additionally, since a primary issue in research and development contracting is obtaining the best scientific and industrial sources, contracting professionals handling research and development requirements should conduct market research for potential additional sources capable of competent performance. In addition, they should encourage potential sources to exchange information with internal technical experts.

Statement of Work

The statement of work should be as clear and complete as possible, notwithstanding the general level of uncertainty that exists in the research and development environment, and should detail the area of exploration for basic research or the end objectives for development and applied research. The statement of work should provide contractors with the freedom required to be innovative and creative, while adhering to the overall objectives of the research and development effort. Research and development statements of work often include some or all of the following elements:

- The research and development effort's objectives, including a statement of the area of exploration and tasks to be performed;
- The background information necessary to help the contractor understand the requirement;
- The factors that might constrain the results of the effort, including personnel, environment, or interface issues;
- The items that the contractor will be required to furnish as the work progresses, such as reporting requirements;

- The type of contract anticipated and an estimate of the professional and technical effort required for level-of-effort requirements; and
- Any other considerations that relate to the work to be performed.

Contract Method and Type

The fundamental nature of research and development contracting usually precludes using the sealed bid method, and often makes fixed-price contracts inappropriate, notwithstanding periodic political perceptions that fixed-price is more appropriate. Because precise specifications are absent and there are associated difficulties in estimating costs, research and development contracts are often cost-reimbursement contracts, sometimes with appropriate incentives. Contracting professionals should consult extensively with internal technical experts regarding which contract type is appropriate.

Solicitations

Buyers should distribute research and development solicitations only to sources identified after publicizing requirements to companies technically qualified to perform the required work and after consulting with internal technical personnel. Such evaluations of technical competence usually include factors such as:

- Present and past performance of similar work,
- Professional stature and reputation,
- Relative position in a particular field of endeavor,
- Ability to acquire and retain the technical capability required to perform the work, and
- Other relevant factors.

If it is not practical to initially solicit all apparently qualified sources, the buyer should solicit a reasonable number to obtain meaningful competition.

Solicitations should normally require offerors to describe their technical and management approach, identify technical uncertainties, and make specific proposals to resolve the uncertainties. The solicitation should also require the offeror to disclose any planned subcontracting of scientific or technical work and may require the submission of separate technical and cost proposals.

The evaluation factors in research and development solicitations used to determine the most technically competent solicitation usually include:

- The offeror's understanding of the scope of the work;
- The approach proposed to accomplish the scientific and technical objectives of the contract or the merit of the ideas and concepts proposed;
- The availability and competence of experienced technical personnel;
- The offeror's experience;
- The pertinent novel ideas in the specific branch of science and technology involved; and
- The availability, from any source, of necessary research, test, laboratory, or shop facilities.

Evaluation

Generally speaking, research and development contracts are most often awarded to the offeror that proposes the best ideas or concepts and has the highest competence in the specific field involved. However, the contracting professional should be careful and not obtain technical capabilities that clearly exceed those required by the solicitation or those required for successful performance of the requirement. It is also customary to evaluate the offeror's proposed cost or price as a means to verify that the offeror has a clear understanding of the scope of the project, perception of risks involved, and the ability to organize and perform the work.

4.2 Architect-Engineer Services and Construction

Contracts for architect-engineer services and construction services are highly technical in nature and are often awarded by specialized contracting professionals with extensive experience in and knowledge of the skills and abilities required for successful performance. Some of the terminology associated with this type of contracting includes:

- "Design": The process that defines a construction requirement, including the functional relationships and technical systems to be used, producing the technical specifications and drawings, and preparing the construction cost estimate.
- "Design-bid-build": The traditional construction delivery method where design and construction

are sequential and contracted for separately with two contracts and two contractors.

- "Design-build": Combining the design and construction requirements in a single contract with one contractor.
- "Two-phase design-build": A selection procedure that selects a number of offerors (based on qualifications) in the first phase to submit detailed proposals for evaluation and award in the second phase.

Architect-Engineer Services

When acquiring architect-engineer services, the government normally publicizes all requirements for such services and negotiates contracts based on the demonstrated competence and qualifications of prospective contractors to perform the services at fair and reasonable prices. Architect-engineer services are generally defined to include:

- Professional services of an architectural or engineering nature, as defined by applicable state law, which the state law requires to be performed by a registered architect or engineer;
- Professional architectural or engineering services associated with the design or construction of real property;
- Other professional architectural or engineering services related to studies, investigations, surveying, mapping, soils engineering, construction phase conceptual design, and similar tasks that require performance by a registered architect, engineer, or their employees; and
- Professional surveying and mapping services, when the mapping services are associated with the construction or alteration of real property.

Selection Criteria
Normal evaluation and selection criteria for architect-engineer services usually include:

- Professional qualifications necessary for satisfactory performance of the required services;
- Specialized experience and technical competence in the type of work required;
- The capacity to accomplish the work in the required time;
- Past performance in both the government and commercial sectors in terms of cost control, quality of work, and compliance with performance schedules; and
- Proximity to the general geographical area of the project and knowledge of the local conditions.

The selection process usually results in the preparation of a selection report that ranks competent contractors in order of preference. The contracting professional then begins specific negotiations with the contractor(s) to agree upon and award a contract.

Construction Services

In commercial construction contracting, there are both formal and informal policies and procedures used in acquiring construction services. Construction contracts are subject to many outside restraints that have an impact on the successful contract performance, such as inspections, permits, and licenses. Careful planning is necessary to ensure adequate coordination of the acquisition.

In government contracting, sealed bid procedures are normally used for construction contracts. The following processes are also normally part of a construction contracting effort:

- *Pre-solicitation notice*—A notice prior to the solicitation containing sufficient detail to identify the nature, volume, location, and schedule for the requirement. These notices are usually issued well in advance of the invitation to bid in order to stimulate the interest of the greatest number of prospective bidders.
- *Invitation for bids*—The invitation for bids should allow sufficient time for bidders to perform the many tasks and issues associated with the bid process, including site inspection, obtaining required subcontracting bids, examining plans and specifications, and preparing the required estimates.
- *Pre-bid conferences*—Pre-bid conferences are often held to ensure that all prospective bidders have a clear and complete understanding of all aspects of the requirement.
- *Notice of award.*
- *Preconstruction orientation*—A preconstruction conference is often held with the successful offeror before the construction effort begins to again ensure that there is a complete understanding of all issues related to the effort.

4.3 Information Technology

Information technology requirements often present a unique set of challenges for the contracting professional. The rapid pace of technological advancements often makes it difficult to acquire state-of-the-art information technology items without exposing the buying organization to a significant amount of inherent risk.

Common risk elements include:

- Schedule risk,
- Risk of technical obsolescence,
- Cost risk,
- Technical feasibility,
- Dependencies between new projects and existing projects or systems,
- The number of simultaneous high-risk projects to be monitored,
- Funding availability, and
- Program management risk.

Typical techniques to manage and mitigate risks associated with information technology acquisitions include:

- Prudent project management,
- Thorough acquisition planning related to budget planning,
- Continuous collection and evaluation of risk-based assessment data,
- Prototyping systems before implementation,
- Post-implementation reviews to determine actual costs and benefits,
- Using quantifiable measures to assess risks and returns, and
- The use of modular contracting.

Modular Contracting

"Modular contracting" is intended to reduce program risk and incentivize contractor performance while providing for the timely access to rapidly changing technology. Modular contracting consists of dividing the information technology acquisition into smaller increments. The benefits of modular contracting include:

- Smaller increments are easier to manage than would be possible in one comprehensive acquisition;
- Complex information technology objectives are addressed incrementally, enhancing the likelihood of achieving workable solutions for each of the objectives;
- Each increment can be tested and implemented, resulting in a functional system or solution that is not dependent upon any subsequent increment in order to perform its principal functions;
- Subsequent increments can take advantage of evolutionary enhancements in technology or changes in needs that occur during the implementation and use of preceding increments; and
- Potential adverse consequences can be isolated, mitigated, or resolved without potentially affecting the entire project.

4.4 Major Systems

The Office of Management and Budget Circular A-109 outlines policies and procedures for the acquisition of government major systems. "Major systems" are defined as those programs that, as determined by the agency head, are directed at and critical to fulfilling an agency mission need, entail allocating relatively large resources for the particular agency, and warrant special management attention, including specific agency head decisions.

Major systems acquisition policies are designed to ensure that agencies acquire major systems in the most effective, economical, and timely manner. The policies require agencies to promote innovation and full and open competition in the development of major system concepts by:

- Expressing agency needs and program objectives in terms of the agency's mission and not in terms of specified systems to satisfy needs,
- Focusing agency resources and special management attention on activities conducted in the initial stage of major programs, and
- To sustain effective competition between alternative system concepts and sources for as long as it is beneficial.

As it relates to major systems acquisition, "effective competition" is defined as a market condition that exists when two or more contractors, acting independently, actively contend for the government's business in a manner that ensures that the government will be offered the lowest cost or price alternative or best technical design meeting its minimum needs. Major systems acquisition requires the direct involvement of senior agency management (including the agency head) in the planning, execution, and continuing evaluation of the status of the program.

4.5 Service Contracts

Many organizations have increased the number and scope of service contacts in recent years. With increasing frequency, organizations are contracting for a variety of services rather than performing the related functions with internal resources, especially when the functions are not part of the core mission or purpose of the organization. The increase in the use of service contracts, particularly in government contracting, brings with it the need for additional skills and knowledge.

As it relates to contracting for general services, the government's policy includes the following precepts:

- Performance-based acquisition is the preferred method for obtaining services;
- Government agencies shall generally rely on the private sector for commercial services;
- Agencies shall not award a contract for the performance of inherently governmental functions;
- Program officials are responsible for accurately describing the service contracting requirement in a manner that ensures full understanding and performance by contractors; and
- Services should be obtained in the most cost-effective manner, without barriers to full and open competition, and free of any potential conflicts of interest.

Key concepts related to service contracts include:

- *Service contract*—A contract that directly engages the time and effort of a contractor to perform an identifiable task, rather than to furnish an end item or good. Service contracts can be personal or nonpersonal, professional or nonprofessional.
- *Personal services contract*—A contract under which the personnel providing the services are subject, either by the contract's terms or the manner in which it is administered, to the supervision and control usually prevailing in relationships between employers and employees.
- *Nonpersonal services contract*—A contract under which the personnel providing the services are not subject, either by the contract's terms or the manner in which it is administered, to the supervision and control usually prevailing in relationships between employers and employees.

Personal services contracts in government contracting are of particular concern to contracting professionals. A personal services contract is characterized by the employer-employee relationship it creates between the government agency and the contractor's personnel. The government is normally required to obtain its employees under direct hire under competitive appointment or other procedures required by civil service law. Obtaining personal services by contract, rather than by direct hire, can circumvent those laws. Accordingly:

- Agencies are prohibited from awarding personal service contracts, except when specifically authorized by statute to do so.
- A nonpersonal services contract can, in effect, become a personal services contract, based on the manner in which the contract is administered after award. This can occur when contractor personnel are subject to the relatively continuous supervision and control of a government manager or employee.
- Certain aspects of the contract and its administration can be used as a guide in assessing whether a proposed contract is personal in nature, including:
  o Performance on site;
  o Principal tools and equipment furnished by the government;
  o Services are applied directly to the integral effort of the agency in furtherance of assigned mission or functions;
  o Comparable services, meeting comparable needs, are performed in the same or similar agency using government personnel;
  o The need for the service is expected to last for more than one year; and
  o The nature of the service, or the manner in which it is provided, requires the direct or indirect government direction or supervision of contractor employees.

Determining Inherently Governmental and Commercial Functions

The Office of Management and Budget has issued guidance in an effort to define "inherently governmental" and "commercial functions." Unfortunately, there is no precise method to determine what constitutes an inherently governmental function and what constitutes a commercial function; their determination is often based on facts in each case. One position in a specific job series could be "commercial" while another in the same job series could be classified as "inherently governmental," because of such things as performance of supervisory duties or holding a contracting warrant. Determining whether a function is inherently governmental or commercial is often a difficult choice and making an appropriate decision often depends upon knowledge of the position's duties, which may or may not be contained in the position description.

Examples to help in making this important decision are listed below. Office of Management and Budget Circular A-76 states:

> [An *inherently governmental function* is one that is] so intimately related to the public interest as to mandate performance by government employees. These functions include those that require either the exercise of discretion in applying government authority or the making of value judgments in making decisions for the government. Inherently governmental functions normally fall into two categories: the exercise of sovereign government authority or the establishment of procedures and processes related to the oversight of monetary transactions or entitlements. An inherently governmental function involves:
>
> - Determining, protecting, and advancing U.S. economic, political, territorial, property, or other interests by military or diplomatic action, civil or criminal judicial proceedings, contract management, or otherwise.
> - Significantly affecting the life, liberty, or property of private persons.
> - Commissioning, appointing, directing, or controlling officers or employees of the United States.
> - The determination of agency policy, such as determining the content and application of regulations, among other things.

Inherently governmental functions, by definition, necessarily involve the exercise of (substantial) discretion, although not every exercise of discretion means that a function is inherently governmental. The discretion must commit the government to a course of action when two or more alternatives exist. Examples include:

- Approving the purchase of a minicomputer rather than a mainframe computer;
- Hiring a statistician rather than an economist;
- Supporting proposed legislation rather than opposing it;
- Devoting more resources to prosecuting one type of criminal case than another;
- Awarding a contract to one firm rather than another;
- Adopting one policy over another; or
- Binding the government to take, or not to take, some action by contract, policy, regulation, authorization, or order.

Below are some examples of inherently governmental functions by specific area.

Budget
- Exerting ultimate control over the acquisition, use, or disposition of the property, real or personal, tangible or intangible, of the United States, including the collection, control, or disbursement of appropriated and other federal funds;
- Determining federal program priorities or budget requests; and
- Determining budget policy, guidance, and strategy.

Administrative (Including Acquisition)
- Determining what government property is to be disposed of and on what terms (although an agency may give contractors authority to dispose of property at prices with specified ranges and subject to other reasonable conditions deemed appropriate by the agency);
- In federal procurement activities with respect to prime contracts;
- Determining what supplies or services are to be acquired by the government (although an agency may give contractors authority to acquire supplies at prices within specified ranges and subject to other reasonable conditions deemed appropriate by the agency);

- Participating as a voting member on source selection boards;
- Approval of any contractual documents, to include documents defining requirements, incentive plans, and evaluation criteria;
- Awarding contracts;
- Administering contracts, including ordering changes in contract performance or contract quantities, taking action based on evaluations of contractor performance, and accepting or rejecting contractor products or services;
- Terminating contracts;
- Determining whether contract costs are reasonable, allocable, and allowable;
- Approving agency responses to Freedom of Information Act requests (other than routine responses that, because of statute, regulation, or agency policy, do not require the exercise of judgment in determining whether documents are to be released or withheld), and the approval of agency responses to the administrative appeals of denials of Freedom of Information Act requests;
- Approving federal licensing actions and inspections; and
- Conducting administrative hearings to determine the eligibility of any person for a security clearance, or involving actions that affect matters of personal reputation or eligibility to participate in government programs.

Contracting

Procuring contracting officers holding a contracting warrant should be designated as inherently governmental. Certain contracting positions may also be inherently governmental if duties include contract project management responsibilities and for positions whose duties include serving as a contracting officer's technical representative.

Examples of Commercial Functions

The Office of Management and Budget's guidance on the use of inherently governmental classification emphasizes that certain functions, although contributing to or supporting an inherently governmental function result (e.g., issuance of a budget, publication of a regulation, entering into a contract, etc.), do not constitute inherently governmental classification; however, they may potentially be, or be closely associated with, inherently governmental functions. Examples include:

- Budget, management, and program analysis work, including cost analysis, workload modeling, manpower and equipment requirements determination, operational audit, efficiency reviews, and fact-finding;
- Conducting reorganization and planning functions;
- Analyses, feasibility studies, and strategy options to be used by agency personnel in developing policy;
- Development of regulations;
- Support of acquisition planning;
- Financial management transactional work, such as invoice payment processing;
- Transacting certain human resources administrative actions, such as processing Standard Form 50, "Notification of Personnel Actions," and maintaining official personnel folders;
- Assistance in the development of performance work statements and statements of work;
- Supporting preparation of responses to Freedom of Information Act requests;
- Providing information regarding agency policies or regulations, such as attending conferences on behalf of an agency, conducting community relations campaigns, or conducting agency training courses;
- Participating as technical advisors to a source selection board or participating as non-voting members of a source evaluation board;
- Serving as arbitrators or providing alternative methods of dispute resolution;
- Providing certain inspection services;
- Providing legal advice and interpretations of regulations and statutes to government officials;
- Providing special non-law-enforcement security functions that do not directly involve criminal investigations, such as prisoner detention or transport and non-military national security details;
- Gathering information for or providing advice, opinions, recommendations, or ideas to government officials;
- Providing support functions, such as building security, mail operations, operation of cafeterias, housekeeping, facilities operations and maintenance, warehouse operations, motor vehicle fleet management and operations, routine

electrical or mechanical services, and recurring information technology–related services such as help-desk services; and

- Development of options to inform an agency decision-maker, or to develop or expand decisions already made by federal officials.[63]

Service Contract Act

The Service Contract Act of 1965 provides for minimum wages and fringe benefits, as well as other conditions of work, under certain types of service contracts. Contracting professionals need to be aware of the potential impact of this law on potential service contracts, such as the need to incorporate Service Contract Act wage determinations in contractual documents.

Government Use of Private Sector Temporaries

Government contracting professionals may enter into contracts with temporary help service firms for brief or intermittent periods without having these contracts regarded or treated as personal services contracts or staff augmentation, which is forbidden. Temporary help service contracts may not be used in lieu of regular recruitment under civil service laws or to replace a federal employee. Detailed information regarding the authority, criteria, and conditions for the use of private sector temporaries is contained in 5 C.F.R. 300.

Advisory and Assistance Services

The acquisition of advisory and assistance services is sometimes used to help government managers achieve maximum effectiveness or economy in their operations. Advisory and assistance service contracts can be used to:

- Obtain outside points of view to avoid limited judgment on critical issues;
- Obtain advice regarding developments in industry, university, or foundation research;
- Obtain the opinions, special knowledge, or skills of noted experts;
- Enhance the understanding of, and develop alternative solutions to, complex issues;
- Support and improve the operation of organizations; and
- Ensure the more efficient or effective operation of managerial or hardware systems.

Advisory and assistance service contracts may not be used to:

- Perform work of a policy, decision-making, or managerial nature, which is the direct responsibility of agency officials;
- Bypass or undermine personnel ceilings, pay limitations, or competitive employment procedures;
- Contract for, on a preferential basis, former federal employees;
- Specifically aid in influencing or enacting legislation; or
- Obtain professional or other technical advice, which is readily available within the agency or another federal agency.

4.6 International Contracting

Contracting domestically is sometimes a difficult process, as evidenced by the misunderstandings, lack of compliance with terms and conditions, late delivery, and payment issues that can develop. When contracting internationally, the potential for problems can expand almost exponentially. Whether functioning as a buyer or seller, contracting professionals who operate in the international market require an enhanced set of skills and knowledge to be effective. International contracting can sometimes result in lower costs and improved quality for buyers, and increased sales and profitability for sellers. However, there are many significant differences between operating in the domestic market and the international market. Some of those differences include the following.

Language

There are obvious potential issues when multiple languages are introduced into the contracting process. Some international firms have personnel who are multilingual. In other cases, the use of third-party interpreters may be appropriate. Regardless, the contracting professional needs to ensure that the sometimes subtle context and nuances inherent in one language are accurately reflected in the translation to a different language.

Location

Dealing with organizations located abroad can present a number of challenges related to time differences and distance. Buyers and sellers may need to adjust their work hours to be able to converse directly with international firms, or they may have to accept the fact that most communication will be indirect, e.g., electronic.

Different Meanings of Common Business Terms

Common business terms, such as "bimonthly" or "relationship," often have different meanings in different countries and can be the source of unintended issues.

Currency Differences

Currency differences, and the constantly changing exchange rates, can have impacts on the business relationship and feasibility of doing business in certain countries.

More Third Party Involvement

Buying and selling internationally often requires the use of various third-party entities, such as trading companies, local representatives, foreign banks, freight forwarders, customs brokers, etc. Some foreign countries require an in-country firm on the company team.

Social Customs

Business, cultural, and social customs and norms, to the degree that they are different from one's experience and expectations, can present significant obstacles to the successful completion of business agreements.

Different Processes

Some companies in less-developed countries may be less sophisticated and knowledgeable in various production, quality control, or management processes, and may be unable or reluctant to modify their systems and procedures to conform to one's expectations.

Legal Processes

Legal terms and processes may differ significantly in various countries, and can inject additional risk in the contracting process. Local laws vary widely from country to country in the areas of employment, labor, and severance. In the cases where contract performance will be done in country, this can impose substantial financial burden on a company.

Tax Implications

The tax-cost implications of doing business in foreign countries can be tremendous; for example, the foreign country may have a right to assess its own income or value-added tax on the company's global earnings that have a connection to that country. There may be personal tax implications for company employees who are temporarily transferred to the country for contract performance.

Export Issues

"Export" is defined as the transfer of commodities, technical data, articles, or services from the United States to a foreign person, corporation, or other entity. The company may be required to obtain export permission from the Bureau of Export Administration within the Department of Commerce or the Office of Defense Trade Controls within the U.S. Department of State.

Political Climate

The political and social climate in many countries is sometimes subject to abrupt and significant change. Contracting professionals must have a thorough understanding of past, present, and future trends that may influence the degree to which business in a foreign country may be affected by changes in the political and social climate.

International contracting presents many positive opportunities, but also presents many challenges that are not present in the domestic sector. Contracting professionals should ensure they have a complete understanding of this more dynamic environment, and use appropriate caution to avoid mistakes.

4.7 State and Local Governments

When viewed as a single entity, the purchasing power of state and local governments represents a huge and often untapped source of business for commercial contracting professionals. However, the unfortunate reality is that state and local government is not a homogenous market segment, but rather a somewhat artificial category that, in fact, is comprised of literally thousands of buying entities, often with their own unique processes, procedures, and challenges. Nonetheless, there are definite advantages to both the seller and the government entity in pursuing business in the state and local government sector, which include:

- State and local governments tend to be more commercially oriented than their federal counterparts since many potentially new customers already exist for firms that deal in commercial goods and services;
- The local government can benefit from the close proximity of a company that can provide high-quality goods and services at competitive prices and that can be available for consultation and advice;
- The success of local businesses generates additional tax revenue for the state and local governments, which can be used to help provide additional government services and to reinvest in the local business community and infrastructure to create more businesses and economic growth; and
- Dealing locally tends to help both the buyer and the seller by developing personal, long-term relationships based on mutual need and mutual benefit.

There are also some disadvantages inherent in dealing with the state and local government segment, including:

- A lack of standardized processes, procedures, and regulatory guidance since many state and local government entities have unique requirements, forms, and local ordinances that may increase the cost to the seller of doing business with multiple entities simultaneously;
- Many local governments seek out the best value, which may make some local businesses, particularly smaller ones, less competitive; and
- Local and regional politics often influence purchasing decisions, and vendors should be aware that sometimes buying decisions are made based on facts or perceptions that have little or nothing to do with price, quality, or service.

Organizations seeking to do business with state and local governments can enhance their chances for success by following several simple rules, which include:

- Learn the rules and procedures for each government entity you wish to do business with and follow them, since trying to get a local government purchasing official to change his or her procedures to accommodate your standard corporate policies is probably a waste of time;
- Whenever possible, standardize and be consistent regarding the interpretation of terms, conditions, clauses, and similar issues;
- Understand the standard business practices of each government entity you wish to do business with, since it is not uncommon to discover that one entity's processes are slightly different than another's, particularly in the billing and payment functions; and
- Take the time to develop personal relationships with the buyers' purchasing personnel, since purchasing decisions are frequently made based on a level of trust and confidence that must be developed and nurtured over time, particularly at the local government level.

4.8 Supply Chain Management

The concept of "supply chain management" as a natural, evolutionary managerial advancement over the traditional purchasing function is much more prevalent and commonly accepted than in the past and has become the norm. Traditional supply chain management theory holds that an organization can reduce procurement costs, reduce procurement cycle time, and add value to the procurement process by taking actions such as:

- *Reducing the number of suppliers used*—Many organizations have found that maintaining large numbers of suppliers for the same or similar products or services and attempting to manage that supplier base was more expensive than the savings potentially realized from extensive competition among the suppliers for orders. Having many suppliers also introduced quality and consistent performance issues that were more difficult to manage.
- *Negotiating long-term contracts with the few preferred suppliers*—Cost savings can be realized by making significant commitments to a few suppliers as opposed to making only short-term commitments to many suppliers.
- *Conducting more rigorous and detailed timelines and quality tracking of the preferred supplier base*—The significant purchase commitments made to a few suppliers are coupled with increased requirements for quality and performance.
- *Analyze and seek to improve every action and link in the supply chain, from the end customer to the lowest-level supplier, with involvement, input, and cooperation from all stakeholders.*

Supply chain management concepts recognize that the acquisition function does not operate in a reactive vacuum, but rather is a component in a larger management system that provides value and profitability by merging customer needs and supplier capabilities with the value-added processes of the organization. Supply chain management also recognizes the interdependencies and interrelationships between and among all members of the supply chain and seeks to maximize the power and competitiveness of the entire supply chain through collaboration, cooperation, continuous improvement, and the maintenance of long-term relationships that benefit all members of the chain.

4.9 Performance-Based Acquisition

Commercial contracting has included performance-based acquisition as a standard practice. However, for government contracting, these methods have seemed more difficult to achieve. Performance-based acquisition is intended to ensure that required outcome quality levels are achieved and that total payment is related to the degree that outcomes achieved meet contract standards. Performance-based contracts should:

- Describe the requirements in terms of results required, rather than the methods of performing the work;

- Use measurable performance standards and quality assurance plans;

- Specify procedures for reductions of fees or for reductions to the price of fixed-price contracts when services are not performed or do not meet certain specified requirements; and

- Include performance incentives where appropriate.

4.10 Government Property

When the U.S. government contracts for supplies and services, the contractor is generally required to provide all necessary resources to successfully meet the terms and conditions of such a contract. These resources also include all property necessary to perform the work required under government contracts. Reutilization of government property promotes cost savings and efficiency for the government. The government also has a responsibility to protect the public trust, and serves as the guardian of the property with public funds.

"Government property" means all property owned by, leased to, or acquired by the U.S. government under the terms of a contract. It includes property delivered or otherwise made available to the contractor (e.g., government-furnished property) and property provided by the contractor (i.e., property purchased by the contractor for use in performance of the contract); title in the latter case depends on the type of contract used and the specific provisions of the contract.

"Government-furnished property" refers to any property in the possession of or directly acquired by the government and subsequently made available to a contractor. The *Federal Acquisition Regulation* distinguishes between government-furnished property and contractor-acquired property under contracts. A simple definition of "government-furnished property" is any property the government makes available or provides to a contractor for use in performance of a contract.

"Contractor-acquired property" is defined as property that is acquired or otherwise provided by the contractor for performing a contract and to which the government has title. Under the terms of a contract, a contractor may be required to buy certain materials, equipment, or other property to perform the contract. The rights to title for such property purchased for use in performing a contract are generally placed (vested) in the government.

"Ownership" means the collection of rights to use and enjoy property, including the right to transmit or convey these rights to others. "Title" defines the right to control and dispose of property.

FAR Part 45 classifies property into five categories:

- Facilities,
- Material,
- Special tooling,
- Special test equipment, and
- Agency-peculiar property.

Facilities

The term "facilities" refers to property used in production, maintenance, research, development, or testing. It includes plant equipment (such as machine tools, test equipment, and furniture) and real property (such as land, buildings, and other structures). It does not include any of the other categories of property mentioned above. It may also include computers and other automatic data processing equipment; therefore, exercise caution when a contractor wants to buy such items, since certain approvals for facilities are required.

Material

The term "material" means property that may be incorporated into or attached to a deliverable end item (e.g., steel used to make bolts) or that may be consumed or expended in performing a contract (e.g., solvents, cleansers, paint). It also includes assemblies, components, parts, raw and processed materials, and small tools and supplies that may be consumed while performing a contract.

Special Tooling

"Special tooling" means jigs (devices used to guide a tool or for holding a machine in place), dies (devices used for cutting out, forming, or stamping material), fixtures, molds, patterns, taps (tools for cutting internal screw threads), gauges, other equipment and manufacturing aids, all components of these items, and replacement of these items, all of which are of such a specialized nature that without substantial modification or alteration, their use is limited to the development or production of particular supplies or parts thereof or to the performance of particular services. In other words, special tooling must be used only for the manufacture of specialty items.

Special Test Equipment

"Special test equipment" refers to either single or multipurpose integrated test units engineered, designed, fabricated, or modified to accomplish special purpose testing in performing a contract. It consists of items or assemblies of equipment, including standard or general purpose items, or components that are interconnected and interdependent so as to become a new factional entity for special testing purposes. In other words, although special test equipment may consist of components that are used for normal testing purposes, it must be used only for special testing purposes as required in performing a contract.

Agency-Peculiar Property

Finally, "agency-peculiar property" means government-owned property that is peculiar to the mission of one agency (e.g., military hardware, such as an aircraft carrier, or space equipment, such as a space shuttle).

Major Phases and Key Activities

If the government plans to award a contract requiring the use of such property, there are formal procedures for the incorporation of such property based on some fundamental considerations. There are four major phases and key activities associated with property:

- Solicitation;
- Delivery of property;
- Control, accountability, and use; and
- Disposition.

Solicitation

During the solicitation phase, property is identified and made available for inspection or used "as is." Existing government-furnished property is also identified, and a determination is made whether to include it in the procurement. If such property is included, it is made available for inspection and is offered either "as-is" or with a guarantee of suitability for use in the procurement. Contractors are allowed to inspect property in order to verify the suitability or the "as-is" condition of such for use in performance of the contract.

Delivery of Property

The government is responsible for providing the property in accordance with the contract schedule, or in such time to allow the contractor to reasonably meet delivery requirements. The contractor may receive an equitable adjustment due to the late delivery or other circumstances that may jeopardize performance in accordance with the agreed-upon terms of the contract.

Control, Accountability, and Use

The contractor is generally responsible for having a property control system, as required by the contract and *Federal Acquisition Regulation* Part 45. The contractor is generally required to maintain property in good condition, less normal wear and tear, while also keeping custodial records that include information regarding the location, cost, allocability to contracts, condition, and disposition of government property.

Disposition

Upon completion or termination of a contract, the contractor is generally responsible for requesting disposition instructions and disposing of any property as directed by the government.

4.11 Other Specialized Areas

As contracting becomes more complex, there are many more areas the contracting professional needs to be familiar with. While they may not have in-depth knowledge of these specialties (they are often managed by other offices), they need to have a working knowledge of the basic concepts as far as they may "touch" their duties. Some examples, in no particular order, include:

- Security (industrial, physical, personal, information assurance);
- Contingency contracting;
- Spend analysis;
- Environmental contracting;
- Inter-agency contracting;
- Contractor system reviews;
- Foreign military sales;
- Government purchase cards; and
- Undefinitized contract actions.

5.0 Business

The following brief descriptions discuss some of the key general business competencies that contracting professionals might reasonably be expected to possess. While no one person will be an expert in all of these areas, a seasoned contracting professional should at least have a basic understanding of each general business competency. These competencies include:

- Management,
- Operations management,
- Accounting,
- Budgeting,
- Economics,
- Finance,
- Information technology and systems, and
- Marketing (see **FIGURE 16**).

5.1 Management

The ability to manage is essential for successful contract management because it determines the success or failure of a contract. Management consists of the processes used to accomplish the

FIGURE 16. General Business Competencies

goals of a contract organization. The basic and commonly accepted functions of contract management include:

- Planning,
- Organizing,
- Directing, and
- Controlling.

The size of an organization and the complexity of its business normally dictates the size of the contract management staff. A small business may have only one person in charge of all contract organization management activities. A large corporation or government agency may have hundreds, or even thousands of managers, each being responsible for some segment of the organization's contract activities. Regardless of the entity's size and business purpose, and at all levels within the contract management organization team, the four key functions of management noted above are essential.

Managerial Skills and Competencies

In addition to the four basic functions of management discussed above, there are a number of other direct and indirect (hard and soft) skills that are most valuable in ensuring managerial effectiveness. These skills include the following.

Technical Skills
Although it may seem intuitively obvious, the need for managers to be technically competent cannot be overemphasized. It is imperative that managers possess the knowledge required to perform the work they require of their subordinates. Though it is likely that a manager will be less proficient than his or her subordinates in actually performing the work on a day-to-day basis, the ability to manage well has a direct relationship to the manager's level of technical knowledge.

Communication Skills
The ability to effectively communicate is an essential skill to effective management. Effective communication is a two-way street and has multiple facets, including:

- The ability to speak clearly and concisely to individuals, small groups, and large groups;
- The ability to listen and understand others at all levels within an organization;
- The ability to plan, conduct, and control formal and informal meetings; and
- The ability to convey information in written form in a format and at a level appropriate to the intended recipient.

Human Relations Skills
Effective managers must be able to work with a wide variety of other individuals and groups with differing social, educational, and experiential backgrounds and varying capabilities to ensure that goals are accomplished. These human relations skills, often more art than science, are of increasing importance as the workforces of most organizations continue to become more and more diverse.

Time Management Skills
Time is one resource that most managers wish they had more of. The ability to structure one's time in a hierarchical manner; to know what is important now and what can be deferred; to recognize "time wasting" activity masquerading as productive effort; to be accessible when needed and alone when required; to organize, plan, and execute the expenditure of time; and to know when to modify the plans are all vital to a manager's ability to succeed.

Technology Skills
The continuing advancements in information technology and communications technology provide significant opportunities for managers to increase their effectiveness. It is important that all managers, particularly those who were educated and began their careers before such technology was widely available, become familiar with and appropriately incorporate the use of technological advances into their arsenal of skills.

The generation gap at work is wide, with vast discrepancies when it comes to the appropriate use of technology. A recent survey by LexisNexis compared technology and software usage among generations of working professionals, including Baby Boomers (ages 44–60+), Generation X (ages 29–43), and Generation Y (ages 28 and younger).

According to the survey, two-thirds of all Boomers agreed that smart phones contribute to a decline in proper workplace etiquette, and believe the use of laptops during in-person meetings is "distracting," while less than half of Generation Y workers agreed with them. Only 17 percent of Boomers believed using laptops or smart phones during in-person meetings was "efficient," while more than one-third of Generation Y believed so. Only 28 percent of Boomers thought that blogging about work-related issues was acceptable, while 40 percent of Generation Y workers believed it was.

5.2 Marketing

"Marketing" is the business process that develops, prices, places, and promotes goods, ideas, or services to enhance exchanges between buyers and sellers. It is also the process of planning and executing the conception, pricing, promotion, and distribution of ideas, goods, and services to create exchanges that satisfy individual and organizational goals. The contracting professional may interact with marketing professionals during the acquisition planning and pre-award phases of the contract life cycle. Marketing professionals typically identify business opportunities during these phases. It is important for the contracting professional to give equal treatment to each vendor during these acquisition planning and pre-award phases to ensure the integrity of the procurement process.

5.3 Operations Management

"Operations management" is a subset of management activity that is primarily concerned with actions related to the directing and controlling functions of management. Operations management is attuned to ensuring the following:

- The function has the correct quantity of necessary inputs (such as materials, labor, etc.) required to perform the desired tasks;
- The transformation process—the way or system in which inputs are changed into something of desired value (e.g., an accounting report)—is valid and efficient;
- Outputs are what were in fact desired initially, and that they conform to the quality and quantity originally planned for; and
- Appropriate feedback occurs, whether it is:
  o Informational feedback—a two-way exchange between management and workers to seek clarification, discuss improvements, and share status;
  o Corrective feedback—an exchange from the manager to workers to point out mistakes and redirect effort toward improvement; or
  o Reinforcing feedback—an exchange from the manager that includes praise for a job well done or for exceeding standards to promote continued improvements.

5.4 Financial Analysis

"Financial analysis" is an aspect of the overall business finance function that involves examining historical data to gain information about the current and future financial health of a company. Financial analysis can be applied in a wide variety of situations to give business managers the information they need to make critical decisions. Business goals and objectives are set in financial terms and their outcomes are measured in financial terms. Finance involves analyzing the data contained in financial statements in order to provide valuable information for management decisions.

Finance

Corporate or business financial analysis relates to the methodology employed to allocate financial resources with a financial value in such a manner as to optimize their benefits to the organization or agency. Contracting professionals need to have a basic understanding of how finance interacts with the other business competencies in their organization.

5.5 Accounting

"Accounting" encompasses a body of principles and conventions and is an established process for capturing financial information related to an organization's resources and using that information to meet the organization's goals. Contract professionals need to consider the accounting function very early in the acquisition planning process. The pricing structure of the resultant contract, payment terms and provisions, and an understanding of overhead rates are key accounting issues that will have a direct impact on successful contract performance.

Budgeting

"Budgeting" is the process of generating a quantitative plan of operations that identifies the resources needed to accomplish the organization's goals and objectives. It can include both financial and non-financial aspects. Contracting professionals need to interact with budgeting personnel throughout the contracting life cycle to ensure that sufficient funding exists for the resultant contract.

5.6 Economics

"Economics" is the social science that studies how a society solves the human issues of unlimited wants and limited resources. Economics makes distinctions between "needs" (those things that are required) and "wants" (those things that are desired but in excess of a need). Economics also recognizes that resources are scarce to the extent that there are never enough resources to completely satisfy all wants. The issue of scarce resources forces individuals, organizations, governments, and society at large to study the relationships between needs, wants, and resources; to prioritize how needs and wants might be satisfied; and to make economic trade-offs and choices in order to maximize the utilization of scarce resources. Contracting professionals need to conserve scarce resources by ensuring maximum competition on each contracting action.

5.7 Information Science or Information Technology

"Information science" is the study, design, development, implementation, support, or management of computer-based information systems and technology, particularly software applications and computer hardware.[64] While the contracting professional is not expected to be an expert in information technology, a basic understanding of the field is highly desirable in today's contracting environment. In addition, contracting professionals that are involved in acquiring and/or administering information technology contracts need to have a good working knowledge of information technology.

5.8 Leadership Skills

Buying and Selling—Leadership Competencies

Traditionally, when people think about what it takes to become a buying and selling team leader, they focus on who they need to know and impress to get promoted. Rather, let us focus on the following five specialized skill areas to truly improve leadership performance and team results:

- Decision-making,
- Integrity,
- Communications (verbal and nonverbal),
- Buying and selling—business acumen, and
- Interpersonal relations.

Decision-Making Skills
When leading a team of business professionals, especially those involved in buying or selling particularly complex integrated solutions composed of multiple products and/or services, the ability to make timely and accurate business decisions is essential to success.

Integrity Skills
Simply put, an individual of integrity is an individual who has principles and lives by them. Said differently, an individual of integrity is an individual who builds trust by managing expectations and honoring commitments on a consistent basis. One of the biggest challenges in creating and maintaining a successful long-term business partnership is building trust through integrity. Trust is like quality; it is difficult to accurately describe, but you know it when it is there.

Communication (Verbal/Nonverbal) Skills
One of the most important skill areas one must master is to achieve consistent success when leading the buying and selling of products and services is communication. Years of extensive research in communication suggests that nearly 90 percent of the meaning transmitted between two or more people in face-to-face communications is through nonverbal channels. Stated differently, only about 10 percent of your message is transmitted by your spoken words.

Buying and Selling—Business Acumen Skills
Becoming a true buying and selling business professional takes business acumen. Business acumen is the combination of business education, experience, on-the-job training, and expert mentoring across a diverse range of business topics, including:

- Marketing and sales,
- Accounting and finance,
- Strategic planning and economic forecasting,
- Purchasing and supply chain management,
- Operations and project management, and
- Business law and contract management.

Interpersonal Relations Skills
The importance of learning how to get along with others, especially dealing with difficult people, cannot be overstressed. As related to leading buying and selling teams, interpersonal skills are

extremely important, including building trust, forming partnerships, and resolving conflicts. Interpersonal skills are vital to success, both within your organization and with your customers and suppliers.[65]

ENDNOTES

1. Derived from Burton S. Kaliski, *Encyclopedia of Busine$$ and Finance*, Volumes 1 and 2 (Macmillian Reference USA, 2001).

2. The American Law Institute, "Creation of the Institute," available at **www.ali.org**.

3. UCC § 1-103.

4. 31 U.S.C. § 665(a).

5. 31 U.S.C. § 1501.

6. 31 U.S.C. § 3526.

7. *Public Law* 93-400.

8. FAR 1.602-3.

9. *Ibid.*

10. 15 U.S.C. §§78dd-1, *et seq.*

11. Derived from Rene G. Rendon and K.F. Snider (Eds.), *Management of Defense Acquisition Projects* (Reston, VA: American Institute of Aeronautics and Astronautics, 2008).

12. Margaret G. Rumbaugh, "Ethical Decision-Making: Issues for Contract Managers and Educators," *Contract Management* (April 2004): 34–35.

13. *See* Defense Industry Initiative Home Page: **www.dii.org**.

14. John W. Polk, "Turning Square Corners," *Contract Management* (January 2008): 18.

15. FAR 19.202-1.

16. 15 U.S.C. 637(a).

17. *See* FAR Part 22 for more information.

18. 5 U.S.C. § 552a.

19. *Public Law* 89-554, 80 Stat. 383.

20. *See* FAR Part 24 for more information.

21. FAR 16.201.

22. FAR 16.207.

23. *See* FAR 16.203.

24. FAR 16.205.

25. FAR 16.206.

26. FAR 16.301.

27. FAR 16.302.

28. FAR 16.303.

29. FAR 16.306.

30. FAR 16.6.

31. *See* FAR 16.4.

32. FAR 16.403.

33. FAR 16.404.

34. FAR 16.405-1.

35. FAR 16.405-2.

36. FAR 16.702.

37. FAR 16.703.

38. FAR 16.603.

39. FAR 16.5.

40. FAR 16.5.

41. Excerpted from Margaret G. Rumbaugh, *Understanding Government Contract Source Selection* (Management Concepts, Inc., 2010), available at **www.managementconcepts.com/pubs**.

42. FAR 14.5.

43. *See* FAR 2.101.

44. *See* Richard Christou, *Drafting Commercial Agreements*, third edition (London: Sweet & Maxwell, 2005): 104.

45. FAR 2.101.

46. FAR 32.106.

47. FAR 32.5.

48. FAR 32.3.

49. FAR 32.4.

50. FAR 27.4.

51. FAR 2.101.

52. FAR 7.105.

53. Adapted from Rumbaugh, *see* note 41.

54. *Ibid.*

55. *Ibid.*

56. FAR 15.503.

57. *Ibid.*

58. FAR 15.505.

59. FAR 15.506.

60. FAR 52.245-1.

61. *See* Diane K. Whitmoyer, "Managing Organizational Conflicts of Interest," *Contract Management* (June 2004): 16.

62. FAR 35.002.

63. *See* http://management.energy.gov/documents/DeterminingIGandCommercialFunctions.pdf.

64. As per the Information Technology Association of America.

65. Derived from Gregory A. Garrett and William C. Pursch, "Building High-Performance Buying and Selling Teams," *Contract Management* (April 2006): 52.

The CMBOK Lexicon

chapter four

The CMBOK lexicon contains an explanation of the terms that are used directly or indirectly in this volume. Multiple sources were consulted. However, where applicable, the terms were taken from the operational definitions published in NCMA's *Desktop Guide to Basic Contracting Terms*, sixth ed. (2006). These definitions reflect the collective opinion of the contract management community. In some instances, the definitions are excerpts with examples added for clarification. The purpose is to clearly convey the intended content of each CMBOK element. Definitions have been taken from the *Federal Acquisition Regulation* (FAR), the Uniform Commercial Code (UCC) dictionaries, websites, official documents (e.g., Office of Management and Budget [OMB] circulars and legal casework), textbooks, and accepted contract management practice.

A&E Selection Process—The unique process used to select architect-engineer firms pursuant to the Brooks Act.

Acceptance—That act of an authorized buyer representative by which the buyer assents to ownership of existing and identified supplies or approves specific services rendered as partial or complete performance of a contract.

Accessibility—The availability of public conveyances, facilities, utilities, technologies, and other designated resources to all persons. In the United States, accessibility considerations are the purview of the Access Board, an independent federal agency devoted to accessibility for people with disabilities. The Access Board develops and maintains accessibility requirements for the built environment, transit vehicles, telecommunications equipment, and electronic and information technology; provides technical assistance and training on these guidelines and standards; and enforces accessibility standards for federally funded facilities.

Accounting—The principles and practices of systematically recording, presenting, and interpreting financial data.

Acquisition Methodology—Requesting or inviting offerors to submit offers, usually by issuing a solicitation. Solicitations consist of 1) a draft contract and 2) provisions on preparing and submitting offers.

Acquisition Plan—A plan for an acquisition that serves as the basis for initiating the individual contracting actions necessary to acquire a system or support a program.

Acquisition Planning—The process by which efforts of all personnel responsible for an acquisition are coordinated and integrated through a comprehensive plan for fulfilling the organization's need in a timely manner at a reasonable cost. It includes developing the overall strategy for managing the acquisition. Simply put, it is the activities and events required for both buyers and sellers to prepare for, negotiate, and form a binding contractual arrangement.

Acquisition Strategy—The conceptual framework for conducting an acquisition. It encompasses the broad concepts and objectives that direct and control the overall acquisition process.

Adequacy of Offer/Conformance to Requirements—Purchasing techniques that enable buyers to solicit input from multiple suppliers and create a solicitation document, taking the best from each. Accordingly, sellers are able to develop a compliance matrix that lists all solicitation and functional requirements, along with an assessment of the firm's competitive strengths and weaknesses.

Administrative Changes—Unilateral contract changes, in writing, that do not affect the substantive rights of the parties, such as a change in the paying office.

Administrative Closeout—Process of ensuring that all documentation—including releases, audits, reports, and final invoices—has been completed and that contract files have been properly stored or disposed of.

Advisory and Assistance Services—Services acquired to support or improve agency policy development, decision-making, management, and administration, or to support or improve the operation of management systems.

Agency—A relationship whereby the principal authorizes another (the agent) to act for and on behalf of the principal and to bind the principal in contract.

Agreements and Restrictions—Agreements exist between the United States and its trading partners regarding international procurement. These include the General Agreement on Tariffs and Trade (GATT), the GATT Government Procurement Code, the North American Free Trade Agreement (NAFTA), as well as bilateral agreements that have been negotiated between the United States and other countries (such as the U.S.-Canada Free Trade Agreement). Congress has routinely included in appropriation acts restrictions on the procurement of certain foreign items, usually to protect domestic industries.

Alternate Disputes Resolution—Any procedure that is used, in lieu of litigation, to resolve issues in controversy, including but not limited to settlement negotiations, conciliation, facilitation, mediation, fact-finding, mini-trials, and arbitration.

Apparent Authority—The right by an agent for a principal to exercise power where the principal knowingly permits the agent to exercise authority, though not actually granted.

Applications Software—Software applications relevant to contract management, including enterprise resource planning, customer relationship management, supply chain automation, sales force automation, and electronic contract management.

Arbitration—The use of an impartial third party to whom the parties to an agreement refer their disputes for resolution. Some contracts contain provisions that provide for binding arbitration of unsettled grievances.

Architect-Engineer Services and Construction—Includes professional services of an architectural or engineering nature that are required to be performed or approved by a person licensed, registered, or certified to provide such services; are associated with research, planning, development, design, construction, alteration, or repair of real property; or involve other related professional services such as studies and surveys. "Construction" means alteration or repair, including dredging, excavating, and painting of buildings, structures, or other real property.

Architect and Design Services—Professional services of an architectural or engineering nature that are required to be performed or approved by a person licensed, registered, or certified to provide such services; are associated with research, planning, development, design, construction, alteration, or repair of real property; or involve other related professional services such as studies and surveys.

Auditing—The examination and review of operations for compliance with corporate policies.

Audits—The systematic examination of records and documents and/or the securing of other evidence by confirmation, physical inspection, or otherwise for one or more of the following purposes:

- Determining the propriety or legality of proposed or completed transactions,
- Ascertaining whether all transactions have been recorded and are reflected accurately in accounts,
- Determining the existence of recorded assets and inclusiveness of recorded liabilities,
- Determining the accuracy of financial or statistical statements or reports and the fairness of the facts they represent,
- Determining the degree of compliance with established policies and procedures in terms of financial transactions and business management, and
- Appraising an account system and making recommendations concerning it.

Authority—The sources from which entities or people receive their empowerment to engage in procurement activities and which set forth the framework and parameters and extend to their empowerment. Such authority includes:

- State statutes,
- State and local regulations charters,
- Local ordinances, and
- Administrative resolutions, policies, or edicts.

Basic Agreement—A written instrument of understanding negotiated between an agency or contracting activity and a contractor that contains contract clauses applying to future contracts between the parties during its term and contemplates separate future contracts that will incorporate, by reference or attachment, the required and applicable clauses agreed on in the basic agreement. A basic agreement is not a contract.

Basic Ordering Agreement—A written instrument of understanding negotiated between an agency, contracting activity, or contracting office and a contractor that contains terms and clauses applying to future contracts (orders) between the parties during its term; a description, as specific as practicable, of supplies or services to be provided; and methods for pricing, issuing, and delivering future orders under the basic ordering agreement. A basic ordering agreement is not a contract.

Bid or No-Bid Decision—Determination made by seller's management whether or not to submit an offer, usually in response to a customer request.

Bilateral and Unilateral—A "bilateral" contract is formed by the exchange of promises to perform reciprocal obligations for the other party. A "unilateral" contract is formed by the exchange of a promise of one party for an action by the other party.

Bilateral/Notice—Termination of a contract by mutual consent. Typically initiated by one party by notice of the exercise of a contractual right to termination based on particular circumstances. Generally, both the circumstances permitting the termination and the process for termination are predetermined in the contract.

Break Even Analysis—A means of determining the number of goods or services that must be sold at a given price to generate sufficient revenue to cover costs.

Budgeting—The planning, scheduling, and budgeting of organizational expenses for the fiscal period.

Buyer-Seller Relationship—Encompasses more than just the procurement process because relationships are developed throughout the supply chain. The buyer-seller relationship affects quality of materials and parts, customer satisfaction, and competitive advantages of both parties.

Capital Budgeting—The process of planning for the best selection and financing of long-term investment proposals, taking into account the time value of money.

Cardinal Change—Change that is not within the contract's general scope. When a contractor is faced with an out-of-scope change to its contract, it generally will not refuse the effort but, rather, will seek additional compensation. Generally, if the work performed is reasonably "within the contemplation of the parties when the contract was entered into," it is considered to be within the scope of the contract.

Cash Budgeting—A schedule of expected cash receipts and disbursements for a designated period. The primary reason for a cash budget is to forecast a company's future financing needs. A cash budget is also used to avoid either unnecessary idle cash or possible cash shortages. In case of cash shortage, it indicates whether the shortage is temporary or permanent (i.e., whether short-term or long-term borrowing is needed).

Change Orders—Written orders signed by the contracting officer or buyer that are authorized by contract clause to modify contractual requirements within the scope of the contract.

Commodity Warehousing, Just in Time—The physical holding of raw materials and commodities units against the time of use. Although the storage of materials for use in the production process is basically the same as storing finished products, raw-materials storage and finished-goods storage differ in terms of the type of facility each requires, the value of the stored items, and product perishability.

Common Law—A body of law common to the whole population, produced primarily by the efforts of the judiciary to harmonize their decisions with precedent decisions and changes in law or regulation.

Competitive Bidding/Negotiation—A method of contracting involving a request for proposal that states the buyer's requirements and criteria for evaluation, submission of timely proposals by a maximum number of offerors, discussions with those offerors found to be within the competitive range, and award of a contract to the one offeror whose offer, price, and other consideration factors are most advantageous to the buyer.

Compliance System—Information technology system that translates contract requirements (such as pricing, warranty, service requirements, and product changes) into executable instructions to internal systems. It includes connectivity to enterprise resource planning tools and other customer-resource management tools that the organization uses to communicate internally and externally.

Conflict of Interest—Term used in connection with public officials and fiduciaries and their relationship to matters of private interest or gain to them. Ethical problems connected therewith are covered by statutes in most jurisdictions and by federal statutes on the federal level. A conflict of interest arises when an employee's personal or financial interests conflict or appear to conflict with his or her official responsibility.

Consent to Subcontract—Situation in which the government must consent to a prime contractor's subcontract. Consent is required when subcontract work is complex, the dollar value is substantial, or the government's interest is not adequately protected by competition and the type of prime or subcontract.

Construction Contracts—The traditional method of construction contracting that uses the phases of design, bid, and build for construction projects. Also means alteration of the landscape, assembly and fitting out of structures, installation of furnishings and fixtures, decoration, or repair of real property.

Constructive Changes—Verbal or written acts or omissions by an authorized government official that are of such a nature that they have the same effect as written change orders.

Consulting—The process of providing subject matter expertise to one who needs such knowledge. The knowledge may be provided in the form of either verbal or written advice. In addition, the consulting may provide the customer with some form of deliverable (e.g., written report, project plans, or—in the case of information technology consulting—a program that addresses a particular need of the client). Consulting services may be paid for in a number of ways. Two common means for determining a consultant's fee are: 1) time and materials, and 2) fixed fee.

Contract Administration—Management of issues that arise during the performance of a contract.

Contract Changes/Modifications—Any written alteration in the specification, delivery point, rate of delivery, contract period, price, quantity, or other provision of an existing contract accomplished in accordance with a contract clause. This alteration may be unilateral or bilateral.

Contract Closeout—The process of declaring that the obligations under a contract have been satisfied and that a procurement file is both physically and administratively complete. A closeout can occur when: 1) the contractor's supplies or services have been accepted and paid for, and 2) all documentation on the procurement is finalized and properly assembled.

Contract Financing—Obtaining the funds necessary for performing the contract, including payment methods, loan guarantees, advanced payments, progress payments, and contract funding.

Contract Formation—The elements of offer, acceptance, mutuality of consideration, competent parties, legal subject matter, and mutuality of agreement.

Contract Performance/Quality Assurance—A planned and systematic pattern of actions necessary to provide adequate confidence that material, data, supplies, and services conform to established technical requirements, and to achieve satisfactory performance.

Contract Principles—Fundamentals of contract management that all contracting professionals must comprehend.

Contract Structures—Specific pricing arrangements employed for the performance of work under the contract.

Contract Termination—Action taken pursuant to a contract clause in which the contracting officer unilaterally ends all or part of the work.

Contracting Methods—The process employed for soliciting offers, evaluating offers, and awarding a contract.

Contractor's Purchasing Systems Review—An evaluation of the efficiency and effectiveness with which the prime contractor spends government funds and complies with government policy when subcontracting.

Convenience Termination—Right reserved to the government, under the standard "Termination for Convenience" clause, to bring an end to contracts that are made obsolete by technological and other developments or that are otherwise no longer advantageous to the government.

Cooperative Agreement—Legal instrument used principally for transferring money, property, or services between or among the parties to accomplish a specific purpose of support or stimulation where substantial involvement and cooperation are expected between or among the parties.

Copyright—Royalty-free, nonexclusive, and irrevocable license to reproduce, translate, publish, use, and dispose of written or recorded material and to authorize others to do so.

Corporate Responsibility and Personal Conduct—Laws and standards governing both corporate and individual behavior, including standards of ethics and conduct, social responsibility, law, regulation, and public policy.

Cost—Concerned with the accounting system design for recording, accumulating, and reporting costs for specific products and services.

Cost Accounting Standards (CAS)—Federal standards designed to provide consistency and coherency in defense and other government contract accounting.

Cost-Based Contracts—Implementation of cost-based methods in commercial contracts, including time-and-materials contracts, indexed pricing, and any other arrangements subject to audit or independent verification.

Cost Contract—Cost-reimbursement contract in which the contractor receives no fee.

Cost Incentives—Most incentive contracts include only cost incentives, which take the form of a profit or fee adjustment formula and are intended to motivate the contractor to effectively manage costs. No incentive contract may provide for other incentives without also providing a cost incentive (or constraint). Except for award fee contracts, incentive contracts include a target cost, a target profit or fee, and a profit or fee adjustment formula. These targets and the formula provide that (within the constraints of a price ceiling or minimum and maximum fee):

- The actual cost that meets the target will result in the target profit fee,
- The actual cost that exceeds the target will result in downward adjustment of target profit or fee, and
- The actual cost that is below the target will result in upward adjustment of target profit or fee.

Cost-Plus-Award-Fee Contract—A cost-reimbursement contract that provides for a fee consisting of: 1) a base amount (which may be zero), fixed at inception of the contract, and 2) an award amount, based on a judgmental evaluation by the government, sufficient to provide motivation for excellence in contract performance.

Cost-Plus-Fixed-Fee Contract—A cost-reimbursement contract that provides for payment to the contractor of a negotiated fee that is fixed at the inception of the contract. The fixed fee does not vary with actual cost, but may be adjusted as a result of changes in the work to be performed under the contract. This contract type permits contracting for efforts that might otherwise present too great a risk to contractors, but it provides the contractor only a minimum incentive to control costs.

Cost-Plus-Incentive-Fee Contract—A cost-reimbursement contract that provides for the initially negotiated fee to be adjusted later by a formula based on the relationship of total allowable costs to total target costs.

Cost/Price Analysis—A review to determine and evaluate the cost elements in an offeror's or contractor's proposal to determine how well the proposed costs represent what the cost of the contract should be, assuming reasonable economy and efficiency. Also, factors to be considered in determining pricing and financial impact of a procurement include commodity markets, price lists, price quotations, negotiated pricing, input costs, transaction costs, relational costs, and landed costs.

Cost Principles—The regulations that establish rules and policies relating to the general treatment of costs in government contracting, particularly the allowability of costs.

Cost Proposal—The instrument required of an offeror for the submission or identification of cost or pricing data by which an offeror submits to the buyer a summary of estimated (or incurred) costs suitable for detailed review and analysis.

Cost Reimbursement—A form of pricing arrangement that provides for payment of allowable, allocable, and reasonable costs incurred in the performance of a contract to the extent that such costs are prescribed or permitted by the contract. This family of contracts includes cost-plus-award-fee, cost-plus-fixed-fee, cost-plus-incentive-fee, and cost-sharing contracts.

Cost-Sharing Contract—Cost-reimbursement contract in which the contractor receives no fee and is reimbursed only for an agreed-on portion of its allowable costs.

Customer Service—Interaction with the designated end users of the contracted products and services;

includes actions to resolve customer complaints and facilitates use of products or access to services.

Data—Recorded information, regardless of form or the media on which it may be recorded. Rights to use technical data developed by the contractor vary depending on the source of funds used to develop the item, component, process, software, or software documentation.

Data Management—Use of commercially available software tools to manage contract information, including repositories for contract documents, reporting systems, contracting process management, and portfolio management.

Data Rights—Rights of ownership of data under any contract. In any contract that may involve the production of scientific or technical data, the rights to those data must be clearly ascribed. Generally, a "Rights in Data" clause will protect the government's right to use and distribute—without limitation, free from payment of royalties, and with immunity against lawsuits for copyright infringement or misuse of data—any data produced under a contract funded by the government.

Database Management—Includes data modeling, query languages database design, and transaction processing.

Debriefings—An explanation given by the buyer to an offeror detailing the reasons its proposal was unsuccessful.

Default Termination—An action that the government may impose under the standard default clause for a contractor's failure to perform.

Defense Priorities and Allocations System (DPAS)—A Department of Commerce system controlling the use of critical material and facilities. Its goals are to ensure the timely availability of industrial resources to meet current defense requirements and to provide a framework for rapid industrial expansion in case of a national emergency.

Defense Production Act—An act passed in 1950 (50 U.S.C. app 2061 and the following ones) that authorizes the president to require the priority performance of contracts and orders necessary or appropriate to promote the national defense over other contracts or orders; to allocate materials, services, and facilities as necessary or appropriate to promote the national defense; and to require the allocation of, or the priority performance under contracts or orders relating to, supplies of materials, equipment, and services to ensure domestic energy supplies for national defense needs.

Defining Requirements—Process for defining and expressing requirements that meet the needs of the purchaser and representing those needs through measurable criteria.

Definite Quantity Contract—Provides for delivery of a definite quantity of specific supplies or services for a fixed period, with deliveries or performance to be scheduled at designated locations upon order.

Delays—Late delivery of products and services and implications to contract management; includes time requirements of obligations, impracticability, and other standards of delivery performance. "Delays" are also contractual provisions designed to protect the contractor from sanctions for late performance. To the extent that it has been excusably delayed, the contractor is protected from default termination, liquidated damages, or excess costs of procurement or completion. Excusable delays (e.g., acts of God or the public enemy, acts of the government in either its sovereign or contractual capacity, fire, flood, quarantines, strikes, epidemics, unusually severe weather, or freight embargoes) also may lead to recovery of additional compensation if the government constructively accelerates performance.

Delegation of Authority—The conferring of authority from one organization or representative to another to accomplish specified tasks, such as contract administrative tasks. Such authority may be shared or recalled.

Delivery Incentives—Should be considered when improvement from a required delivery schedule is a significant government objective. It is important to determine the government's primary objectives in a given contract.

Delivery Order Contract—A contract for supplies that does not procure or specify a firm quantity of supplies (other than a minimum or maximum quantity) and that provides for the issuance of orders for the delivery of supplies during the period of the contract.

Design/Build—A method of construction contracting that combines the architectural, engineering, and construction services required for a project into a single agreement.

Discussions—Any verbal or written communication between the buyer and seller other than communications conducted for the purpose of minor clarification, whether or not initiated by the government, that: 1) involves information essential for determining the acceptability of the proposals, or 2) provides the offeror an opportunity to revise or modify its proposal.

Disputes—Disagreements between the parties regarding their rights under a contract that will originate when a claim is denied by the party against which it is made.

Diversity—Multicultural issues in the conduct of business and trade that include cultural diversity, workplace diversity, and supplier diversity. "Diversity" also refers to programs designed to encourage a diverse workforce or education and training group, such as programs that prohibit employment or workplace discrimination based on race, color, religion, sex, national origin, age, or disability.

Documenting Requirements—Process for documenting requirements, validating requirements, and communicating to prospective suppliers; includes make-or-buy decisions and creation of solicitations.

Earned Value—A management technique that relates resource planning to schedules and to technical cost and schedule requirements. All work is planned, budgeted, and scheduled in time-phased "planned value" increments constituting a cost and schedule measurement baseline. There are two major objectives of an earned-value system: 1) to encourage contractors to use effective internal cost and schedule management control systems, and 2) to enable the customer to rely on timely data produced by those systems for determining product-oriented contract status.

Economics—The study of the problems arising when goods and services are scarce relative to human desires for those goods and services.

Electronic Commerce—Marketing goods and services over the Internet by exchanging information between buyers and sellers while in the process minimizing paperwork and simplifying payment procedures; includes both "business-to-consumer" and "business-to-business" transactions. "Electronic commerce" also refers to a paperless process, including e-mail, electronic bulletin boards, electronic funds transfer, electronic data interchange, and similar techniques for accomplishing business transactions.

Electronic, Web-based, Clickware—Contracts for sale accomplished electronically using the Internet where the offer is displayed via an Internet site and the acceptance is accomplished electronically. The terms are the sellers' terms associated with the website, and obligations of the parties with regard to disclosure of terms and acceptance of liabilities are governed by law and regulation.

Employment Agreement—A contract by which one person, called "the employer," engages another person, called "the employee," to do something for the benefit of the employer or a third person for which the employee receives compensation. The contract may be verbal or written.

Enterprise Resource Planning (ERP) System—A set of integrated business applications or modules to carry out most common business functions, including inventory control, general ledger accounting, accounts payable, accounts receivable, material requirements planning, order management, purchasing, and human resources. ERP modules are integrated, primarily through a common set of definitions and a common database, and the modules have been designed to reflect a particular way of doing business (i.e., a particular set of business processes). An "ERP system" also refers to any software system designed to support and automate the business processes of medium and large businesses. This may include manufacturing, distribution, personnel, project management, payroll, and financials. ERP systems are accounting-oriented information systems for identifying and planning the enterprisewide resources needed to take, make, distribute, and account for customer orders.

Environmental Issues—Policies and procedures supporting the government's program for ensuring a drug-free workplace and of protecting and improving the quality of the environment through pollution control, energy conservation, identification of hazardous material, and use of recovered materials.

E-Procurement—Use of information technology and systems in the procurement process. Focuses on the four basic types of e-commerce business models used in procurement:

- Sell-side system,
- Electronic marketplace,

- Buy-side system, and
- Online trading community.

Ethics—Of or relating to moral action, conduct, motive, or character as ethical emotion; professionally right or benefiting; and conforming to professional standards of conduct.

Evaluation Factors—Factors that are tailored to each acquisition and the consideration of each proposal that establish a baseline for proposal evaluation for recommendations regarding the source selection decision. Price, or cost to the government, and quality are addressed in every source selection. Other relevant factors may also be included.

Evaluation Procedures—The process used to evaluate offers against established selection criteria in accordance with the source selection plan.

Export Controls—The comprehensive set of controls that have been established to protect national security interests and to foster foreign policy initiatives. The Department of State monitors and controls the export and re-export of goods and services in accordance with the *International Traffic in Arms Regulations* and the *Department of Commerce Export Administration Regulation* enforces the Export Administration Act.

Export Financing—Financing of international transactions in the exporting or importing of products and services. Addresses factors such as transit times, customs regulations, banking rules and regulations, buyer and seller credit, exchange rates, and political risk.

Extraordinary Contractual Relief—Form of relief for contractors under federal law giving the president the power to authorize federal agencies to enter into contracts, or amendments or modifications of contracts, without regard to other revisions of law relating to the making, performance, amendment, or modification of contracts when the president believes the action will facilitate national defense.

Facilities Contract—A contract under which government facilities are provided to a contractor or subcontractor by the government for use in connection with performing one or more related contracts for supplies or services. It is used occasionally to provide special tooling or special test equipment. Facilities contracts are cost contracts; contractors receive no fee.

Fact Finding—The process of identifying and obtaining information necessary to complete the evaluation of proposals.

Fair Value—Examines product or service features that enhance profits for the final product and the ability of a commercial firm to maintain a competitive advantage in the marketplace.

Federal Regulations—Applicable directives and instructions issued by the several departments and agencies that establish and implement acquisition policies. Examples include the *Federal Acquisition Regulation (FAR)*, agency *FAR* supplements, and Office of Management and Budget circulars.

Federal Statutes—Applicable laws enacted by the legislative branch and signed by the president that affect acquisition. Examples include the Armed Services Procurement Act of 1947, the Federal Property and Administrative Services Act of 1949, the Competition in Contracting Act of 1984, and the Federal Acquisition Streamlining Act of 1994.

Federal Supply Schedules—A program directed and managed by the General Services Administration that provides federal agencies with a simplified process for obtaining commonly used supplies and services at prices associated with volume buying.

Federally Funded Research and Development Corporation (FFRDC)—An activity sponsored under a broad charter by a government agency (or agencies) for the purpose of performing, analyzing, integrating, supporting, and/or managing basic or applied research and/or development, and which receive 70 percent or more of its financial support from the government. If a long-term relationship is contemplated, most or all of the facilities are owned or funded by the government and the FFRDC has access to government and supplier data, employees, and facilities beyond that which is common in a normal contractual relationship. The operation, management, and administration of an FFRDC is performed by a university, consortium of universities, nonprofit organization, or industrial firm as an identifiable and separate operating unit of a parent organization. The National Science Foundation maintains the master list of FFRDCs.

Finance—The process of managing the money matters of the organization.

Financial Analysis—Includes international financial analysis, assets, return on investment, asset turnover, and variance analysis.

Financial Reporting—Includes financial statements, sales forecasting, planning, and control.

Firm-Fixed-Price Contract—Provides for a price that is not subject to any adjustment on the basis of the contractor's cost experience in performing the contract. This contract type places on the contractor maximum risk and full responsibility for all costs and resulting profit or loss. It provides maximum incentives for the contractor to control costs and perform effectively and imposes a minimum administrative burden on the contracting parties.

Firm-Fixed-Price, Level-of-Effort Term Contract—A contract that requires the contractor to provide a specified level of effort, over a stated period of time, on work that can be stated only in general terms and requires the government to pay the contractor a fixed dollar amount.

Fixed Price—A type (family) of contracts providing for a firm pricing arrangement established by the parties at the time of contracting. This family of contracts includes:

- Firm-fixed-price,
- Fixed-price with economic price adjustment,
- Fixed-price incentive,
- Fixed-price re-determination (prospective and retroactive), and
- Firm-fixed-price, level-of-effort.

Fixed-Price Contract with Award Fees—A contract used when the government wishes to motivate a contractor and other incentives cannot be used because contractor performance cannot be measured objectively. Such contracts shall establish a fixed price (including normal profit) for the effort that will be paid for satisfactory contract performance. Such contracts shall establish that the award fee earned (if any) will be paid in addition to that fixed price and provide for periodic evaluation of the contractor's performance against an award fee plan.

Fixed-Price Contract with Economic Price Adjustment—A contract that provides for upward and downward revision of the stated contract price on the occurrence of specified contingencies. There are three general types of economics price adjustments:

- Adjustments based on established prices where price adjustments are based on increases or decreases from an agreed-on level in published or otherwise established prices of specific items or the contract end items,
- Adjustments based on actual costs of labor or material where price adjustments are based on increases or decreases in specified costs of labor or material that the contractor actually experiences during contract performance, and
- Adjustments based on cost indexes of labor or material where price adjustments are based on increases or decreases in labor or material cost standards or indexes that are specifically identified in the contract.

Fixed-Price Contract with Prospective Price Re-determination—A contract that provides for a firm-fixed-price for an initial period of contract deliveries or performance and prospective re-determination at a stated time or times during performance of the price for subsequent periods of performance.

Fixed-Price Contract with Retroactive Price Re-determination—A contract that provides for a fixed ceiling price and retroactive price re-determination within the ceiling after completion of the contract.

Fixed-Price Incentive Contract—A contract that provides for adjusting profit and establishing the final contract price by a formula based on the relationship of final negotiated total cost to total target cost. Fixed-price incentive contracts are covered in *Federal Acquisition Regulation* (*FAR*) 16.4, "Incentive Contracts." See FAR 16.403 for more complete descriptions, application, and limitations for these contracts. Prescribed clauses are found at FAR 16.406. The final price is subject to a price ceiling, which is negotiated at the outset. The two forms of fixed-price incentive contracts—firm target and successive target contracts—are discussed below.

Fixed-Price Incentive (Firm Target) Contract—A contract that specifies a target cost, a target profit, a price ceiling (but not a profit ceiling or floor), and a profit adjustment formula. These elements are all negotiated at the outset.

Fixed-Price Incentive (Successive Targets) Contract—A contract that specifies the following elements, all of which are negotiated at the outset: an initial target cost, an initial target profit, and an initial profit adjustment formula. These targets and formula are used to establish:

- The firm target profit, including a ceiling and floor for the firm target profit;
- The production point at which the firm target cost and firm target profit will be negotiated (usually before delivery or shop completion of the first item); and
- A ceiling price that is the maximum that may be paid to the contractor, except for any adjustment under other contract clauses providing for equitable adjustment or other revision of the contract price under stated circumstances.

Forecasting—An estimate of financial position, results of operations, and changes in cash flows for one or more future periods based on a set of assumptions representing the most probable outcomes. If the assumptions are not necessarily the most likely outcomes, the estimate is called a "projection."

Foreign Military Sales (FMS)—That portion of the U.S. security assistance authorized by the Foreign Assistance Act of 1961, as amended, and the Arms Export Control Act, as amended, where the recipient provides reimbursement for defense articles and services transferred. FMS includes Department of Defense (DOD) cast sales from stocks, DOD guarantees covering financing by private or Federal Financing Bank sources for credit sales of defense articles and defense services, sales financed by appropriated direct credits, and sales funded by grants under the Military Assistance Program.

Formal and Informal Contracts—A "formal" contract is one to which the law gives special effect because of the form used in creating it (e.g., negotiable instruments). An "informal" contract is one for which the law does not require a particular set of formalities.

Forums—The administrative and judicial bodies that adjudicate protests.

Framework Pricing Arrangement—A contract that is definitive in all respects except pricing. The agreement or contract specifies a predetermined index, formula, or algorithm (i.e., the "framework") for the calculation of price at the point of sale.

Fraud—Unethical conduct in the creation of the contract. Such conduct may take place in the offer or acceptance of a contract. Such conduct communicates a promise on the part of one party and a manifestation to the terms of the offer by the other party. Conduct of both parties represents capacity to contract, good faith dealings (honesty in fact and reasonable standard of fair dealing), and legality of purpose. This includes apparent authority: the authority that, although not actually granted, the principal knowingly permitted an agent to exercise or the principal holds the agent out as possessing. Fraud includes such acts or attempts to defraud the government or its agents and acts violating the False Claims Act or the Anti-Kickback Act.

Free-on-Board (FOB)—A term used in conjunction with a physical point to determine the responsibility and basis for payment of freight charges and, unless otherwise agreed, the point at which title for goods passes to the buyer or consignee. FOB includes domestic transportation of goods in the United States, including documentation necessary to govern, direct control of, and provide information about a shipment (includes bill of lading, freight bills, claims, and FOB terms of sale).

Gap Fillers—Interim agreements that define the rights and obligations of the parties and establish the basis for the conduct of business before the establishment of a long-term contractual relationship. Includes memorandums of understanding, letter contracts, teaming agreements, and other short-term agreements.

General and Administrative (G&A)—A subcategory of overhead that includes costs necessary for overall management and operations but which are not directly associated with a specific cost objective or business segment. Typical G&A costs include sales staff salaries, insurance, executive compensation, and central office expenses.

General Business—Portions of other disciplines relevant to contract management.

Generally Accepted Accounting Principles (GAAP)—A term encompassing conventions, rules, and procedures of accounting that are "generally accepted" and have "substantial authoritative support." The GAAP have been developed by agreement on the basis of experience, reason, custom, usage, and, to a certain extent, practical necessity, rather than being derived from a formal set of theories.

Global Issues—A corporate framework for conducting international business, including evaluation of objectives, strengths, and weaknesses, as well as development of strategies for product development and marketing.

Grant—A legal instrument for transferring money, property, or services to the recipient to accomplish a specific purpose of support or stimulation where there is no substantial involvement between the grantor and the recipient during performance.

Historically Underutilized Business Zone (HUBZone)—A historically underutilized business zone or area that is located within one or more qualified census tracts, qualified non-metropolitan counties, or lands within the boundaries of an Indian reservation. "Indian" means any person who is a member of any Indian tribe, band, group, pueblo, or community that is recognized by the U.S. federal government as eligible for services from the Bureau of Indian Affairs in accordance with 25 U.S.C. 1452 and any "Native" as defined in the Alaska Native Claims Settlement Act (43 U.S.C. 1601).

Human Relations—Individual behavior, interpersonal relationships, group behavior, and human problems in the work environment.

Implied, Express, Quasi Contracts—An "implied" contract (sometimes called "implied in fact") is one in which the terms of the contract are wholly or partly inferred from conduct or surrounding circumstance. An "express" contract is one in which the terms of the contract are stated in words, either written or spoken. "Quasi" contracts (sometimes called "implied in law") are obligations imposed by law to prevent the unjust enrichment of one person at another's expense.

Improper Practices—A broad range of activities forbidden or limited by the *Federal Acquisition Regulation* with regard to the award and performance of government contracts.

Incentive Contracts—Contracts that are appropriate when a firm-fixed-price contract is not appropriate, the required supplies or services can be acquired at lower costs, and, in certain instances, when they will improve delivery or technical performance by relating the amount of profit or fee payable under the contract to the contractor's performance. Incentive contracts are designed to obtain specific acquisition objectives by establishing reasonable and attainable targets that are clearly communicated to the contractor and include appropriate incentive arrangements designed to motivate contractor efforts that might not otherwise be emphasized and discourage contractor inefficiency and waste.

INCO Terms—Internationally recognized terms of sale that define responsibilities of both the buyer and the seller in any international transaction, codified into 13 distinct categories.

Indefinite Delivery/Indefinite Quantity (IDIQ) Contract/Governmentwide Acquisition Contract (GWAC)—IDIQ contracts provide for an indefinite quantity within stated limits of supplies or services to be furnished within a fixed period with deliveries or performance to be scheduled by placing orders with the contractor. Examples of these contracts include:

- Delivery order,
- Task order,
- Definite quantity,
- Requirements, and
- Indefinite quantity.

GWACs are governmentwide acquisition contracts available to multiple buyers.

Indefinite Quantity Contract—Provides for an indefinite quantity, within stated limits, of supplies or services during a fixed period. The government places orders for individual requirements. Quantity limits may be stated as number of units or as dollar values.

Indemnification—Protections provided by the parties to each other; also to restore a loss, either in whole or in part, by payment, repair, or replacement. "Indemnification" also refers to contract provisions whereby one party engages to secure another against an anticipated loss resulting from an act or forbearance on the part of one of the parties or some third party.

Independent Research and Development (IR&D)—Effort that is neither sponsored by a grant nor required in performing a contract and that falls within any of the following four areas:

- Basic research,
- Applied research,
- Development, and
- Systems and other concept formulation studies.

Information Management—The applications of information science to the practical aspects of specifying, designing, implementing, and managing information systems.

Information Science—The technical, managerial, and policy issues associated with computer-based information systems in modern organizations.

Information Technology (IT)—The collection of technologies that deal specifically with processing, storing, and communicating information; includes all types of computer and communication systems. It involves those special policies and procedures applicable to the acquisition and use of computers, telecommunications, and related resources.

Inherently Governmental—An activity that is so intimately related to the public interest that it mandates performance by federal employees. Activities that meet these criteria are not in competition with commercial sources, are not generally available from commercial sources, and, therefore, are not subject to the Office of Management and Budget.

Innovative Contracting Methods—Contracting methods focusing on an alternative aspect of cost-effective contract management that ensure total fulfillment of the contract goals. Examples of such innovative contracting methods are warranty flexibility, multi-parameter, and best-value contracting. "Warranty" contracting includes an extended warranty that places responsibility for product performance on the contractor, generating a longer-lasting product and lower overall maintenance costs. In "multi-parameter" contracting, agencies determine contract winners based on the lowest combination of cost, time, and other parameters. "Best-value" contracting focuses on such factors as technical excellence, management capability, past performance, and personnel qualifications and makes tradeoffs for lowest price.

Inspection—The examination (including testing) of supplies and services (including, when appropriate, raw materials, components, and intermediate assemblies) to determine whether the supplies and services conform to the contract requirements.

Insurance Law—Law governing the transfer of risk from one person (either the insured person or the policy owner) to another (the insurer). This transfer of risk is accomplished by a two-party contract called an "insurance policy."

Integrated Project/Product Team (IPT)—A team composed of representatives from appropriate functional disciplines working together to build successful programs, identify and resolve issues, and make sound and timely recommendations to facilitate decision-making. There are three types of IPTs:

- Overarching IPTs (OIPTs), which focus on strategic guidance, program assessment, and issue resolution;
- Working-level IPTs (WIPTs), which identify and resolve program issues, determine program status, and seek opportunities for acquisition reform; and
- Program-level IPTs (PIPTs), which focus on program execution and may include representatives from both government and, after contract award, industry.

Intellectual Property—The kind of property that results from the fruits of mental labor. Intellectual property rights include any or all of the following: patent, trademark, copyright, trade secret, trade name, service mark, and the like.

Intergovernmental Relations—A range of cooperative activities between governments, including various forms of intergovernmental cooperative purchasing, joint or shared use of facilities and supplies, and procurements made by one government from another.

International Contracting—The policies and procedures that govern the acquisition and sale of goods and services with foreign nationals and governments.

International Organization for Standardization (ISO) Standards—The ISO Standards are families of standards consisting of standards and guidelines that relate to management systems and related supporting standards on terminology and specific tools, such as auditing (the process of checking that the management system conforms to the standard).

Invitation for Bids (IFB)—Solicitation used in the sealed-bid method of procurement.

Labor Laws—Policies and procedures for implementing labor laws such as the Davis-Bacon Act, Contract Work Hours and Safety Standards Act, and the Service Contract Act.

Labor Surplus Area—A geographical area identified by the Department of Labor as an area of concentrated unemployment or underemployment or an area of labor surplus.

Labor-Hour Contract—Variation of the time-and-materials contract, differing only in that materials are not supplied by the contractor.

Laws and Regulations—Refers to the statutes and regulations that provide the legal and regulatory framework for the acquisition of goods and services.

Leases—Rental agreements in which the lessor conveys to the lessee the right to use the lessor's personal or real property, usually in exchange for a payment of money.

Letter Contract—A written preliminary contractual instrument that authorizes the contractor to begin immediately manufacturing supplies or performing services.

Liability Costs, Warranty, Service Life, Protection, Risk—Remedies and recourse in resolution of contract performance issues, including limitations of remedies, liquidated damages, limitation of liability, breach, and damages.

Licensing—The sale of a license permitting the use of patents, trademarks, or other technology to another firm. A license also covers a patent, technical or proprietary data, technical assistance, know-how, or any combination of these—granted by a U.S. firm to a foreign firm or government—to produce, co-produce, or sell a defense article or service within a given sales territory. An exclusive license grants this right without competition from any other licensees or from the licensor. For a nonexclusive license, competition may be permitted with other licensees and/or the licensor. Licensing involves the many procedures administrative agencies perform in conjunction with issuance of various types of licenses.

Logistics—Inventory management, transportation and traffic, and distribution supporting the product/service mission of the organization.

Major Systems—A combination of elements that will function together to produce the capabilities required to fulfill a mission need, including hardware, equipment, software, or any combination of these, but excluding construction.

Make-or-Buy Program—That part of a contractor's written plan for the development or production of an end item outlining the subsystems, major components, assemblies, subassemblies, and parts intended to be manufactured, test-treated, or assembled by the seller (make) and those the seller intends to procure from another source (buy).

Management—The art and science of the processes of planning, organizing, directing, and controlling the affairs of the organization.

Market Price—The exchange value of a good or service, calculated with due consideration to market conditions, legal constraints, competitive pressures, and changes in market factors.

Market Research—The process used for collecting and analyzing information about the entire market available to satisfy an agency's needs for the minimum information required to establish the most suitable approach to acquiring, distributing, and supporting supplies and services.

Market Strategy—The action plan of how a company will sell its services or products. The strategy must consider the company's business environment, its abilities and competencies, the desires of top management, and overall mission objectives. Market strategy consists of four basic concepts:

- Market segmentation,
- Market positioning,
- Market entry, and
- Marketing mix.

Marketing—Activities that direct the flow of goods and services from the producer to the consumers.

Master Agreements—Business arrangements in which the parties determine the underlying commercial arrangement governing the relationship (e.g., terms and conditions) but defer specific negotiation of elements of the contract to specific events or transactions (e.g., price).

Modes of Transportation—Means of moving freight traffic utilizing transportation methods such as bills of lading, parcel post, bus service, air cargo, rail freight, carload and less than carload, motor freight, freight forwarder, and pipeline.

Modular Contracts—Use of one or more contracts to acquire information technology systems in successive, interoperable increments.

Multiple-Incentive Contracts—Such contracts should motivate the contractor to strive for outstanding results in all incentive areas and compel tradeoff decisions among the incentive areas consistent with the government's overall objectives for the acquisition.

NCMA CMBOK—The "Contract Management Body of Knowledge" (CMBOK). A definitive description of the elements making up the body of professional knowledge that applies to contract management.

Negotiation—The process of entering into or modifying a contract to the mutual agreement of the parties to the contract.

Negotiations—A method of contracting that uses either competitive or other-than-competitive proposals and (usually) discussions. It is a flexible process that includes the receipt of proposals from offerors, permits bargaining, and usually affords offerors an opportunity to revise their offers before award of a contract. Contract negotiations may be conducted formally or informally and may involve many people or just two—a representative for the buyer and a representative for the seller. Contract negotiation may take a few minutes or may involve lengthy discussions.

Negotiation Objectives—Determining the issues to be negotiated and the minimum and maximum positions for each issue. Includes both "win-lose" and "win-win" strategies and all tactics and counter-tactics necessary to achieve the desired result.

Network Systems—Computer equipment or interconnected systems or subsystems of equipment used in the automatic acquisition, storage, manipulation, management, movement, control, display, switching interchange, transmission, or reception of data or information. These systems include computers, servers, ancillary equipment, software, and related services. They are systems that transmit any combination of voice, video, and/or data between users. The network includes the network operating system in the client and server machines, the cables connecting them, and all the supporting hardware in between, such as bridges, routers, and switches. In wireless systems, antennas and towers are also part of the network. In general, the network is a collection of terminals, computers, servers, and components that function in relation to each other to allow for the easy flow of data and use of resources among the interrelated entities.

Non-Disclosure Agreement—A legally binding document setting forth the conditions under which proprietary information is offered and received between the parties.

OMB Circular A-76—Establishes federal policy regarding the performance of commercial activities. It implements the statutory requirements of the Federal Activities Inventory Reform Act of 1998 (*Public Law* 105-270).

Operations Management—The concepts, techniques, and practices used in managing the operations of an organization.

Organization—The administrative and personnel structure of a business or government that reflects the organizational patterns, procurement authority, and scope of activities or its various elements. It may include boards, commissions, or committees and may reflect a delegation's exemptions, as well as full or limited authority to act.

Organizational Behavior—Human behavior as it influences organizational efficiency and effectiveness.

Organizational Communication—Focuses on the processes of communication ranging from that between two persons to that of the total organization.

Organizational/Industrial Marketing—Activities of marketing directed toward organizations rather than individual consumers and includes research, product planning and development, distribution, promotion, and pricing.

Other Types—Miscellaneous contracts that use a form of pricing arrangement (such as time-and-materials, labor-hour, and letter contracts) or are described by the terms governing ordering (indefinite-delivery contracts).

Outsourcing—A version of the make-or-buy decision, commonly used for services, in which a firm elects to purchase an item/service that was previously made/performed in-house. It is also a specialized form of consulting. When a client elects to outsource, the client generally turns a specific task over to a consultant. In the computer industry, this task might be to run a data center. The client is concerned with "what" is outsourced (in this example, running a data center). The client is typically not concerned with "how" the operation occurs. The client is hiring the consultant to provide this service based on the consultant's expertise in the process, people, and technology to perform the outsourced task. This type of service is normally contracted for on a fixed-fee basis in which the client pays a flat fee per month for a given service. Therefore, the vast majority of the financial risk is shifted from the client to the consultant. If the consultant can effectively and efficiently provide the service, the consultant will realize a profit. Conversely, if the consultant is either ineffective or inefficient, the consultant still has to deliver the contracted deliverable for service; however, the consultant will be doing so at the consultant's loss.

Outsourcing of Contract Management—Contract administration and other business processes through long-term agreements; includes business process outsourcing of functional responsibilities for human resources, finance and accounting, procurement, and information technology.

Overhead—Indirect costs other than those related to general and administrative expense and selling expenses; a general term often used to identify an indirect cost, production, or sale of identifiable goods or services.

Ownership, Royalties, Escrow Agreement—Legal title or right to something. Mere possession is not ownership. With ownership comes the potential of royalties for use. These include royalties and rights delegated (as to an individual or corporation) by a sovereign party, including a share of the profit or product reserved by the grantor. They also include payments made to an author or composer for each copy of a work sold or to an inventor for each article sold under a patent. An owner may also escrow assets, creating an instrument and especially a deed of money or property held by a third party to be turned over to the grantee and become effective only upon the fulfillment of some condition; a fund or deposit designed to serve as an escrow. Includes source code escrow agreements, which allow the licensee to obtain access to the software's source code under certain circumstances, as when the licensor goes out of business or fails to make required modifications to the software.

Past Performance—Evaluating how well offerors performed in the past in the performance of similar contracts.

Patents—A government grant of exclusive rights to an inventor that prohibits others from making, using, or selling an invention.

Payments—The amount payable under the contract, supporting data required to be submitted with invoices, and other payment terms such as time for payment and retention. Includes consideration, exchanges, compromise, and release of claims, part-payment, and forbearance.

Performance-Based Contract—A contract that is structured around the purpose of the work to be performed as opposed to either the manner in which the work is to be performed or a broad statement of work.

Performance Incentives—May be considered in connection with specific product characteristics (e.g., a missile range, an aircraft speed, an engine thrust, or a vehicle maneuverability) or other specific elements of the contractor's performance. These incentives should be designed to relate profit or fee to results achieved by the contractor compared with specified targets.

Personal Services—A contact that by its express terms or as administered, makes the contractor personnel appear, in effect, as government employees.

Physical Completion—When the contractor has completed required deliveries and/or performed all services, all options have expired, or the contractor has given a notice that the contract has been terminated.

Point of Sale Transactions—Business arrangements in which the entire business arrangement between the parties is executed in a single event.

Pre-Award Process: Buyer—Process by which buyers develop a comprehensive plan for fulfilling requirements for products or services in a timely manner at a reasonable price; includes developing an overall strategy for the purchase, which is accomplished through market research, strategy development, initiating the procurement, and selecting a supplier.

Pre-Award Process: Seller—Process by which sellers develop and execute a strategy for obtaining the award of a contract, including market strategies, pricing strategies, and responding to the procurement.

Pre-Award Surveys—An evaluation of a prospective contractor's ability to perform a specific contract, performed by the contract administration office or the purchasing office, with assistance from an audit organization, at the request of either office. The evaluation addresses the physical, technical, managerial, and financial capability of the prospective contractor. The adequacy of the contractor's systems and procedures and past performance record are also addressed.

Prequalification—The buyer's announcement of interest, including criteria for selecting proposals and soliciting the participation of all offerors capable of meeting requirements.

Pricing—Concerned with strategies for pricing products such as market-based pricing or cost-based pricing.

Principles—The explanation of the methods and operation of the processes of management.

Privity of Contract—The legal relationship between two parties to the same contract. The buyer has "privity of contract" with the prime contractor. Therefore, the buyer's relationship with subcontractors is indirect in nature.

Process and Results Management—Joint buyer-seller actions taken to successfully perform and administer a contractual agreement, including effective change management and timely contract closeout. It also includes maintaining open and effective communication, timely delivery of quality products and services, responsive corrective actions to problems, compliance with all agreed-on terms, and management of conditions and effective changes.

Procurement—Acquiring the goods and services supporting the missions of the organization, including the development and maintenance of relationships with suppliers and internal customers.

Production Planning and Control—Coordination of product supply with product demand. The manufacturer must forecast customer demand and provide the finished product supply either from available inventory or by producing additional product.

Product/Service Planning—Defining the product or service that satisfies the needs of clients and customers.

Program Management—The process whereby a single leader and team are responsible for planning, organizing, coordinating, directing, and controlling the combined efforts of participating and assigned personnel and organizations in accomplishment of program objectives. This special management approach provides centralized authority and responsibility for the management of a specific program.

Program Manager-Contracting Officer Relationship—The authority and responsibility of the program manager, who is in charge of executing the program, and the contracting officer, who has a fiduciary responsibility to ensure that all laws and regulations are complied with before signing the contract, requires a close working relationship.

Programming—The data structures and algorithms applied in programming solutions to problems.

Promotion—Publicizing the attributes of the product/service through media and personal contacts and presentations (e.g., technical articles/presentations, news releases, advertising, and sales calls).

Property Administration—The processes used by prime contractors to account for and manage all property, both real and personal. It includes facilities, material, special tooling, special test equipment, and agency-peculiar property.

Property Control System—Procedures that meet the requirements of government property clauses to control, protect, and maintain all government property.

Proposal Preparation—Activities and events required to submit an offer or quotation, usually in response to a customer request.

Protests—A written objection by an interested party to:

- A solicitation or other request by an agency for offers for a contract for the procurement of property or services,
- The cancellation of the solicitation or other request,
- An award or proposed award of the contract, or
- A termination or cancellation of an award of the contract if the written objection contains an allegation that the termination or cancellation is based in whole or in part on improprieties concerning the award of the contract.

Research and Development Contract—A contract for basic research (directed toward improving or expanding new scientific discoveries, technologies, materials, processes, or techniques), or development (directed production of, or improvements in, useful products to meet specific performance requirements through the systematic application of scientific knowledge).

Records and Reports—Procedures to maintain official records of government property and periodic reports required in accordance with contract clauses.

Records Retention—After contract closeout is completed, *Federal Acquisition Regulation* 4.805 establishes retention periods for contract files. The record retention requirements apply to both prime contracts and subcontracts. Contractors must make books, records, documents, and other supporting evidence available to the comptroller general and contracting agencies for a certain period after final payment. The calculation of a retention period starts at the end of the contractor's fiscal year in which an entry is made that charges a cost to a government contract.

Relationship Management—Actions of the contracting parties to mutually resolve disagreements about the correct interpretation of terms and conditions without recourse to litigations or arbitration.

Reporting—Contractually required reports provided by the seller during contract fulfillment to observe performance, collect information, and measure actual contract achievement.

Request for Information (RFI)—Tool used for gathering information from independent vendors for the purpose of determining availability of products and services and gathering market information on capabilities to perform.

Request for Proposals (RFP)—Solicitation document used in other-than-sealed-bid procurements. RFPs are used in negotiated procurements to communicate government requirements to prospective contractors and to solicit proposals from them.

Request for Quotations (RFQ)—Solicitation document used in other-than-sealed-bids procurements. Because an RFQ is merely a request for information, quotes submitted in response to it are not offers and consequently may not be accepted by the government to form a binding contract.

Request for Technical Proposals (RFTP)—A solicitation document used in two-step sealed bidding. Normally in letter form, it asks only for technical information; price and cost breakdowns are forbidden. It also asks for technical information only; price and cost breakdowns are either budgetary or omitted at the RFTP stage. It is used to pre-qualify bidders.

Requirements Contract—A contract that provides for filling all actual purchase requirements of designated government activities for supplies or services during a specified contract period, with deliveries or performance to be scheduled by placing orders with the contractor.

Research and Development (R&D)—Effort that constitutes research, development, or both.

Revenue Recognition—The process of formally recording or incorporating a revenue item in the accounts and financial statements of an entity. The revenue recognition principle provides that revenue is recognized when it is realized or realizable and it is earned. Revenues are realized when goods and services are exchanged for cash or claims to cash (receivables). Revenues are realizable when assets received in exchange are readily convertible to known amounts of cash or claims to cash. Revenues are earned when the entity has substantially accomplished what it must do to be entitled to the benefits represented by the revenues; that is, when the earnings process is complete or virtually complete.

Risk Analysis—Management of factors that create the possibility of loss or injury in the performance of a contract; includes all activities necessary to identify, analyze, plan, track, or control risk management activities. It also includes communication of risks and risk management internally and externally.

Risk Management—The process for identification, analysis, and treatment of loss exposure, as well as the administration of techniques to accomplish the goal of minimizing potential financial loss from such exposure. The methodical process used to enhance opportunities and reduce risks by identifying potential opportunities and risks, assessing associated probabilities of occurrence and impacts, and determining courses of action.

Royalties—Any costs or charges in the nature of royalties, license fees, patent or license amortization costs, or the like that are paid for the use of or for rights in patents and patent applications in connection with performing a contract or subcontract.

Sales Contracts—Business arrangements in which all elements of the transaction are determined and defined between the parties at the time of contract formation, including mutual assent, exchange of consideration, capacity to contract, and legal purpose.

Sealed Bidding—A method involving the unrestricted solicitation of bids, a public opening, and award of a contract to the lowest responsive and responsible bidder.

Seat Management (SEAT)—A customer-selected set of desktop and networking functions that may include contractor-provided personal computers and network hardware, desktop and network software, the management of the hardware and software assets, help desk, training, and the maintenance of the hardware and software. SEAT is an integrated approach to delivering end-user computing services under a single offering. It is a method of coordinating all of the workstations in an enterprise network and includes the installation, operation, and maintenance of hardware and software at each workstation. It offers desktop computers, servers, peripherals, networking, and support services for general purpose and scientific and engineering environments. SEAT is typically provided on a fixed monthly fee per user, or "per seat," basis for the equipment and services selected. A "seat" is a workstation or terminal that can be operated by one user at a time. The service also creates efficiencies and mitigates risk through standardization and unification of procedures.

Service Contracts—Contracts that directly engage the time and effort of a contractor whose primary purpose is to perform an identifiable task rather than furnish an end item of supply.

Shop Rights—The right of an employer to use, without payment of royalties, an invention conceived by an employee in the course of employment or through the use of the employer's facilities, the employee not having been hired to perform such work.

Simplified Acquisitions—Methods for entering into contracts without elaborate and formal solicitation techniques (i.e., invitation for bids and request for proposals) that are restricted to purchases under a low dollar threshold.

Single-Source Negotiation—A negotiation with a single provider, because either the provider is the sole supplier of the product or service or the relationship with the provider is of strategic importance, based on long-term relationships, and built on mutual trust.

Small and Disadvantaged Business Concerns—A small business that is owned (at least 51 percent) by members of socially and economically disadvantaged groups (i.e., groups that have been subjected to racial or ethnic prejudice or cultural bias).

Small Business—A business that is independently owned and operated, and is not dominant in its field; a business concern meeting government size standards for its particular industry type.

Small Business Innovation Research (SBIR) Program—The SBIR Program is a highly competitive three-phase award system that provides qualified small business concerns with opportunities to propose innovative ideas that meet the specific research and development needs of the federal government. Federal agencies that have research and development budgets in excess of $100 million must set aside a fixed percentage of their budgets strictly for small businesses.

Socioeconomic Programs—Programs designed to benefit particular groups. They represent a multitude of program interests and objectives unrelated to procurement objectives. Some examples of these are preferences for small business and for American products, required sources for specific items, and minimum labor pay levels mandated for contractors.

Sole-Source Negotiations—The process for entering into or modifying a contract after soliciting and negotiating with only one source.

Source Selection—The process wherein the requirements, facts, recommendations, and policies relevant to an award decision in a competitive procurement of a system/project are examined and the decision made.

Source Selection Board/Team—Any board, team, council, or other group that evaluates bids or proposals for the purpose of selecting a contract/contractor. It is also a multidisciplinary team responsible for evaluating offers and identifying the most advantageous offer through proposal evaluation, to include an assessment of both the proposal and the offeror's ability to successfully accomplish the prospective contract.

Source Selection Plan—The document that describes the selection criteria, process, and organization to be used in evaluating proposals for competitively awarded contracts.

Specialized Knowledge Areas—Additional professional skills that are necessary for contract managers to either perform efficiently and effectively in a specific industry or work environment (e.g., construction) or interact productively with other specialized professionals (e.g., finance).

Specialized, Long Lead Items—Lead time management of critical materials and deliverables. Procurement lead time starts when a material requirement is identified and spans the time until a significant portion of the material is delivered. Procurement lead time has two components: 1) administrative lead time and 2) production lead time. Administrative lead time begins with the identification of a material requirement and continues until a contract is awarded for the creation of the material. Production lead time is the time from contract award until material delivery. Lead time risk, therefore, is the program impact associated with the failure of material to arrive when required.

Specifications—A description of the technical requirements for a material, product, or service that includes the criteria for determining whether the requirements have been met. As used in the law relating to patents, for manufacturing, and contracting contracts, these are a particular order or detailed statement, account description, or listing of various events.

Standards of Conduct—Refers to the ethical conduct of personnel involved in the acquisition of goods and services. Within the federal government, business shall be conducted in a manner above reproach and, except as authorized by law or regulation, with complete impartiality and without preferential treatment. They refer to the ethical conduct of personnel involved in the purchase or sale of goods and services. They include personal conduct and also compliance with laws, regulations, and corporate standards.

State and Local Government—The policies and procedures that govern the acquisition and sale of goods and services at the state and local government levels.

State Differences and Jurisdictional Issues—Differences and distinctions between state laws and factors in determining appropriate law and regulation governing business dealings, including law of the forum, conflicts of laws, domicile, and center of gravity.

Statement of Work (SOW)—That portion of a contract describing the actual work to be done by means of specifications or other minimum requirements, quantities, performance or delivery date, and a statement of the requisite quality. The SOW defines the scope of the overall contract in the case of task order contracts.

Statistics—Tools that include descriptive statistics, probability theory, probability and sampling distribution, inference estimation, and hypothesis testing.

Stop-Work Order—Under a negotiated fixed-price supply, cost-reimbursement supply, research and development, or service contract, a "stop-work order" is a contract clause that permits the contracting officer to order the contractor to stop work if a work stoppage is required for reasons such as state-of-the-art advancements, production or engineering breakthroughs, or realignment of programs. It includes instruction served on the seller by the buyer requiring that the seller cease to perform the contract and take alternative steps to limit the risk and liabilities of the parties. This is usually governed by predetermined protocols set forth in the contract. In the event of such termination, the contractor must immediately stop all work and immediately cause any and all of its suppliers and subcontractors to stop all work.

Strategy and Tactics—Specific methods used during negotiations to reach agreement.

Subcontract Management—A concept that addresses subcontracting issues and the buyer's role in ensuring successful prime contractor interaction with subcontractors in order to satisfy prime contract requirements.

Supplemental Agreements—Contract modifications that are accomplished by the mutual consent of the parties.

Supplier Goods, Services—Management of any contract, agreement, or purchase order (and any preliminary contractual instrument other than a prime contract) calling for the performance of any work or the making or furnishing of any material required for the performance of a prime contract; includes managing the purchase of supplies that are consumed in use or become incorporated in other property, thus losing their identity.

Supply Chain—Sum total of all functions, operations, and facilities that are involved in the procurement and delivery of goods to a customer; includes manufacturers, warehouses, transportation, distribution centers, retail outlets, and inventory at stages from raw materials to finished package that flows between and among facilities.

Supply Chain Function—Management of the flow and storage of materials (raw materials, semi-finished goods, and finished products) from vendor sources through to the ultimate customer. It includes both inbound logistics (materials management and procurement) and outbound logistics (customer service and channels of distribution).

Supply Chain Management—Management of flows between and among all stages and facilities in a supply chain to maximize profitability.

System Acquisition Process (Life Cycle)—The sequence of acquisition activities—starting with the agency's reconciliation of its mission needs with its capabilities, priorities, and resources—and extending through the introduction of a system into operational use or the otherwise successful achievement of program objectives.

Systems and Processes—The arrangement of things so connected or related to form a whole, generally involving a number of steps or operations.

Task Order Contract—A services contract that does not procure or specify a firm quantity of services (other than a minimum or maximum quantity) and that provides for the issuance of orders for the performance of tasks during the period of the contract.

Teaming—Agreement among two or more prospective offerors to participate jointly in a business venture.

Technical/Management Proposal—That part of the offer that describes the seller's approach to meeting the buyer's requirement.

Telecommunications—Equipment used for such modes of transmission as telephone, data, facsimile, video, radio, and audio, and such corollary items as switches, wire, cable, access arrangements, and communications security facilities and related services. It is also the branch of electrical engineering concerned with the technology of electronic communication at a distance. It includes systems of hardware and software used to carry voice, video, and/or data; includes telephone wires, satellite signals, cellular links, coaxial cables, and related devices.

Time-and-Materials (T&M) Contract—A contract that provides for acquiring supplies or services on the basis of specified fixed hourly rates that include wages, overhead, general and administrative expenses, profit, and materials cost, including, if appropriate, material handling costs as part of material costs. T&M contracts are also a common way to pay for consulting services. When using this method of calculating payment, the consultant is paid for any time he or she devotes to the needs of a client. The consultant is typically paid for each hour he or she logs to a client's project. In addition, the consultant is generally paid for any expenses he or she incurs on behalf of the client (e.g., travel, engagement-specific tools or materials, copy services, etc.). All of the aforementioned items may either be limited or expanded (e.g., authorization of air travel in first class versus coach) by the specific contract entered into between the consultant and the client. This form of consulting places virtually all the risk on the client (as opposed to the consultant). That is to say, the client typically has a budget for a specific task. The client is betting that the consultant can complete the assigned work within that budget. However, the consultant is typically under no such obligation, and the bill for the consultant's time may well exceed the client's projected budget.

Trade—Law in the United States, including the Robinson-Patman Act, unfair-trade laws, fair-trade laws, and other legal and regulatory restrictions on the conduct of business, especially with respect to pricing.

Trade Secrets—Any information, process, or procedure used in business that may give the owner some advantage over its competitors.

Trademark—Distinctive mark of authenticity. It includes words, symbols, devices, or designs affixed to or placed on an article or its container to identify an article offered for sale. It also includes "service marks," which designate particular manners or modes of service delivery protected as intellectual property.

Transportation—Applying transportation and traffic management considerations in the acquisition of supplies and acquiring transportation-related services.

Transportation-Related Services—Procedures for the acquisition of related services such as stevedoring, storage, packing, marking, and ocean freight forwarding.

Two-Step Sealed Bidding—A combination of competitive procedures designed to obtain the benefits of sealed bidding when adequate specifications are not available. Step one consists of the request for the submission of technical proposals, evaluation, and discussion without pricing. Step two involves the submission of sealed-priced bids by those who submitted acceptable technical proposals in step one.

Uniform Commercial Code (UCC)—Uniform law governing commercial transactions, developed by the National Conference of Commissioners on Uniform State Laws and the American Law Institute, which has been adopted by all states in the United States except Louisiana, and is sometimes used to aid in the interpretation and enforcement of government subcontracts.

Unilateral and Bilateral Contracts—A "unilateral contract" is one in which only one party (promissor) makes a promise; in contrast, a "bilateral contract" is one in which both parties make promises.

Unilateral/Nonperformance—Termination of a contract by one of the parties. Right to terminate, notice required, and procedures for termination are typically specified in the contract. Most commonly, this is available as a remedy for nonperformance by the seller or failure to pay by the buyer.

Unsolicited Proposal—A research or developmental proposal that is made by a prospective contractor without prior formal or informal solicitation from a purchasing activity.

U.S. Securities and Exchange Commission (SEC)—The SEC regulates securities markets. The SEC requires public companies to disclose meaningful financial and other information to the public, which provides a common pool of knowledge for all investors. The SEC also oversees other key participants in the securities world, including stock exchanges, broker-dealers, investment advisors, mutual funds, and public utility holding companies. The SEC is concerned primarily with promoting disclosure of important information, enforcing the securities laws, and protecting investors who interact with these various organizations and individuals. As a regulatory agency, the SEC frequently exercises its enforcement authority. Each year the SEC brings between 400 and 500 civil enforcement actions against individuals and companies that break the securities laws. Typical infractions include insider trading, accounting fraud, and providing false or misleading information about securities and the companies that issue them.

Use of Trade/Course of Dealing—Any practice or method of dealing having such regularity of observance in a place, vocation, or trade as to justify an expectation that it will be observed with respect to the transaction in question; a pattern of prior business transactions that can establish a background for the interpretation of the immediate transaction.

Warranty—A promise or affirmation given by a seller to a buyer regarding the nature, usefulness, or condition of the supplies or performance of services furnished under the contract. Generally, a warranty's purpose is to delineate the rights and obligations for defective items and services, and to foster quality performance.

Woman-Owned, Native American–Owned, Veteran-Owned Business—A firm that is at least 51-percent owned by a woman, Native American, or veteran. In the case of a publicly owned business, at least 51 percent of the stock must be controlled by a woman, Native American, or veteran, and its management and daily business must be controlled by one or more women, Native Americans, or veterans.

Working Capital—The excess of current assets over current liabilities that represents a company's financial liquid resources to meet demands of the operating cycle.

NCMA Certification Exams

chapter five

In conjunction with the CMBOK updates, NCMA is developing certification examinations to ensure they are reflective of actual practice. The current examination format consists of multiple-choice questions.

Many people assume multiple-choice questions are easy to answer because they have had experience with tests that are not psychometrically sound. This means that every test question has undergone the full rigor of educational and statistical testing necessary to ensure that it elicits the exact response desired, that it is unambiguous, and that it has only one correct answer. However, three other plausible possible answers will separate those who know and understand the material from those who don't. Furthermore, multiple-choice testing can test more than simple recall of facts and recognition of words. It can test for understanding of content and for responses that indicate application of principles to a situation.

The benefits of multiple-choice examination lie in the objective assessment of question answers. There is no scope for alternative interpretation of results. That is not to say that every question is perfect. Rather, the multiple-choice format has the flexibility that allows NCMA, working in conjunction with psychometricians, or test developers, to change the examination and make every question a fair, valid, and reliable one.

Using a computer-based multiple-choice examination allows NCMA to provide candidates with their results before they leave the testing site, improving immeasurably on the four-month wait for results that Certified Professional Contract Manager (CPCM) candidates used to have to endure. In addition, multiple-choice questions allow for a wider sampling of the body of knowledge. On the one hand, this means that candidates are bound to find areas with which they are familiar. On the other hand, it means that candidates may be unsure exactly where to concentrate their study. However, candidates should feel confident that the examination will ask only those questions that determine whether a contract manager has the knowledge to be a good practitioner. NCMA will not be testing on extraneous or trivial matters.

The computer has hastened the acceptance of multiple-choice examinations. Familiarity with this style of testing begins as early as elementary school. Because the future contract management community is in the hands of the demographic strata of the population that has either grown up with or grown familiar with computers, this style of testing will gain even wider acceptance. Furthermore, because multiple-choice examinations lend themselves to computer delivery, test developers can readily discern trends and make judgments about the examination or the underlying practice. In either case, the examination can be changed to correct or reflect the practice.

An examination delivered via computer can be delivered to many more people than can an examination that is graded by hand and by volunteer experts. In the latter case, the population can avail itself of an examination opportunity that is constrained by limited resources. With computers, examinations can be delivered and scored continuously, with the limiting factor being the number of computers to which the exam is delivered. The new program, while unable to offer worldwide 24-7 testing opportunities, will vastly increase the capacity of the program. This will allow NCMA to bring the Certification Program to those outside the membership community who may not previously have been aware of the program. This expansion will increase the influence of NCMA, increase the testing pool, and improve the chance that changes to the practice will be readily noticed. And, thus, it will change the examinations to reflect the practice, which will increase the validity, reliability, and influence of the program.

Using the results of the testing program, NCMA will be better positioned to provide its membership, and the entire contract management community, with the education and information they need almost as soon as they need it.

The Anatomy of a Multiple-Choice Question

A multiple-choice question has its own terminology. The question itself is called the "stem." The stem should contain all the information needed to provide the correct answer. The stem should be phrased in clear, unambiguous language that will leave no doubt as to what is being asked. A knowledgeable candidate should be able to discern the correct answer upon reading only the stem.

The answers also have specific terminology. The correct answer is the "key," and the other possible answers are the "distracters." The key is the only correct answer; plausible answers only to those who don't know the correct answer.

How to Study

Given that the examinations sample a wider slice of the body of knowledge, how should a candidate prepare? First of all, candidates should relax. Examinations do not include "everything but the kitchen sink." Rather, the examinations will reflect the sum of the eligibility requirements and current contract management practice.

Self-assessment is the first step to a study program. Does the candidate work well in a group or alone? Given the CMBOK, are there areas about which the candidate has little or no knowledge? Are there areas that the candidate is confident enough to teach others? In a review program, the areas where the candidate is confident would be areas of less intense concentration.

Even working alone, it is good to have a study plan. For example, candidates might plan to study one hour on a weekend for the next eight weeks, or three hours per week for the next six weeks. Even as little as half an hour of study can help candidates gain knowledge and increase comprehension.

An alternative study method would be to join a group—for example, a group of office colleagues or a study group at the chapter level. NCMA chapters have provided study groups to hundreds of examination candidates. Study groups successfully allow for multiple points of view, as well as for sharing information and resources. Furthermore, chapter study group sessions are often led by experts in the field. In terms of time spent, expert information beats informed research almost any day. Candidates may contact their local chapters for study group information. Chapters may be accessed through the NCMA website by clicking on the "Membership" button and selecting "Chapter Information" from the menu list.

Test Specifications for Certification Examination

Certification candidates must take and pass examinations consisting of multiple-choice questions. The distribution of certification examination questions is explained below. The NCMA Certification and Accreditation Board developed this distribution with the aid of a team of psychometricians and from the results of the body of knowledge revision. This includes research, the input of subject matter experts, and the results of surveys.

The answers to the questions in the examination are based on common terms and concepts found in publications, including this guide, readily available and normally found in public libraries, websites, or through NCMA.

When constructing an exam, the number of items or questions devoted to a task or topic is determined by the relative importance of a task or topic.

How to Approach the Certification Examinations

For the mental side of examinations, here are a few good test-taking techniques:

- Relax. The examination is based on your profession.

- Read the questions carefully, answering those you can easily and quickly answer. It is usually a good idea to go with your first impression when answering a question; second-guessing can cause you to change a correct answer to an incorrect one.

- Skip over or flag questions that appear too difficult and return to them later.

- Don't stop. Keep going. Keep reading questions until you find one you can answer. The questions you've read will be in the back of your mind; when you return to them, you'll have a fresh perspective. Avoid overanalyzing and second-guessing the question. Choose the correct answer for the question as it is written. Do not make assumptions about what the question means. Don't regard questions as being "trick questions" or concentrate on the exceptions to normal practice.

- Keep an eye on the clock. Judge the time you have so you don't spend a lot of time puzzling over one question to the detriment of being able to answer several others. Flag questions you are having trouble with and move on.

- Don't try to "game" the system by choosing answers to ensure that an equal number of As, Bs, Cs and so on are selected. In the long run (over a lifetime), this may be a good technique, but in the short run (for one examination) the statistical underpinning for this myth has not been proven.

- Try to answer the question in your mind before you read the choices. Good test questions are constructed to allow the knowledgeable examination candidate to do this.

- If you can't readily identify the correct answer, make an educated guess. Eliminate the choices you know to be false and select from those remaining.
- Look over your answers, if time permits. However, avoid trying to second-guess your answers.
- Don't worry about the examination. You may feel wrung out and exhausted at the end of the exam, but that is not an indication of how well or how poorly you may have performed.

Lifetime Certification

For those currently certified individuals who have been continuously certified for a period of at least 20 years, or who reach the age of 60 during their recertification period, a "Lifetime Certification" is available. Applicants for Lifetime Certification based on age alone must submit verification of age in addition to their application and application processing fee.

Once awarded Lifetime Certification, the designee is no longer required to meet the five-year recertification requirements. This improvement allows those who maintain their certification over a 20-year period to apply for Lifetime Certification regardless of age.

appendices

Uniform Commercial Code—Article 1

Part 1. General Provisions

- § 1-101. Short Titles.
- § 1-102. Scope of Article.
- § 1-103. Construction of [Uniform Commercial Code] to Promote its Purposes and Policies: Applicability of Supplemental Principles of Law.
- § 1-104. Construction Against Implied Repeal.
- § 1-105. Severability.
- § 1-106. Use of Singular and Plural; Gender.
- § 1-107. Section Captions.
- § 1-108. Relation to Electronic Signatures in Global and National Commerce Act.

Part 2. General Definitions and Principles of Interpretation

- § 1-201. General Definitions.
- § 1-202. Notice; Knowledge.
- § 1-203. Lease Distinguished from Security Interest.
- § 1-204. Value.
- § 1-205. Reasonable Time; Seasonableness.
- § 1-206. Presumptions.

Part 3. Territorial Applicability and General Rules

- § 1-301. Territorial Applicability; Parties' Power to Choose Applicable Law.
- § 1-302. Variation by Agreement.
- § 1-303. Course of Performance, Course of Dealing, and Usage of Trade.
- § 1-304. Obligation of Good Faith.
- § 1-305. Remedies to be Liberally Administered.
- § 1-306. Waiver or Renunciation of Claim or Right After Breach.
- § 1-307. Prima Facie Evidence by Third-Party Documents.
- § 1-308. Performance or Acceptance Under Reservation of Rights.
- § 1-309. Option to Accelerate at Will.
- § 1-310. Subordinated Obligations.

Uniform Commercial Code—Article 2

Part 1. Short Title, General Construction, and Subject Matter

- § 2-101. Short Title.
- § 2-102. Scope; Certain Security and Other Transactions Excluded From This Article.
- § 2-103. Definitions and Index of Definitions.
- § 2-104. Definitions: "Merchant"; "Between Merchants"; "Financing Agency."
- § 2-105. Definitions: "Transferability"; "Goods"; "Future" Goods; "Lot"; "Commercial Unit."
- § 2-106. Definitions: "Contract"; "Agreement"; "Contract for Sale"; "Sale"; "Present Sale"; "Conforming" to Contract; "Termination"; "Cancellation."
- § 2-107. Goods to Be Severed From Realty: Recording.

Part 2. Form, Formation, and Readjustment of Contract

- § 2-201. Formal Requirements; Statute of Frauds.
- § 2-202. Final Written Expression: Parol or Extrinsic Evidence.
- § 2-203. Seals Inoperative.
- § 2-204. Formation in General.
- § 2-205. Firm Offers.
- § 2-206. Offer and Acceptance in Formation of Contract.
- § 2-207. Additional Terms in Acceptance or Confirmation.
- § 2-209. Modification, Rescission, and Waiver.
- § 2-210. Delegation of Performance; Assignment of Rights.

Part 3. General Obligation and Construction of Contract

- § 2-301. General Obligations of Parties.
- § 2-302. Unconscionable Contract or Clause.
- § 2-303. Allocation or Division of Risks.
- § 2-304. Price Payable in Money, Goods, Realty, or Otherwise.

- § 2-305. Open Price Term.
- § 2-306. Output, Requirements, and Exclusive Dealings.
- § 2-307. Delivery in Single Lot or Several Lots.
- § 2-308. Absence of Specified Place for Delivery.
- § 2-309. Absence of Specific Time Provisions; Notice of Termination.
- § 2-310. Open Time for Payment or Running of Credit; Authority to Ship Under Reservation.
- § 2-311. Options and Cooperation Respecting Performance.
- § 2-312. Warranty of Title and Against Infringement; Buyer's Obligation Against Infringement.
- § 2-313. Express Warranties by Affirmation, Promise, Description, Sample.
- § 2-313A. Obligation to Remote Purchaser Created by Record Packaged With or Accompanying Goods.
- § 2-313B. Obligation to Remote Purchaser Created by Communication to the Public.
- § 2-314. Implied Warranty: Merchantability; Usage of Trade.
- § 2-315. Implied Warranty: Fitness for Particular Purpose.
- § 2-316. Exclusion or Modification of Warranties.
- § 2-317. Cumulation and Conflict of Warranties Express or Implied.
- § 2-318. Third-Party Beneficiaries of Warranties Express or Implied.
- § 2-319. F.O.B. and F.A.S. Terms.
- § 2-320. C.I.F. and C. & F. Terms.
- § 2-321. C.I.F. or C. & F.: "Net Landed Weights"; "Payment on Arrival"; Warranty of Condition on Arrival.
- § 2-322. Delivery "Ex-Ship."
- § 2-323. Form of Bill of Lading Required in Overseas Shipment; "Overseas."
- § 2-324. "No Arrival, No Sale" Term.
- § 2-325. "Letter of Credit" Term; "Confirmed Credit."
- § 2-326. Sale on Approval and Sale or Return; Consignment Sales and Rights of Creditors.
- § 2-327. Special Incidents of Sale on Approval and Sale or Return.
- § 2-328. Sale by Auction.

Part 4. Title, Creditors, and Good Faith Purchasers

- § 2-401. Passing of Title; Reservation for Security; Limited Application of This Section.
- § 2-402. Rights of Seller's Creditors Against Sold Goods.
- § 2-403. Power to Transfer; Good Faith Purchase of Goods; "Entrusting."

Part 5. Performance

- § 2-501. Insurable Interest in Goods; Manner of Identification of Goods.
- § 2-502. Buyer's Right to Goods on Seller's Repudiation, Failure to Deliver or Insolvency.
- § 2-503. Manner of Seller's Tender of Delivery.
- § 2-504. Shipment by Seller.
- § 2-505. Seller's Shipment Under Reservation.
- § 2-506. Rights of Financing Agency.
- § 2-507. Effect of Seller's Tender; Delivery on Condition.
- § 2-508. Cure by Seller of Improper Tender or Delivery; Replacement.
- § 2-509. Risk of Loss in the Absence of Breach.
- § 2-510. Effect of Breach on Risk of Loss.
- § 2-511. Tender of Payment by Buyer; Payment by Check.
- § 2-512. Payment by Buyer Before Inspection.
- § 2-513. Buyer's Right to Inspection of Goods.
- § 2-514. When Documents Deliverable on Acceptance; When on Payment.
- § 2-515. Preserving Evidence of Goods in Dispute.

Part 6. Breach, Repudiation, and Excuse

- § 2-601. Buyer's Rights on Improper Delivery.
- § 2-602. Manner and Effect of Rightful Rejection.
- § 2-603. Merchant Buyer's Duties as to Rightfully Rejected Goods.
- § 2-604. Buyer's Options as to Salvage of Rightfully Rejected Goods.
- § 2-605. Waiver of Buyer's Objections by Failure to Particularize.
- § 2-606. What Constitutes Acceptance of Goods.

- § 2-607. Effect of Acceptance; Notice of Breach; Burden of Establishing Breach After Acceptance; Notice of Claim or Litigation to Person Answerable Over.
- § 2-608. Revocation of Acceptance in Whole or in Part.
- § 2-609. Right to Adequate Assurance of Performance.
- § 2-610. Anticipatory Repudiation.
- § 2-611. Retraction of Anticipatory Repudiation.
- § 2-612. "Installment Contract"; Breach.
- § 2-613. Casualty to Identified Goods.
- § 2-614. Substituted Performance.
- § 2-615. Excuse by Failure of Presupposed Conditions.
- § 2-616. Procedure on Notice Claiming Excuse.

Part 7. Remedies

- § 2-701. Remedies for Breach of Collateral Contracts Not Impaired.
- § 2-702. Seller's Remedies on Discovery of Buyer's Insolvency.
- § 2-703. Seller's Remedies in General.
- § 2-704. Seller's Right to Identify Goods to the Contract Notwithstanding Breach or to Salvage Unfinished Goods.
- § 2-705. Seller's Stoppage of Delivery in Transit or Otherwise.
- § 2-706. Seller's Resale Including Contract for Resale.
- § 2-707. "Person in the Position of a Seller."
- § 2-708. Seller's Damages for Non-acceptance or Repudiation.
- § 2-709. Action for the Price.
- § 2-710. Seller's Incidental Damages.
- § 2-711. Buyer's Remedies in General; Buyer's Security Interest in Rejected Goods.
- § 2-712. "Cover"; Buyer's Procurement of Substitute Goods.
- § 2-713. Buyer's Damages for Non-delivery or Repudiation.
- § 2-714. Buyer's Damages for Breach in Regard to Accepted Goods.
- § 2-715. Buyer's Incidental and Consequential Damages.
- § 2-716. Buyer's Right to Specific Performance or Replevin.
- § 2-717. Deduction of Damages From the Price.
- § 2-718. Liquidation or Limitation of Damages; Deposits.
- § 2-719. Contractual Modification or Limitation of Remedy.
- § 2-720. Effect of "Cancellation" or "Rescission" on Claims for Antecedent Breach.
- § 2-721. Remedies for Fraud.
- § 2-722. Who Can Sue Third Parties for Injury to Goods.
- § 2-723. Proof of Market Price: Time and Place.
- § 2-724. Admissibility of Market Quotations.
- § 2-725. Statute of Limitations in Contracts for Sale.

Uniform Commercial Code—Article 2A

Part 1. General Provisions

- § 2A-101. Short Title.
- § 2A-102. Scope.
- § 2A-103. Definitions and Index of Definitions.
- § 2A-104. Leases Subject to Other Law.
- § 2A-105. Territorial Application of Article to Goods Covered by Certificate of Title.
- § 2A-106. Limitation on Power of Parties to Consumer Lease to Choose Applicable Law and Judicial Forum.
- § 2A-107. Waiver or Renunciation of Claim or Right After Default.
- § 2A-108. Unconscionability.
- § 2A-109. Option to Accelerate at Will.

Part 2. Formation and Construction of Lease Contract

- § 2A-201. Statute of Frauds.
- § 2A-202. Final Written Expression: Parol or Extrinsic Evidence.
- § 2A-203. Seals Inoperative.
- § 2A-204. Formation in General.

- § 2A-205. Firm Offers.
- § 2A-206. Offer and Acceptance in Formation of Lease Contract.
- § 2A-208. Modification, Rescission, and Waiver.
- § 2A-209. Lessee Under Finance Lease as Beneficiary of Supply Contract.
- § 2A-210. Express Warranties.
- § 2A-211. Warranties Against Interference and Against Infringement; Lessee's Obligation Against Infringement.
- § 2A-212. Implied Warranty of Merchantability.
- § 2A-213. Implied Warranty of Fitness for Particular Purpose.
- § 2A-214. Exclusion or Modification of Warranties.
- § 2A-215. Cumulation and Conflict of Warranties Express or Implied.
- § 2A-216. Third-Party Beneficiaries of Express and Implied Warranties.
- § 2A-217. Identification.
- § 2A-218. Insurance and Proceeds.
- § 2A-219. Risk of Loss.
- § 2A-220. Effect of Default on Risk of Loss.
- § 2A-221. Casualty to Identified Goods.

Part 3. Effect of Lease Contract

- § 2A-301. Enforceability of Lease Contract.
- § 2A-302. Title to and Possession of Goods.
- § 2A-303. Alienability of Party's Interest Under Lease Contract or of Lessor's Residual Interest in Goods; Delegation of Performance; Transfer of Rights.
- § 2A-304. Subsequent Lease of Goods by Lessor.
- § 2A-305. Sale or Sublease of Goods by Lessee.
- § 2A-306. Priority of Certain Liens Arising by Operation of Law.
- § 2A-307. Priority of Liens Arising by Attachment or Levy on, Security Interest in, and Other Claims to Goods.
- § 2A-308. Special Rights of Creditors.
- § 2A-309. Lessor's and Lessee's Rights when Goods Become Fixtures.
- § 2A-310. Lessor's and Lessee's Rights when Goods Become Accessions.
- § 2A-311. Priority Subject to Subordination.

Part 4. Performance of Lease Contract: Repudiated, Substituted, and Excused

- § 2A-401. Insecurity: Adequate Assurance of Performance.
- § 2A-402. Anticipatory Repudiation.
- § 2A-403. Retraction of Anticipatory Repudiation.
- § 2A-404. Substituted Performance.
- § 2A-405. Excused Performance.
- § 2A-406. Procedure on Excused Performance.
- § 2A-407. Irrevocable Promises: Finance Leases.

Part 5. Default

A. In General

- § 2A-501. Default: Procedure.
- § 2A-502. Notice After Default.
- § 2A-503. Modification or Impairment of Rights and Remedies.
- § 2A-504. Liquidation of Damages.
- § 2A-505. Cancellation and Termination and Effect of Cancellation, Termination, Rescission, or Fraud on Rights and Remedies.
- § 2A-506. Statute of Limitations.
- § 2A-507. Proof of Market Rent: Time and Place.

B. Default by Lessor

- § 2A-508. Lessee's Remedies.
- § 2A-509. Lessee's Rights on Improper Delivery; Rightful Rejection.
- § 2A-510. Installment Lease Contracts: Rejection and Default.
- § 2A-511. Merchant Lessee's Duties as to Rightfully Rejected Goods.
- § 2A-512. Lessee's Duties as to Rightfully Rejected Goods.
- § 2A-513. Cure by Lessor of Improper Tender or Delivery; Replacement.
- § 2A-514. Waiver of Lessee's Objections.

- § 2A-515. Acceptance of Goods.
- § 2A-516. Effect of Acceptance of Goods; Notice of Default; Burden of Establishing Default After Acceptance; Notice of Claim or Litigation to Person Answerable Over.
- § 2A-517. Revocation of Acceptance of Goods.
- § 2A-518. Cover; Substitute Goods.
- § 2A-519. Lessee's Damages for Non-Delivery, Repudiation, Default, and Breach of Warranty in Regard to Accepted Goods.
- § 2A-520. Lessee's Incidental and Consequential Damages.
- § 2A-521. Lessee's Right to Specific Performance or Replevin.
- § 2A-522. Lessee's Right to Goods on Lessor's Insolvency.

C. Default by Lessee

- § 2A-523. Lessor's Remedies.
- § 2A-524. Lessor's Right to Identify Goods to Lease Contract.
- § 2A-525. Lessor's Right to Possession of Goods.
- § 2A-526. Lessor's Stoppage of Delivery in Transit or Otherwise.
- § 2A-527. Lessor's Rights to Dispose of Goods.
- § 2A-528. Lessor's Damages For Non-Acceptance, Failure to Pay, Repudiation, or Other Default.
- § 2A-529. Lessor's Action for The Rent.
- § 2A-530. Lessor's Incidental Damages.
- § 2A-531. Standing to Sue Third Parties for Injury to Goods.
- § 2A-532. Lessor's Rights to Residual Interest.

Uniform Commercial Code—Article 3

Part 1. General Provisions and Definitions

- § 3-101. Short Title.
- § 3-102. Subject Matter.
- § 3-103. Definitions.
- § 3-104. Negotiable Instrument.
- § 3-105. Issue of Instrument.
- § 3-106. Unconditional Promise or Order.
- § 3-107. Instrument Payable in Foreign Money.
- § 3-108. Payable on Demand or at Definite Time.
- § 3-109. Payable to Bearer or to Order.
- § 3-110. Identification of Person to Whom Instrument is Payable.
- § 3-111. Place of Payment.
- § 3-112. Interest.
- § 3-113. Date of Instrument.
- § 3-114. Contradictory Terms of Instrument.
- § 3-115. Incomplete Instrument.
- § 3-116. Joint and Several Liability; Contribution.
- § 3-117. Other Agreements Affecting Instrument.
- § 3-118. Statute of Limitations.
- § 3-119. Notice of Right to Defend Action.

Part 2. Negotiation, Transfer, and Indorsement

- § 3-201. Negotiation.
- § 3-202. Negotiation Subject to Rescission.
- § 3-203. Transfer of Instrument; Rights Acquired by Transfer.
- § 3-204. Indorsement.
- § 3-205. Special Indorsement; Blank Indorsement; Anomalous Indorsement.
- § 3-206. Restrictive Indorsement.
- § 3-207. Reacquisition.

Part 3. Enforcement of Instruments

- § 3-301. Person Entitled to Enforce Instrument.
- § 3-302. Holder in Due Course.
- § 3-303. Value and Consideration.
- § 3-304. Overdue Instrument.
- § 3-305. Defenses and Claims in Recoupment.
- § 3-306. Claims to an Instrument.
- § 3-307. Notice of Breach of Fiduciary Duty.
- § 3-308. Proof of Signatures and Status as Holder in Due Course.
- § 3-309. Enforcement of Lost, Destroyed, or Stolen Instrument.

- § 3-310. Effect of Instrument on Obligation for Which Taken.
- § 3-311. Accord and Satisfaction by Use of Instrument.
- § 3-312. Lost, Destroyed, or Stolen Cashier's Check, Teller's Check, or Certified Check.

Part 4. Liability of Parties

- § 3-401. Signature.
- § 3-402. Signature by Representative.
- § 3-403. Unauthorized Signature.
- § 3-404. Impostors; Fictitious Payees.
- § 3-405. Employer's Responsibility For Fraudulent Indorsement by Employee.
- § 3-406. Negligence Contributing to Forged Signature or Alteration of Instrument.
- § 3-407. Alteration.
- § 3-408. Drawee Not Liable on Unaccepted Draft.
- § 3-409. Acceptance of Draft; Certified Check.
- § 3-410. Acceptance Varying Draft.
- § 3-411. Refusal to Pay Cashier's Checks, Teller's Checks, and Certified Checks.
- § 3-412. Obligation of Issuer of Note or Cashier's Check.
- § 3-413. Obligation of Acceptor.
- § 3-414. Obligation of Drawer.
- § 3-415. Obligation of Indorser.
- § 3-416. Transfer Warranties.
- § 3-417. Presentment Warranties.
- § 3-418. Payment or Acceptance by Mistake.
- § 3-419. Instruments Signed for Accommodation.
- § 3-420. Conversion of Instrument.

Part 5. Dishonor

- § 3-501. Presentment.
- § 3-502. Dishonor.
- § 3-503. Notice of Dishonor.
- § 3-504. Excused Presentment and Notice of Dishonor.
- § 3-505. Evidence of Dishonor.

Part 6. Discharge and Payment

- § 3-601. Discharge and Effect of Discharge.
- § 3-602. Payment.
- § 3-603. Tender of Payment.
- § 3-604. Discharge by Cancellation or Renunciation.
- § 3-605. Discharge of Indorsers and Accommodation Parties.

Uniform Commercial Code—Article 4

Part 1. General Provisions And Definitions

- § 4-101. Short Title.
- § 4-102. Applicability.
- § 4-103. Variation by Agreement; Measure of Damages; Action Constituting Ordinary Care.
- § 4-104. Definitions and Index of Definitions.
- § 4-105. "Bank"; "Depositary Bank"; "Payor Bank"; "Intermediary Bank"; "Collecting Bank"; "Presenting Bank."
- § 4-106. Payable Through or Payable at Bank; Collecting Bank.
- § 4-107. Separate Office of Bank.
- § 4-108. Time of Receipt of Items.
- § 4-109. Delays.
- § 4-110. Electronic Presentment.
- § 4-111. Statute of Limitations.

Part 2. Collection of Items: Depositary and Collecting Banks

- § 4-201. Status of Collecting Bank as Agent and Provisional Status of Credits; Applicability of Article; Item Indorsed "Pay Any Bank."
- § 4-202. Responsibility for Collection or Return; When Action Timely.
- § 4-203. Effect of Instructions.
- § 4-204. Methods of Sending and Presenting; Sending Directly to Payor Bank.
- § 4-205. Depositary Bank Holder of Unendorsed Item.
- § 4-206. Transfer between Banks.
- § 4-207. Transfer Warranties.

- § 4-208. Presentment Warranties.
- § 4-209. Encoding and Retention Warranties.
- § 4-210. Security Interest of Collecting Bank in Items, Accompanying Documents, and Proceeds.
- § 4-211. When Bank Gives Value for Purposes of Holder in Due Course.
- § 4-212. Presentment by Notice of Item Not Payable By, Through, or at Bank; Liability of Drawer or Indorser.
- § 4-213. Medium and Time of Settlement by Bank.
- § 4-214. Right of Charge-Back or Refund; Liability of Collecting Bank; Return of Item.
- § 4-215. Final Payment of Item by Payor Bank; When Provisional Debits and Credits Become Final; When Certain Credits Become Available for Withdrawal.
- § 4-216. Insolvency and Preference.

Part 3. Collection of Items: Payor Banks.

- § 4-301. Deferred Posting; Recovery of Payment by Return of Items; Time of Dishonor; Return of Items by Payor Bank.
- § 4-302. Payor Bank's Responsibility for Late Return of Item.
- § 4-303. When Items Subject to Notice, Stop-Payment Order, Legal Process, or Setoff; Order in Which Items May be Charged or Certified.

Part 4. Relationship between Payor Bank and its Customer

- § 4-401. When Bank May Charge Customer's Account.
- § 4-402. Bank's Liability to Customer for Wrongful Dishonor; Time of Determining Insufficiency of Account.
- § 4-403. Customer's Right to Stop Payment; Burden of Proof of Loss.
- § 4-404. Bank Not Obliged to Pay Check More Than Six Months Old.
- § 4-405. Death or Incompetence of Customer.
- § 4-406. Customer's Duty to Discover and Report Unauthorized Signature or Alteration.
- § 4-407. Payor Bank's Right to Subrogation on Improper Payment.

Part 5. Collection of Documentary Drafts

- § 4-501. Handling of Documentary Drafts; Duty to Send for Presentment and to Notify Customer of Dishonor.
- § 4-502. Presentment of "On Arrival" Drafts.
- § 4-503. Responsibility of Presenting Bank for Documents and Goods; Report of Reasons for Dishonor; Referee in Case of Need.
- § 4-504. Privilege of Presenting Bank to Deal With Goods; Security Interest For Expenses.

Uniform Commercial Code—Article 4A

Part 1. Subject Matter and Definitions

- § 4A-101. Short Title.
- § 4A-102. Subject Matter.
- § 4A-103. Payment Order—Definitions.
- § 4A-104. Funds Transfer—Definitions.
- § 4A-105. Other Definitions.
- § 4A-106. Time Payment Order is Received.
- § 4A-107. Federal Reserve Regulations and Operating Circulars.
- § 4A-108. Exclusion of Consumer Transactions Governed by Federal Law.

Part 2. Issue and Acceptance of Payment Order

- § 4A-201. Security Procedure.
- § 4A-202. Authorized and Verified Payment Orders.
- § 4A-203. Unenforceability of Certain Verified Payment Orders.
- § 4A-204. Refund of Payment and Duty of Customer to Report With Respect to Unauthorized Payment Order.
- § 4A-205. Erroneous Payment Orders.
- § 4A-206. Transmission of Payment Order through Funds-Transfer or Other Communication System.
- § 4A-207. Misdescription of Beneficiary.
- § 4A-208. Misdescription of Intermediary Bank or Beneficiary's Bank.
- § 4A-209. Acceptance of Payment Order.
- § 4A-210. Rejection of Payment Order.

- § 4A-211. Cancellation and Amendment of Payment Order.
- § 4A-212. Liability and Duty of Receiving Bank Regarding Unaccepted Payment Order.

Part 3. Execution of Sender's Payment Order by Receiving Bank

- § 4A-301. Execution and Execution Date.
- § 4A-302. Obligations of Receiving Bank in Execution of Payment Order.
- § 4A-303. Erroneous Execution of Payment Order.
- § 4A-304. Duty of Sender to Report Erroneously Executed Payment Order.
- § 4A-305. Liability for Late or Improper Execution or Failure to Execute Payment Order.

Part 4. Payment

- § 4A-401. Payment Date.
- § 4A-402. Obligation of Sender to Pay Receiving Bank.
- § 4A-403. Payment by Sender to Receiving Bank.
- § 4A-404. Obligation of Beneficiary's Bank to Pay and Give Notice to Beneficiary.
- § 4A-405. Payment by Beneficiary's Bank to Beneficiary.
- § 4A-406. Payment by Originator to Beneficiary; Discharge of Underlying Obligation.

Part 5. Miscellaneous Provisions

- § 4A-501. Variation by Agreement and Effect of Funds-Transfer System Rule.
- § 4A-502. Creditor Process Served on Receiving Bank; Setoff by Beneficiary's Bank.
- § 4A-503. Injunction or Restraining Order With Respect to Funds Transfer.
- § 4A-504. Order in Which Items and Payment Orders May be Charged to Account; Order of Withdrawals from Account.
- § 4A-505. Preclusion of Objection to Debit of Customer's Account.
- § 4A-506. Rate of Interest.
- § 4A-507. Choice of Law.

Uniform Commercial Code—Article 5

- § 5-101. Short Title.
- § 5-102. Definitions.
- § 5-103. Scope.
- § 5-104. Formal Requirements.
- § 5-105. Consideration.
- § 5-106. Issuance, Amendment, Cancellation, and Duration.
- § 5-107. Confirmer, Nominated Person, and Adviser.
- § 5-108. Issuer's Rights and Obligations.
- § 5-109. Fraud and Forgery.
- § 5-110. Warranties.
- § 5-111. Remedies.
- § 5-112. Transfer of Letter of Credit.
- § 5-113. Transfer by Operation of Law.
- § 5-114. Assignment of Proceeds.
- § 5-115. Statute of Limitations.
- § 5-116. Choice of Law and Forum.
- § 5-117. Subrogation of Issuer, Applicant, and Nominated Person.
- § 5-118. Security Interest of Issuer or Nominated Person.

Uniform Commercial Code—Article 6

Alternative A

- § 1. Repeal.
- § 2. Amendment.
- § 3. Amendment.
- § 4. Savings Clause.

Alternative B

Part 1. Subject Matter and Definitions

- § 6-101. Short Title.
- § 6-102. Definitions and Index of Definitions.
- § 6-103. Applicability of Article.
- § 6-104. Obligations of Buyer.
- § 6-105. Notice to Claimants.
- § 6-106. Schedule of Distribution.

- § 6-107. Liability for Noncompliance.
- § 6-108. Bulk Sales by Auction; Bulk Sales Conducted by Liquidator.
- § 6-109. What Constitutes Filing; Duties of Filing Officer; Information From Filing Officer.
- § 6-110. Limitation of Actions.

Uniform Commercial Code—Article 7

Part 1. General

- § 7-101. Short Title.
- § 7-102. Definitions and Index of Definitions.
- § 7-103. Relation of Article to Treaty, Statute, Tariff, Classification, or Regulation.
- § 7-104. Negotiable and Non-negotiable Warehouse Receipt, Bill of Lading, or Other Document of Title.
- § 7-105. Construction against Negative Implication.

Part 2. Warehouse Receipts: Special Provisions

- § 7-201. Who May Issue a Warehouse Receipt; Storage Under Government Bond.
- § 7-202. Form of Warehouse Receipt; Essential Terms; Optional Terms.
- § 7-203. Liability for Non-receipt or Misdescription.
- § 7-204. Duty of Care; Contractual Limitation of Warehouseman's Liability.
- § 7-205. Title under Warehouse Receipt Defeated in Certain Cases.
- § 7-206. Termination of Storage at Warehouseman's Option.
- § 7-207. Goods Must Be Kept Separate; Fungible Goods.
- § 7-208. Altered Warehouse Receipts.
- § 7-209. Lien of Warehouseman.
- § 7-210. Enforcement of Warehouseman's Lien.

Part 3. Bills of Lading: Special Provisions

- § 7-301. Liability for Non-receipt or Misdescription; "Said to Contain"; "Shipper's Load and Count"; Improper Handling.
- § 7-302. Through Bills of Lading and Similar Documents.
- § 7-303. Diversion; Reconsignment; Change of Instructions.
- § 7-304. Bills of Lading in a Set.
- § 7-305. Destination Bills.
- § 7-306. Altered Bills of Lading.
- § 7-307. Lien of Carrier.
- § 7-308. Enforcement of Carrier's Lien.
- § 7-309. Duty of Care; Contractual Limitation of Carrier's Liability.

Part 4. Warehouse Receipts and Bills of Lading: General Obligations

- § 7-401. Irregularities in Issue of Receipt or Bill or Conduct of Issuer.
- § 7-402. Duplicate Receipt or Bill; Overissue.
- § 7-403. Obligation of Warehouseman or Carrier to Deliver; Excuse.
- § 7-404. No Liability for Good Faith Delivery Pursuant to Receipt or Bill.

Part 5. Warehouse Receipts and Bills of Lading: Negotiation and Transfer

- § 7-501. Form of Negotiation and Requirements of "Due Negotiation."
- § 7-502. Rights Acquired by Due Negotiation.
- § 7-503. Document of Title to Goods Defeated in Certain Cases.
- § 7-504. Rights Acquired in the Absence of Due Negotiation; Effect of Diversion; Seller's Stoppage of Delivery.
- § 7-505. Indorser Not a Guarantor for Other Parties.
- § 7-506. Delivery Without Indorsement: Right to Compel Indorsement.
- § 7-507. Warranties on Negotiation or Transfer of Receipt or Bill.
- § 7-508. Warranties of Collecting Bank as to Documents.
- § 7-509. Receipt or Bill: When Adequate Compliance With Commercial Contract.

Part 6. Warehouse Receipts and Bills of Lading: Miscellaneous Provisions

- § 7-601. Lost and Missing Documents.
- § 7-602. Attachment of Goods Covered by a Negotiable Document.
- § 7-603. Conflicting Claims; Interpleader.

Uniform Commercial Code—Article 8

Part 1. Short Title and General Matters

- § 8-101. Short Title.
- § 8-102. Definitions.
- § 8-103. Rules for Determining Whether Certain Obligations and Interests are Securities or Financial Assets.
- § 8-104. Acquisition of Security or Financial Asset or Interest Therein.
- § 8-105. Notice of Adverse Claim.
- § 8-106. Control.
- § 8-107. Whether Indorsement, Instruction, or Entitlement Order is Effective.
- § 8-108. Warranties in Direct Holding.
- § 8-109. Warranties in Indirect Holding.
- § 8-110. Applicability; Choice of Law.
- § 8-111. Clearing Corporation Rules.
- § 8-112. Creditor's Legal Process.
- § 8-113. Statute of Frauds Inapplicable.
- § 8-114. Evidentiary Rules Concerning Certificated Securities.
- § 8-115. Securities Intermediary and Others Not Liable to Adverse Claimant.
- § 8-116. Securities Intermediary as Purchaser for Value.

Part 2. Issue and Issuer

- § 8-201. Issuer.
- § 8-202. Issuer's Responsibility and Defenses; Notice of Defect or Defense.
- § 8-203. Staleness as Notice of Defect or Defense.
- § 8-204. Effect of Issuer's Restriction on Transfer.
- § 8-205. Effect of Unauthorized Signature on Security Certificate.
- § 8-206. Completion or Alteration of Security Certificate.
- § 8-207. Rights and Duties of Issuer With Respect to Registered Owners.
- § 8-208. Effect of Signature of Authenticating Trustee, Registrar, or Transfer Agent.
- § 8-209. Issuer's Lien.
- § 8-210. Overissue.

Part 3. Transfer of Certificated and Uncertificated Securities

- § 8-301. Delivery.
- § 8-302. Rights of Purchaser.
- § 8-303. Protected Purchaser.
- § 8-304. Indorsement.
- § 8-305. Instruction.
- § 8-306. Effect of Guaranteeing Signature, Indorsement, or Instruction.
- § 8-307. Purchaser's Right to Requisites For Registration of Transfer.

Part 4. Registration

- § 8-401. Duty of Issuer to Register Transfer.
- § 8-402. Assurance that Indorsement or Instruction is Effective.
- § 8-403. Demand that Issuer not Register Transfer.
- § 8-404. Wrongful Registration.
- § 8-405. Replacement of Lost, Destroyed, or Wrongfully Taken Security Certificate.
- § 8-406. Obligation to Notify Issuer of Lost, Destroyed, or Wrongfully Taken Security Certificate.
- § 8-407. Authenticating Trustee, Transfer Agent, and Registrar.

Part 5. Security Entitlements

- § 8-501. Securities Account; Acquisition of Security Entitlement from Securities Intermediary.
- § 8-502. Assertion of Adverse Claim against Entitlement Holder.

- § 8-503. Property Interest of Entitlement Holder in Financial Asset Held by Securities Intermediary.
- § 8-504. Duty of Securities Intermediary to Maintain Financial Asset.
- § 8-505. Duty of Securities Intermediary With Respect to Payments and Distributions.
- § 8-506. Duty of Securities Intermediary to Exercise Rights as Directed by Entitlement Holder.
- § 8-507. Duty of Securities Intermediary to Comply With Entitlement Order.
- § 8-508. Duty of Securities Intermediary to Change Entitlement Holder's Position to Other Form of Security Holding.
- § 8-509. Specification of Duties of Securities Intermediary by Other Statute or Regulation; Manner of Performance of Duties of Securities Intermediary and Exercise of Rights of Entitlement Holder.
- § 8-510. Rights of Purchaser of Security Entitlement from Entitlement Holder.
- § 8-511. Priority among Security Interests and Entitlement Holders.

Uniform Commercial Code—Article 9

Part 1. General Provisions

[Subpart 1. Short Title, Definitions, and General Concepts]

- § 9-101. Short Title.
- § 9-102. Definitions and Index of Definitions.
- § 9-103. Purchase-Money Security Interest; Application of Payments; Burden of Establishing.
- § 9-104. Control of Deposit Account.
- § 9-105. Control of Electronic Chattel Paper.
- § 9-106. Control of Investment Property.
- § 9-107. Control of Letter-of-Credit Right.
- § 9-108. Sufficiency of Description.

[Subpart 2. Applicability of Article]

- § 9-109. Scope.
- § 9-110. Security Interests Arising Under Article 2 or 2A.

Part 2. Effectiveness of Security Agreement; Attachment of Security Interest; Rights of Parties to Security Agreement

[Subpart 1. Effectiveness and Attachment]

- § 9-201. General Effectiveness of Security Agreement.
- § 9-202. Title to Collateral Immaterial.
- § 9-203. Attachment and Enforceability of Security Interest; Proceeds; Supporting Obligations; Formal Requisites.
- § 9-204. After-Acquired Property; Future Advances.
- § 9-205. Use or Disposition of Collateral Permissible.
- § 9-206. Security Interest Arising in Purchase or Delivery of Financial Asset.

[Subpart 2. Rights And Duties]

- § 9-207. Rights and Duties of Secured Party Having Possession or Control of Collateral.
- § 9-208. Additional Duties of Secured Party Having Control of Collateral.
- § 9-209. Duties of Secured Party if Account Debtor Has Been Notified of Assignment.
- § 9-210. Request for Accounting; Request Regarding List of Collateral or Statement of Account.

Part 3. Perfection and Priority

[Subpart 1. Law Governing Perfection and Priority]

- § 9-301. Law Governing Perfection and Priority of Security Interests.
- § 9-302. Law Governing Perfection and Priority of Agricultural Liens.
- § 9-303. Law Governing Perfection and Priority of Security Interests in Goods Covered by a Certificate of Title.
- § 9-304. Law Governing Perfection and Priority of Security Interests in Deposit Accounts.
- § 9-305. Law Governing Perfection and Priority of Security Interests in Investment Property.
- § 9-306. Law Governing Perfection and Priority of Security Interests in Letter-of-Credit Rights.

- § 9-307. Location of Debtor.
- § 9-308. When Security Interest or Agricultural Lien is Perfected; Continuity of Perfection.
- § 9-309. Security Interest Perfected Upon Attachment.
- § 9-310. When Filing Required to Perfect Security Interest or Agricultural Lien; Security Interests and Agricultural Liens to which Filing Provisions do not Apply.
- § 9-311. Perfection of Security Interests in Property Subject to Certain Statutes, Regulations, and Treaties.
- § 9-312. Perfection of Security Interests in Chattel Paper, Deposit Accounts, Documents, Goods Covered by Documents, Instruments, Investment Property, Letter-of-Credit Rights, and Money; Perfection by Permissive Filing; Temporary Perfection Without Filing or Transfer of Possession.
- § 9-313. When Possession by or Delivery to Secured Party Perfects Security Interest Without Filing.
- § 9-314. Perfection by Control.
- § 9-315. Secured Party's Rights on Disposition of Collateral and in Proceeds.
- § 9-316. Continued Perfection of Security Interest Following Change in Governing Law.

[Subpart 3. Priority]

- § 9-317. Interests That Take Priority Over or Take Free of Unperfected Security Interest or Agricultural Lien.
- § 9-318. No Interest Retained in Right to Payment That is Sold; Rights and Title of Seller of Account or Chattel Paper With Respect to Creditors and Purchasers.
- § 9-319. Rights and Title of Consignee With Respect to Creditors and Purchasers.
- § 9-320. Buyer of Goods.
- § 9-321. Licensee of General Intangible and Lessee of Goods in Ordinary Course of Business.
- § 9-322. Priorities Among Conflicting Security Interests in and Agricultural Liens on Same Collateral.
- § 9-323. Future Advances.
- § 9-324. Priority of Purchase-Money Security Interests.
- § 9-325. Priority of Security Interests in Transferred Collateral.
- § 9-326. Priority of Security Interests Created by New Debtor.
- § 9-327. Priority of Security Interests in Deposit Account.
- § 9-328. Priority of Security Interests in Investment Property.
- § 9-329. Priority of Security Interests in Letter-of-Credit Right.
- § 9-330. Priority of Purchaser of Chattel Paper or Instrument.
- § 9-331. Priority of Rights of Purchasers of Instruments, Documents, and Securities Under Other Articles; Priority of Interests in Financial Assets and Security Entitlements Under Article 8.
- § 9-332. Transfer of Money; Transfer of Funds from Deposit Account.
- § 9-333. Priority of Certain Liens Arising by Operation of Law.
- § 9-334. Priority of Security Interests in Fixtures and Crops.
- § 9-335. Accessions.
- § 9-336. Commingled Goods.
- § 9-337. Priority of Security Interests in Goods Covered by Certificate of Title.
- § 9-338. Priority of Security Interest or Agricultural Lien Perfected by Filed Financing Statement Providing Certain Incorrect Information.
- § 9-339. Priority Subject to Subordination.

[Subpart 4. Rights Of Bank]

- § 9-340. Effectiveness of Right of Recoupment or Set-Off Against Deposit Account.
- § 9-341. Bank's Rights and Duties with Respect to Deposit Account.
- § 9-342. Bank's Right to Refuse to Enter into or Disclose Existence of Control Agreement.

Part 4. Rights of Third Parties

- § 9-401. Alienability of Debtor's Rights.

- § 9-402. Secured Party Not Obligated on Contract of Debtor or in Tort.
- § 9-403. Agreement Not to Assert Defenses Against Assignee.
- § 9-404. Rights Acquired by Assignee; Claims and Defenses Against Assignee.
- § 9-405. Modification of Assigned Contract.
- § 9-406. Discharge of Account Debtor; Notification of Assignment; Identification and Proof of Assignment; Restrictions on Assignment of Accounts, Chattel Paper, Payment Intangibles, and Promissory Notes Ineffective.
- § 9-407. Restrictions on Creation or Enforcement of Security Interest in Leasehold Interest or in Lessor's Residual Interest.
- § 9-408. Restrictions on Assignment of Promissory Notes, Health-Care-Insurance Receivables, and Certain General Intangibles Ineffective.
- § 9-409. Restrictions on Assignment of Letter-of-Credit Rights Ineffective.

Part 5. Filing

[Subpart 1. Filing Office; Contents and Effectiveness of Financing Statement]

- § 9-501. Filing Office.
- § 9-502. Contents of Financing Statement; Record of Mortgage as Financing Statement; Time of Filing Financing Statement.
- § 9-503. Name of Debtor and Secured Party.
- § 9-504. Indication of Collateral.
- § 9-505. Filing and Compliance with Other Statutes and Treaties for Consignments, Leases, Other Bailments, and Other Transactions.
- § 9-506. Effect of Errors or Omissions.
- § 9-507. Effect of Certain Events on Effectiveness of Financing Statement.
- § 9-508. Effectiveness of Financing Statement if New Debtor Becomes Bound by Security Agreement.
- § 9-509. Persons Entitled to File a Record.
- § 9-510. Effectiveness of Filed Record.
- § 9-511. Secured Party of Record.
- § 9-512. Amendment of Financing Statement.
- § 9-513. Termination Statement.
- § 9-514. Assignment of Powers of Secured Party of Record.
- § 9-515. Duration and Effectiveness of Financing Statement; Effect at Lapsed Financing Statement.
- § 9-516. What Constitutes Filing; Effectiveness of Filing.
- § 9-517. Effect of Indexing Errors.
- § 9-518. Claim Concerning Inaccurate or Wrongfully Filed Record.

[Subpart 2. Duties and Operation of Filing Office]

- § 9-519. Numbering, Maintaining, and Indexing Records; Communicating Information Provided in Records.
- § 9-520. Acceptance and Refusal to Accept Record.
- § 9-521. Uniform Form of Written Financing Statement and Amendment.
- § 9-522. Maintenance and Destruction of Records.
- § 9-523. Information from Filing Office; Sale or License of Records.
- § 9-524. Delay by Filing Office.
- § 9-525. Fees.
- § 9-526. Filing Office Rules.
- § 9-527. Duty to Report.

Part 6. Default

[Subpart 1. Default and Enforcement of Security Interest]

- § 9-601. Rights After Default; Judicial Enforcement; Consignor or Buyer of Accounts, Chattel Paper, Payment Intangibles, or Promissory Notes.
- § 9-602. Waiver and Variance of Rights and Duties.
- § 9-603. Agreement on Standards Concerning Rights and Duties.
- § 9-604. Procedure if Security Agreement Covers Real Property or Fixtures.
- § 9-605. Unknown Debtor or Secondary Obligor.
- § 9-606. Time of Default for Agricultural Lien.

- § 9-607. Collection and Enforcement by Secured Party.
- § 9-608. Application of Proceeds of Collection or Enforcement; Liability for Deficiency and Right to Surplus.
- § 9-609. Secured Party's Right to Take Possession after Default.
- § 9-610. Disposition of Collateral after Default.
- § 9-611. Notification Before Disposition of Collateral.
- § 9-612. Timeliness of Notification Before Disposition of Collateral.
- § 9-613. Contents and Form of Notification Before Disposition of Collateral: General.
- § 9-614. Contents and Form of Notification Before Disposition of Collateral: Consumer-Goods Transaction.
- § 9-615. Application of Proceeds of Disposition; Liability for Deficiency and Right to Surplus.
- § 9-616. Explanation of Calculation of Surplus or Deficiency.
- § 9-617. Rights of Transferee of Collateral.
- § 9-618. Rights and Duties of Certain Secondary Obligors.
- § 9-619. Transfer of Record or Legal Title.
- § 9-620. Acceptance of Collateral in Full or Partial Satisfaction of Obligation; Compulsory Disposition of Collateral.
- § 9-621. Notification of Proposal to Accept Collateral.
- § 9-622. Effect of Acceptance of Collateral.
- § 9-623. Right to Redeem Collateral.
- § 9-624. Waiver.

[Subpart 2. Noncompliance With Article]

- § 9-625. Remedies for Secured Party's Failure to Comply with Article.
- § 9-626. Action in Which Deficiency or Surplus is in Issue.
- § 9-627. Determination of Whether Conduct was Commercially Reasonable.
- § 9-628. Nonliability and Limitation on Liability of Secured Party; Liability of Secondary Obligor.

Part 7. Transition

- § 9-701. Effective Date.
- § 9-702. Savings Clause.
- § 9-703. Security Interest Perfected Before Effective Date.
- § 9-704. Security Interest Unperfected Before Effective Date.
- § 9-705. Effectiveness of Action Taken Before Effective Date.
- § 9-706. When Initial Financing Statement Suffices to Continue Effectiveness of Financing Statement.
- § 9-707. Amendment of Pre-Effective-Date Financing Statement.
- § 9-708. Persons Entitled to File Initial Financing Statement or Continuation Statement.
- § 9-709. Priority.

Federal Acquisition Regulation (FAR)

General Structure and Subparts

Subchapter A—General

Part 1—Federal Acquisition Regulations System

1.1 Purpose, Authority, Issuance
1.2 Administration
1.3 Agency Acquisition Regulations
1.4 Deviations from The *FAR*
1.5 Agency and Public Participation
1.6 Career Development, Contracting Authority, and Responsibilities
1.7 Determinations and Findings

Part 2—Definitions of Words and Terms

2.1 Definitions
2.2 Definitions Clause

Part 3—Improper Business Practices and Personal Conflicts of Interest

3.1 Safeguards
3.2 Contractor Gratuities to Government Personnel
3.3 Reports of Suspected Antitrust Violations
3.4 Contingent Fees
3.5 Other Improper Business Practices
3.6 Contracts with Government Employees or Organizations Owned or Controlled by Them
3.7 Voiding and Rescinding Contracts
3.8 Limitation on the Payment of Funds to Influence Federal Transactions
3.9 Whistleblower Protections for Contractor Employees

Part 4—Administrative Matters

4.1 Contract Execution
4.2 Contract Distribution
4.3 Paper Documents
4.4 Safeguarding Classified Information Within Industry
4.5 Electronic Commerce in Contracting
4.6 Contract Reporting
4.7 Contractor Records Retention
4.8 Government Contract Files
4.9 Taxpayer Identification Number Information
4.10 Contract Line Items
4.11 Central Contractor Registration
4.12 Annual Representations and Certifications

Subchapter B—Competition And Acquisition Planning

Part 5—Publicizing Contract Actions

5.1 Dissemination of Information
5.2 Synopses of Proposed Contract Actions
5.3 Synopses of Contract Awards
5.4 Release of Information
5.5 Paid Advertisements
5.6 Publicizing Multi-Agency Use Contracts

Part 6—Competition Requirements

6.1 Full and Open Competition
6.2 Full and Open Competition After Exclusion of Sources
6.3 Other Than Full and Open Competition
6.4 Sealed Bidding and Competitive Proposals
6.5 Competition Advocates

Part 7—Acquisition Planning

7.1 Acquisition Plans
7.2 Planning for the Purchase of Supplies in Economic Quantities
7.3 Contractor Versus Government Performance
7.4 Equipment Lease or Purchase
7.5 Inherently Governmental Functions

Part 8—Required Sources of Supplies and Services

8.1 Excess Personal Property
8.2 [Reserved]
8.3 [Reserved]
8.4 Federal Supply Schedules
8.5 Acquisition of Helium
8.6 Acquisition from Federal Prison Industries, Inc.

8.7 Acquisition from Nonprofit Agencies Employing People who are Blind or Severely Disabled

8.8 Acquisition of Printing and Related Supplies

8.9 [Reserved]

8.10 [Reserved]

8.11 Leasing of Motor Vehicles

Part 9—Contractor Qualifications

9.1. Responsible Prospective Contractors

9.2 Qualifications Requirements

9.3 First Article Testing and Approval

9.4 Debarment, Suspension, and Ineligibility

9.5 Organizational and Consultant Conflicts of Interest

9.6 Contractor Team Arrangements

9.7 Defense Production Pools and Research and Development Pools

Part 10—Market Research

Part 11—Describing Agency Needs

11.1 Selecting and Developing Requirements Documents

11.2 Using and Maintaining Requirements Documents

11.3 Acceptable Material

11.4 Delivery or Performance Schedules

11.5 Liquidated Damages

11.6 Priorities and Allocations

11.7 Variation in Quantity

11.8 Testing

Part 12—Acquisition of Commercial Items

12.1 Acquisition of Commercial Items—General

12.2 Special Requirements for the Acquisition of Commercial Items

12.3 Solicitation Provisions and Contract Clauses for the Acquisition of Commercial Items

12.4 Unique Requirements Regarding Terms and Conditions for Commercial Items

12.5 Applicability of Certain Laws to the Acquisition of Commercial Items

12.6 Streamlined Procedures for Evaluation and Solicitation for Commercial Items

Subchapter C—Contracting Methods and Contract Types

Part 13—Simplified Acquisition Procedures

13.1 Procedures

13.2 Actions at or Below the Micro-Purchase Threshold

13.3 Simplified Acquisition Methods

13.4 Fast Payment Procedure

13.5 Test Program for Certain Commercial Items

Part 14—Sealed Bidding

14.1 Use of Sealed Bidding

14.2 Solicitation of Bids

14.3 Submission of Bids

14.4 Opening of Bids and Award of Contract

14.5 Two-Step Sealed Bidding

Part 15—Contracting by Negotiation

15.1 Source Selection Processes and Techniques

15.2 Solicitation and Receipt of Proposals and Information

15.3 Source Selection

15.4 Contract Pricing

15.5 Preaward, Award, and Postaward Notifications; Protests; and Mistakes

15.6 Unsolicited Proposals

Part 16—Types of Contracts

16.1 Selecting Contract Types

16.2 Fixed-Price Contracts

16.3 Cost-Reimbursement Contracts

16.4 Incentive Contracts

16.5 Indefinite-Delivery Contracts

16.6 Time-and-Materials, Labor-Hour, and Letter Contracts

16.7 Agreements

Part 17—Special Contracting Methods

17.1 Multi-Year Contracting
17.2 Options
17.3 [Reserved]
17.4 Leader Company Contracting
17.5 Interagency Acquisitions Under the Economy Act
17.6 Management and Operating Contracts

Part 18—[Reserved]

Subchapter D—Socioeconomic Programs

Part 19—Small Business Programs

19.1 Size Standards
19.2 Policies
19.3 Determination of Small Business Status for Small Business Programs
19.4 Cooperation with the Small Business Administration
19.5 Set-Asides for Small Business
19.6 Certificates of Competency and Determinations of Responsibility
19.7 The Small Business Subcontracting Program
19.8 Contracting with the Small Business Administration (The 8(a) Program)
19.9 Very Small Business Pilot Program
19.10 Small Business Competitiveness Demonstration Program
19.11 Price Evaluation Adjustment For Small Disadvantaged Business Concerns
19.12 Small Disadvantaged Business Participation Program
19.13 Historically Underutilized Business Zone (HUBZone) Program
19.14 Service-Disabled Veteran–Owned Small Business Procurement Program

Part 20—[Reserved]

Part 21—[Reserved]

Part 22—Application of Labor Laws to Government Acquisitions

22.1 Basic Labor Policies
22.2 Convict Labor
22.3 Contract Work Hours and Safety Standards Act
22.4 Labor Standards for Contracts Involving Construction
22.5 [Reserved]
22.6 Walsh-Healey Public Contracts Act
22.7 [Reserved]
22.8 Equal Employment Opportunity
22.9 Nondiscrimination Because of Age
22.10 Service Contract Act Of 1965, As Amended
22.11 Professional Employee Compensation
22.12 [Reserved]
22.13 Special Disabled Veterans, Veterans of the Vietnam Era, and Other Eligible Veterans
22.14 Employment of Workers with Disabilities
22.15 Prohibition of Acquisition of Products Produced by Forced or Indentured Child Labor
22.16 Notification of Employee Rights Concerning Payment of Union Dues or Fees

Part 23—Environment, Energy and Water Efficiency, Renewable Energy Technologies, Occupational Safety, and Drug-Free Workplace

23.1 [Reserved]
23.2 Energy and Water Efficiency and Renewable Energy
23.3 Hazardous Material Identification and Material Safety Data
23.4 Use of Recovered Materials
23.5 Drug-Free Workplace
23.6 Notice of Radioactive Material
23.7 Contracting for Environmentally Preferable Products and Services
23.8 Ozone-Depleting Substances
23.9 Contractor Compliance with Toxic Chemical Release Reporting
23.10 Federal Compliance with Right-to-Know Laws and Pollution Prevention Requirements

Part 24—Protection of Privacy and Freedom of Information

24.1 Protection of Individual Privacy
24.2 Freedom of Information Act

Part 25—Foreign Acquisition

25.1 Buy American Act—Supplies
25.2 Buy American Act—Construction Materials
25.3 [Reserved]
25.4 Trade Agreements
25.5 Evaluating Foreign Offers—Supply Contracts
25.6 Trade Sanctions
25.7 Prohibited Sources
25.8 Other International Agreements and Coordination
25.9 Customs and Duties
25.10 Additional Foreign Acquisition Regulations
25.11 Solicitation Provisions and Contract Clauses

Part 26—Other Socioeconomic Programs

26.1 Indian Incentive Program
26.2 Disaster or Emergency Assistance Activities
26.3 Historically Black Colleges and Universities and Minority Institutions

Subchapter E—General Contracting Requirements

Part 27—Patents, Data, and Copyrights

27.1 General
27.2 Patents
27.3 Patent Rights Under Government Contracts
27.4 Rights in Data and Copyrights
27.5 [Reserved]
27.6 Foreign License and Technical Assistance Agreements

Part 28—Bonds and Insurance

28.1 Bonds and Other Financial Protections
28.2 Sureties and Other Security for Bonds
28.3 Insurance

Part 29—Taxes

29.1 General
29.2 Federal Excise Taxes
29.3 State and Local Taxes
29.4 Contract Clauses

Part 30—Cost Accounting Standards Administration

30.1 General
30.2 CAS Program Requirements
30.3 CAS Rules and Regulations [Reserved]
30.4 Cost Accounting Standards [Reserved]
30.5 Cost Accounting Standards for Educational Institutions [Reserved]
30.6 CAS Administration

Part 31—Contract Cost Principles and Procedures

31.1 Applicability
31.2 Contracts with Commercial Organizations
31.3 Contracts with Educational Institutions
31.4 [Reserved]
31.5 [Reserved]
31.6 Contracts with State, Local, and Federally Recognized Indian Tribal Governments
31.7 Contracts with Nonprofit Organizations

Part 32—Contract Financing

32.1 Non-Commercial Item Purchase Financing
32.2 Commercial Item Purchase Financing
32.3 Loan Guarantees for Defense Production
32.4 Advance Payments for Non-Commercial Items
32.5 Progress Payments Based on Costs
32.6 Contract Debts
32.7 Contract Funding
32.8 Assignment of Claims
32.9 Prompt Payment
32.10 Performance-Based Payments
32.11 Electronic Funds Transfer

Part 33—Protests, Disputes, and Appeals

33.1 Protests
33.2 Disputes and Appeals

Subchapter F—Special Categories of Contracting

Part 34—Major System Acquisition

34.0 General
34.1 Testing, Qualification, and Use of Industrial Resources Developed Under Title III, Defense Production Act

Part 35—Research and Development Contracting

Part 36—Construction and Architect-Engineer Contracts

36.1 General
36.2 Special Aspects of Contracting for Construction
36.3 Two-Phase Design-Build Selection Procedures
36.4 [Reserved]
36.5 Contract Clauses
36.6 Architect-Engineer Services
36.7 Standard and Optional Forms for Contracting for Construction, Architect-Engineer Services, and Dismantling, Demolition, or Removal of Improvements

Part 37—Service Contracting

37.1 Service Contracts—General
37.2 Advisory and Assistance Services
37.3 Dismantling, Demolition, or Removal of Improvements
37.4 Nonpersonal Health Care Services
37.5 Management Oversight of Service Contracts
37.6 Performance-Based Contracting

Part 38—Federal Supply Schedule Contracting

38.1 Federal Supply Schedule Program
38.2 Establishing and Administering Federal Supply Schedules

Part 39—Acquisition of Information Technology

39.1 General
39.2 Electronic and Information Technology

Part 40—[Reserved]

Part 41—Acquisition of Utility Services

41.1 General
41.2 Acquiring Utility Services
41.3 Requests for Assistance
41.4 Administration
41.5 Solicitation Provision and Contract Clauses
41.6 Forms
41.7 Formats

Subchapter G—Contract Management

Part 42—Contract Administration and Audit Services

42.1 Contract Audit Services
42.2 Contract Administration Services
42.3 Contract Administration Office Functions
42.4 Correspondence and Visits
42.5 Postaward Orientation
42.6 Corporate Administrative Contracting Officer
42.7 Indirect Cost Rates
42.8 Disallowance of Costs
42.9 Bankruptcy
42.10 [Reserved]
42.11 Production Surveillance and Reporting
42.12 Novation and Change-of-Name Agreements
42.13 Suspension of Work, Stop-Work Orders, and Government Delay of Work
42.14 Traffic and Transportation Management
42.15 Contractor Performance Information
42.16 Small Business Contract Administration
42.17 Forward Pricing Rate Agreements

Part 43—Contract Modifications

43.1 General
43.2 Change Orders
43.3 Forms

Part 44—Subcontracting Policies and Procedures

- 44.1 General
- 44.2 Consent to Subcontracts
- 44.3 Contractors' Purchasing Systems Reviews
- 44.4 Subcontracts for Commercial Items and Commercial Components

Part 45—Government Property

- 45.1 General
- 45.2 Competitive Advantage
- 45.3 Providing Government Property to Contractors
- 45.4 Contractor Use and Rental of Government Property
- 45.5 Management of Government Property in the Possession of Contractors
- 45.6 Reporting, Reutilization, and Disposal

Part 46—Quality Assurance

- 46.1 General
- 46.2 Contract Quality Requirements
- 46.3 Contract Clauses
- 46.4 Government Contract Quality Assurance
- 46.5 Acceptance
- 46.6 Material Inspection and Receiving Reports
- 46.7 Warranties
- 46.8 Contractor Liability for Loss of or Damage to Property of the Government

Part 47—Transportation

- 47.1 General
- 47.2 Contracts for Transportation or for Transportation-Related Services
- 47.3 Transportation in Supply Contracts
- 47.4 Air Transportation by U.S.-Flag Carriers
- 47.5 Ocean Transportation by U.S.-Flag Vessels

Part 48—Value Engineering

- 48.1 Policies and Procedures
- 48.2 Contract Clauses

Part 49—Termination of Contracts

- 49.1 General Principles
- 49.2 Additional Principles for Fixed-Price Contracts Terminated for Convenience
- 49.3 Additional Principles for Cost-Reimbursement Contracts Terminated for Convenience
- 49.4 Termination for Default
- 49.5 Contract Termination Clauses
- 49.6 Contract Termination Forms and Formats

Part 50—Extraordinary Contractual Actions

- 50.1 General
- 50.2 Delegation of and Limitations on Exercise of Authority
- 50.3 Contract Adjustments
- 50.4 Residual Powers

Part 51—Use of Government Sources by Contractors

- 51.1 Contractor Use of Government Supply Sources
- 51.2 Contractor Use of Interagency Fleet Management System (IFMS) Vehicles

Subchapter H—Clauses and Forms

Part 52—Solicitation Provisions and Contract Clauses

- 52.1 Instructions for Using Provisions and Clauses
- 52.2 Text of Provisions and Clauses
- 52.3 Provision and Clause Matrix

Part 53—Forms

- 53.1 General
- 53.2 Prescription of Forms
- 53.3 Illustration of Forms

Appendix

Index

Task List from Job Analysis Study

Domain 1: Identify Needs

1.1 Perform Needs Assessment
1.2 Conduct Preliminary Market Research for Capability
1.3 Shape Customer Requirements (e.g., Work With Requiring Activity/Program Office)
1.4 Determine Achievability
1.5 Refine Needs Assessment

Domain 2: Plan Contracting

2.1 Conduct Detailed Market Research Regarding Potential Suppliers
2.2 Conduct A Pre-Proposal Conference
2.3 Select Proper Contract Type
2.4 Formulate Contracting Strategy
2.5 Document Acquisition Plan, Including Supporting Documents (e.g., Justification and Approvals, Determinations and Findings)
2.6 Formulate Proposal Evaluation Plan
2.7 Perform Contract Portfolio Management (e.g., Evaluate Alternative Solutions to Support Requirements, Review Customer Requirements, Return on Investment)
2.8 Perform Requirements Analysis
2.9 Perform Spend Analysis
2.10 Perform Risk Analysis (Identification, Probability, Impact, Mitigation)
2.11 Make Teaming Decisions
2.12 Negotiate Nondisclosure Agreements (NDAs)
2.13 Negotiate Teaming Agreements
2.14 Assess Competition
2.15 Manage Potential Organizational Conflicts of Interest (OCIs), Fraud Identification
2.16 Conduct Bid/No Bid Analysis
2.17 Develop Win Strategies
2.18 Determine Appropriate Clauses and Provisions
2.19 Determine Need for any Pre-Award Reviews (e.g., Integrated Baseline Review, Financial Survey, etc.) and Analyze Results

Domain 3: Select Source

3.1 Prepare Solicitations
3.2 Advertise Solicitations
3.3 Amend Solicitations (When Necessary)
3.4 Respond to Questions from Potential Sources
3.5 Review Solicitations in Order to Understand Unique/Special Requirements
3.6 Review Solicitation and Write Request for Proposal Abstract/Compliance Matrix
3.7 Develop Pricing Strategy
3.8 Write Proposal
3.9 Prepare Independent Government Cost Estimate (IGCE)
3.10 Participate in Pre-Proposal Conference
3.11 Submit Proposal and Verify Receipt
3.12 Conduct Compliance Review of Proposals
3.13 Submit Proposals to Appropriate Audit Agency for Review (e.g., Defense Contract Management Agency [DCMA]/Defense Contract Audit Agency [DCAA]) (if Required)
3.14 Analyze Audits of Proposals (Both Technical and Cost)
3.15 Respond to Audit Questions and Support Position
3.16 Perform Cost Analysis
3.17 Perform Price Analysis
3.18 Prepare/Respond to Clarification Requests/Deficiency Reports
3.19 Conduct Negotiations
3.20 Request/Prepare Final Proposal Revision
3.21 Evaluate Submitted Proposals in Accordance with Evaluation Factors
3.22 Select Source
3.23 Prepare Contract Document
3.24 Review/Approve the Contract Document and Contract File
3.25 Document Selection Process in Contract File (e.g., Price Memorandum, Evaluation Comments)
3.26 Notify Unsuccessful Offerors
3.27 Manage Protests and Appeals
3.28 Execute Contract Document
3.29 Capture, Document, and Share Lessons Learned

Domain 4: Manage Contract

4.1 Debrief Offerors
4.2 Conduct Post-Award Conference Meeting

4.3 Monitor Contract Performance
4.4 Prepare Contract Modifications
4.5 Execute Contract Modifications
4.6 Obtain Consent to Subcontract (if Required)
4.7 Execute Contract Agreements (e.g., Subcontracts, Teaming Arrangements)
4.8 Manage Subcontracts
4.9 Monitor Contractor's Subcontract Management
4.10 Manage Contract Changes (e.g., Modifications, Negotiated Changes, Post-Award Audits, Configuration Control)
4.11 Analyze and Respond to Audit Findings
4.12 Conduct Performance Reviews
4.13 Conduct Contractor Systems Reviews (e.g., Contractor Purchasing Systems, Earned Value Management System [EVMS])
4.14 Deliver Contract Requirements (e.g., Contract Data Requirements List, Contract Line Item Number, Products and Services)
4.15 Inspect and Accept Contract Requirements (e.g., Contract Data Requirements List, Contract Line Item Number, Products and Services)
4.16 Maintain Contract Documentation/Files
4.17 Ensure Compliance with Contract Terms and Conditions
4.18 Track Project Funding and Contract Value
4.19 Manage Contract Payment Process (Submission/Payment of Invoices, Progress Payments, Vouchers, etc.)
4.20 Manage Key Personnel Changes
4.21 Require/Submit a Truth in Negotiations Act (TINA) Certification (When Appropriate)
4.22 Manage Government/Contractor-Furnished Property, Equipment, Information
4.23 Maintain Communications with Requiring Activity/Program Office
4.24 Compile and Maintain Contractors' Past Performance Data
4.25 Reclaim or Rebut Past Performance Information Data

Domain 5: Close Contract

5.1 Verify Contract Completion
5.2 Prepare Contract Completion Documents
5.3 Make Final Payment
5.4 Manage Disposition of Government/Contractor-Furnished Property/Equipment
5.5 Reconcile Contracts (e.g., Funding, Deliverables, Inventories, Payments, Modifications)
5.6 Capture, Document, and Share Lessons Learned

Knowledge Domains From Job Analysis Study

Content Area 1: Pre-Award
Knowledge of:

K1.1 Requirements Identification Techniques
K1.2 Market Research Techniques and Tools to Understand the Competitive Environment, Markets, and Available Information Sources
K1.3 Elements of Planning (e.g., Acquisition Streamlining Techniques, Sources of Supply, Competition, Socioeconomic Policies)
K1.4 Risk Analysis and Mitigation Strategies
K1.5 Portfolio (i.e., Collection of Programs) Management Principles
K1.6 Roles and Responsibilities in Program Management
K1.7 Industry—Commercial Contracting Considerations (e.g., Uniform Commercial Code [UCC], Teaming Agreements, NDAs, Pricing Strategies)
K1.8 Organizational and Personal Conflict of Interest Identification and Mitigation Strategies
K1.9 Methods to Solicit or Invite Offers
K1.10 Contract Incentives (e.g., Cost, Performance, Delivery)
K1.11 Other Contracts, Agreements, and Arrangements (e.g., Basic Agreements, Letter Contracts, Indefinite Delivery/Indefinite Quantity Contacts)
K1.12 Contract Financing Options
K1.13 Elements of a Solicitation Package (e.g., Statement of Work, Contract Type and Method, Terms and Conditions)
K1.14 Elements of a Subcontract Package
K1.15 Government Requirements for Publicizing Solicitations
K1.16 Proposal Evaluation Factors (e.g., Price/Cost, Technical Capabilities, Past Performance)

K1.17 Proposal Evaluation Techniques (e.g., Rating Scales and Weights, Separate Evaluation of Technical and Price/Cost Proposals)

K1.18 Contract Negotiation Strategies and Tactics

K1.19 Pre-Award Practices Unique to Federal Contracting

K1.20 Pricing and Payments (e.g., Prelists, Payment Structures, Milestone Payments, Incentives)

K1.21 Price and Cost Analysis

K1.22 Flow-Down Contract Requirements and Clauses

K1.23 Legal Entity Structures (e.g., Joint Venture, Teaming Agreements)

K1.24 Federal Government Uniform Contract Format

K1.25 Award Practices Unique to Federal Contracting (e.g., Pre and Post-Award Notification, Debriefing, Mistakes and Protests, Small Business Programs, Inspection, Acceptance, Title, Warranties)

K1.26 Appropriate Documentation Techniques to Mitigate Protests

K1.27 Subcontract Flow Down and Applicable Provisions

Content Areas 2: Post-Award Knowledge of:

K2.1 Types of Contract Changes (e.g., Directed, Constructive, Cardinal)

K2.2 Change Management (e.g., Scope Creep, Configuration Control)

K2.3 Subcontract Management Techniques (e.g., Flow Down of Changes)

K2.4 Alternate Dispute Resolution Methods

K2.5 Legal Dispute Resolution (e.g., Claims, Remedies)

K2.6 Forms of Contract Termination (e.g., Termination for Cause, Termination by Mutual Consent, Termination for Convenience)

K2.7 Post-Award Practices Unique to Federal Contracting (e.g., Treatment of Property, Contract Financing Methods and Preferences)

K2.8 Contract Close-Out Procedures

K2.9 Inspection and Acceptance

K2.10 Quality Management Principles

Content Area 3: Business Knowledge of:

K3.1 Oral and Written Communication Techniques

K3.2 Team Leadership Techniques

K3.3 Electronic Contracting Tools

K3.4 Generally Accepted Accounting Principles (e.g., Balance Sheets, Profit and Loss, Cash Flow)

K3.5 Cost Principles (e.g., Overhead, General and Administrative [G&A] Rates, Wrap Rate Calculations)

K3.6 Economic Principles (e.g., Supply and Demand, Forecasting, Inflation, Trade-Offs, Economic Price Adjustments)

K3.7 Principles of Marketing (e.g., Product/Service Planning, Promotion, Pricing)

K3.8 Customer Relationship Management (CRM) Techniques

K3.9 Business Advisory Roles of the Contract Manager

K3.10 Knowledge Management (e.g., Lessons Learned, Benchmarking, Best Practices)

K3.11 Types of Audits (e.g., Pre-Award Surveys, Close-Out, Operations, Financial, Floor Check)

K3.12 Suspension and Debarment Procedures

K3.13 Networking Techniques

K3.14 Life Cycle Management

K3.15 Management Tools (e.g., Earned Value Management Systems [EVMS])

Content Area 4: Legal/Regulatory/Professional Knowledge of:

K4.1 Forms of Legal Relationships (e.g., Consortia, Teaming Agreements, Joint Venture, Memorandum of Agreement [MOA]/Memorandum of Understanding)

K4.2 *Federal Acquisition Regulation* (*FAR*) and Supplements

K4.3 Article 2 of the UCC

K4.4 Non-*FAR* Transactions (e.g., Financial Assistance, Grants, Other Transactions)

K4.5 Cost Accounting Standards (CAS)

K4.6 Sarbanes-Oxley Act

K4.7 Laws Related to International Contracting

K4.8 Professional Standards of Conduct and Codes of Ethics

K4.9 Classes of Agents (e.g., Universal, General, Special)

K4.10 Basis of Authority of Agents to Act (i.e., Expressed, Implied, Apparent)

K4.11 Labor Law (e.g., Service Contract Act, Walsh-Healy Public Contracts Act, Davis-Bacon Act)

K4.12 Appropriations/Fiscal Law as it Relates to Contract Funding (e.g., Color of Money, Bona Fide Needs Rule, Antideficiency Act)

K4.13 Intellectual Property (e.g., Patent, Copyright, Data) and its Legal Treatment (e.g., Licensing, Royalties, Nondisclosure Agreements)

K4.14 Roles of Different Branches of Government in Contract Oversight

Domain 5: Specialized Knowledge of:

K5.1 Research and Development

K5.2 Architect, Engineering, and Construction Services

K5.3 Information Technology

K5.4 Contracting for Services

K5.5 Performance-Based Acquisition

K5.6 Contracts with State and Local Governments

K5.7 Supply Chain Management

K5.8 International Contracting (e.g., Export/Import Control/Offsets, Foreign Corrupt Practices Act

K5.9 *International Traffic in Arms Regulation (ITAR)/Export Administration Regulation (EAR)*

K5.10 Government Property

K5.11 Security (e.g., Industrial, Physical, Personal, Information Assurance)

K5.12 Contingency Contracting

K5.13 Spend Analysis

K5.14 Environmental Contracting

K5.15 Inter-Agency Contracting (e.g., Federal Supply Schedules, Government-wide Acquisition Contracts, Multi-Agency Contracts)

K5.16 Contractor System Reviews (e.g., Earned Value Management Systems, Contractor Purchasing System Reviews)

K5.17 Foreign Military Sales

K5.18 Government Purchase Card (GPC)

K5.19 Undefinitized Contract Action (UCA)

bibliography

American Intellectual Property Association. *An Overview of Intellectual Property.* Arlington, Virginia, 1995. AIPA.

"The American Law Institute," "Creation of the Institute," **www.ali.org**.

Campbell, Kelsey (editor) and Regina Mickells Bova, compiler. *NCMA Desktop Guide to Basic Contracting Terms.* Vienna, Virginia. NCMA, 1994.

Christou, Richard. *Drafting Commercial Agreements*, third edition. (London: Sweet & Maxwell 2005).

Contract Management Institute (CMI). 1999. Survey of Contracting and Purchasing Professional: Emerging Demands on a Changing Profession. Vienna, Virginia: Contract Management Institute.

Contract Management (September): 57–59. 1996b. "The NCMA Body of Knowledge." *Contract Management* (October): 44–54.

Defense Industry Initiative Home Page; **www.dii.org**.

Department of Energy website. **http://management.energy.gov/documents/DetermininglGandCommercialFunctions.pdf** accessed October 3, 2010.

Diamond, Jay and Gerald Pintel, *Principles of Marketing.* Englewood Cliffs, New Jersey. Prentice-Hall, 1986.

Drucker, Peter F. *An Introductory View of Management.* New York: Harper and Row, 1977.

Federal Acquisition Regulation (FAR), U.S. Government website. **www.arnet.gov**.

Fisher, Cynthia D., Lyle F. Schoenfeldt, and James B. Shaw. 1990, 1999. *Human Resource Management.* Boston: Houghton Mifflin Company.

Garrett, Gregory A., and William C. Pursch. "Building High-Performance Buying and Selling Teams." *Contract Management.* April 2006.

Harris, Seymore, and Richard Gill. *Vocabulary for Economics.* Flushing, New York: Data-Guide, Inc.

Hellriegel, Don, John W. Slocum Jr., and Richard W. Woodman. 2001. *Organizational Behavior*, 9th ed. Cincinnati: South-Western College Publishing.

Meneely, Frank T. 1996. "Introducing NCMA's Body of Knowledge." *Contract Management* (September): 56.

Nash, Ralph C., Jr. and Steven L. Schooner. *The Government Contracts Reference Book.* Washington, DC: The George Washington University, 1992.

National Association of Purchasing Management (NAPM). 1999. *Procurement Body of Knowledge.* NCMA and NAPM.

National Contract Management Association (NCMA). 1996a. "The NCMA Body of Knowledge."

The Desktop Guide to Basic Contracting Terms, Revised by Margaret G. Rumbaugh, 6th ed., 2006. Vienna, Virginia: NCMA.

Perez, Sarah. ReadWriteWeb. April 24, 2009. **www.readwriteweb.com/archives/the_technology_generation_gap_at_work_is_oh_so_wide.php**. Accessed October 3, 2010.

Project Management Institute, Inc. (PMI). 1996, 2000. *Guide to the Project Management Body of Knowledge (PMBOK®).* Newton Square, Pennsylvania: PMI.

Rendon, R. G., & Snider, K. F. (eds.). 2008. *Management of Defense Acquisition Projects.* American Institute of Aeronautics and Astronautics, Reston, Virginia.

Rumbaugh, Margaret G. "Ethical Decision-Making: Issues for Contract Managers and Educators;" *Contract Management*; April 2004; pg. 34-35.

Rumbaugh, Margaret G., *Understanding Government Contract Source Selection* © 2010 by Management Concepts, Inc. All rights reserved. **www.managementconcepts.com/pubs**.

Sikula, Andrew F., *Management and Administration.* Columbus: Charles E. Merrill Publishing Co, 1973.

Thornton, Connie L., "Contracting: A Systematic Body of Knowledge." Masters Degree Thesis, Naval Postgraduate School, 1987.

U.S. Department of Defense. *Department of Defense FAR Supplement.* Washington, DC, Government Printing Office, 1995.

Webster's New World Dictionary of American English, 1988.

Whitmoyer, Diane K., *Contract Management*. "Managing Organizational Conflicts of Interest." June 2004.